THE
NAZI AND THE
PSYCHIATRIST

The

NAZI *and the*
PSYCHIATRIST

*Hermann Göring, Dr. Douglas M. Kelley, and a
Fatal Meeting of Minds at the End of WWII*

JACK EL-HAI

PUBLICAFFAIRS
New York

PublicAffairs books are available at special discounts for bulk purchases in the
U.S. by corporations, institutions, and other organizations. For more information, please contact the Special Markets Department at the Perseus Books
Group, 2300 Chestnut Street, Suite 200, Philadelphia, PA 19103, call (800)
810-4145, ext. 5000, or e-mail special.markets@perseusbooks.com.

Book Design by Timm Bryson

Library of Congress Cataloging-in-Publication Data
El-Hai, Jack.
  The Nazi and the psychiatrist : Hermann Göring, Dr. Douglas M. Kelley, and a
fatal meeting of minds at the end of WWII / Jack El-Hai.—First Edition.
    pages cm
  Includes bibliographical references and index.
  ISBN 978-1-61039-156-6 (hardcover)—ISBN 978-1-61039-157-3 (e-book)
  1. Göring, Hermann, 1893–1946—Psychology. 2. Kelley, Douglas M. (Douglas
McGlashan), 1912–1958. 3. Nazis—Psychology. 4. War criminals—Germany—
Psychology. 5. Nuremberg Trial of Major German War Criminals, Nuremberg,
Germany, 1945–1946. 6. Nuremberg War Crime Trials, Nuremberg, Germany,
1946–1949. 7. Nazis—Germany—Biography. 8. Psychiatrists—United States—
Biography. I. Title.
  DD247.G67E4 2014
  341.6'90268—dc23

                                                              2013010730

First Edition
10 9 8 7 6 5 4 3 2 1

TO ESTELLE EL-HAI AND DR. ARNOLD E. ARONSON

with my love and gratitude

CONTENTS

PRINCIPAL CHARACTERS

NUREMBERG JAIL STAFF
Col. Burton Andrus, commandant
Capt. John Dolibois, welfare officer
Lt. Gustave Gilbert, psychologist
Maj. Douglas McGlashan Kelley, psychiatrist
Howard Triest, translator

NUREMBERG DEFENDANTS
Karl Dönitz, admiral and Hitler's designated successor
Hans Frank, governor-general of Nazi-occupied Poland
Wilhelm Frick, head of the radio division, German Propaganda Ministry
Walther Funk, minister of economics
Hermann Göring, Reichsmarschall and Luftwaffe chief
Rudolf Hess, deputy to the Führer
Alfred Jodl, chief of operations for the German High Command
Ernst Kaltenbrunner, chief of security police
Wilhelm Keitel, chief of staff of the German High Command
Robert Ley, head of the German Labor Front
Konstantin von Neurath, minister of foreign affairs (until 1938)
Franz von Papen, German vice chancellor
Erich Raeder, commander in chief of the German navy
Joachim von Ribbentrop, foreign minister
Alfred Rosenberg, Nazi party philosopher and Reichsminister for the Eastern
    Occupied Territories
Fritz Sauckel, chief of slave labor recruitment
Hjalmar Schacht, Reichsbank president and minister of economics (until 1937)
Baldur von Schirach, Hitler Youth leader

Arthur Seyss-Inquart, Austrian chancellor and Reich commissioner for the
     Netherlands
Albert Speer, Reichsminister for armaments and munitions
Julius Streicher, editor of *Der Stürmer*

INTERNATIONAL MILITARY TRIBUNAL OFFICIALS
William "Wild Bill" Donovan, special assistant to the chief prosecutor
Robert Jackson, US chief of counsel for the prosecution
Judge Geoffrey Lawrence, president of the court

FAMILY OF DOUGLAS MCGLASHAN KELLEY
Charles McGlashan, grandfather
June McGlashan Kelley, mother
George "Doc" Kelley, father
Alice Vivienne "Dukie" Hill Kelley, wife
Doug, Alicia, and Allen Kelley, children

1
THE HOUSE

The Kelleys lived in a sprawling, Mediterranean-style villa on Highgate Road in the hills of Kensington, north of Berkeley, California. Its red-tiled roof rose high above the distant, drifting waters of the bay, but closer, beyond the yard's four terraces and stone walks and down a slope of redwood and fruit trees, stood the headstones of Sunset View Cemetery.

A little merry-go-round and a children's swimming pool sat in the center courtyard of the Kelleys' U-shaped house. The front door opened onto a hallway with the kitchen to the left, where the doctor made the family's meals using a large oven, a fast-food griddle, and a meat grinder. The kitchen connected to a pantry with a freezer. The oldest son once sat atop the humming appliance and contemplated killing his father with an ax.

The entry hallway led to a bathroom on the right—the site of a gruesome scene that played out on the first day of 1958—and beyond that to the living room, which contained a fireplace, a long sofa, and the doctor's own green leather chair. The room was carpeted, with the furniture pushed against the walls to open space for guests. Sometimes Dr. Kelley would play a game there with his oldest son. The boy had to leave the room, and in his absence the doctor would move a pencil on the coffee table. When the boy returned, he had to figure out what had changed.

Beyond the living room was Dr. Kelley and Dukie's bedroom, overlooking the rear of the half-acre lot. In a small closet that the children sneaked into through a hallway, they could overhear their parents' fights.

From the living room, black-stained stairs rose to the second level. Up there a bullet hole, hidden beneath a rug, scarred the wooden floor of a hallway drenched with sunlight from tall windows. Before terminating at Dr. Kelley's office, the hallway ran past a closet concealing the magic tricks and props for his shows.

The view from the office window presented a glorious panorama of the Golden Gate bay and the prison tower of Alcatraz Island. When Dr. Kelley turned his desk chair to face the view, he may have settled his gaze on Alcatraz and remembered his months working in another prison, in Nuremberg. His desk was orderly. In cabinets and a small laboratory he kept bone saws, a lab table, mortars, alcohol burners, graduated cylinders and beakers, collections of crystals, botanical samples mounted on glass slides, two human skulls, and a large assortment of chemicals, many of them toxic.

The children slept in the basement bedrooms. They dreaded the unpredictability of Dr. Kelley's goodnight visits. When they heard the creak of his weight on the stairs, they had a few seconds to brace themselves for whatever mood he was in.

The last argument began in the kitchen. Often when Dr. Kelley and Dukie fought, she would pack her purse and leave for the day. This time Dr. Kelley burst out of the kitchen howling and stormed up the stairs to his office. He slammed the door, toppling a porcelain doorstop, its fragments raining down the steps. After a couple of minutes he emerged, concealing something in his hand. He came down the stairs and stopped on the landing, which commanded the living room like a stage. He shouted a statement that terrified and bewildered his wife, father, and children. Then he put something in his mouth and swallowed.

2

MONDORF-LES-BAINS

The airplane, a little Piper L-4, couldn't budge. Its sole passenger, Hermann Göring—former World War I ace, chief of the once fearsome Luftwaffe, and highest-ranking official of the Third Reich left alive—weighed too much for a safe takeoff.

This was an unaccustomed lull for Göring. For weeks he had been in a state of continual movement, uncertainty, and danger. He had evacuated his beloved hunting retreat and party estate, Carinhall. He had endured forced confinement at Adolf Hitler's order after offering, heroically in his view, to take control of the Nazi government. Soon afterward Göring learned of Martin Bormann's command to German forces to murder him, and he scrambled away from the custody of the Schutzstaffel (SS).

Less than forty-eight hours before boarding the Piper, on the day before Germany's surrender, May 7, 1945, Göring had sent a letter across the disintegrating line of battle to the US military command. He acknowledged Nazi Germany's imminent collapse and offered to help the Allies form a new government of the Reich. US Army Brigadier General Robert I. Stack marveled at the sender's audacity and was soon leading a convoy of soldiers in jeeps to capture him. They caught up with Göring's own procession of vehicles near the Austrian town of Radstadt. Göring was riding in a Mercedes-Benz equipped with bulletproof glass.

The chauffeur nudged Göring and said, "Here are the Americans, Herr Reichsmarschall." Leaning toward his wife, Emmy, Göring said, "I have a good feeling about this." Stack emerged from a US Army car, and the men exchanged salutes. Göring and his wife, once one of the most powerful couples in Europe, had reached the end of their war. Emmy was in tears. This meeting with enemy officers on a road congested with refugees "was certainly an extremely painful moment for us," she later wrote.

Stack telephoned the field office of General Dwight D. Eisenhower, Supreme Commander of the Allied forces in Europe, with news of Göring's capture. Göring, who considered himself the most charismatic and internationally admired of the German leaders, believed Eisenhower would soon order his release. American soldiers escorted Göring and his family to Castle Fischorn near Zell am See, where Göring joked with his captors as his family settled into rooms on the second floor and ate dinner with Stack. Göring told Emmy that he would leave the following day for his meeting with Eisenhower, but that he would soon return to her. "Don't worry if I'm away for a day or two longer," he said to her. After some reflection, he added, "To tell the truth, I feel that things will be all right. Don't you think so?"

Göring spent the night at the headquarters of the US Seventh Army at Kitzbühl, where he again asked for safe conduct and a meeting with Eisenhower. His captors told Göring it was unlikely such a meeting would ever happen. Yet Stack and his staff extended many courtesies to Göring: the Nazi leader drank champagne during receptions with American soldiers, posed for photographs and held a press conference, and was treated for one last time as the high-ranking representative of state that he believed himself to be.

● • ●

The following morning Göring, dressed in his gray Luftwaffe uniform, was taken to the edge of a nearby airstrip, to the tight cabin of the Piper, where it became evident that the aircraft could not transport his 270-pound bulk.

Someone found a slightly larger plane, a Piper L-5, which had the horsepower to carry the Nazi prisoner. Göring boarded and settled into the backseat, but another impediment to safe travel arose. He could not stretch the passenger restraint around his belly. Göring held up the loose strap, shrugged, and said, "*Das gut*," to the US Army Air Corps pilot at the controls, Captain Bo Foster. Then, in a gesture of nonchalance, he leaned his elbow out the window and onto the fuselage as Foster taxied the plane onto the runway and it lifted into the air.

The Piper flew for fifty-five minutes to Augsburg, Germany, where American intelligence officers of the Seventh Army waited. Along the way Göring and Foster mixed German and English in a discussion of the sights below them. Göring pointed out airfields and industrial sites that he recognized. They talked about other things, too. Foster asked when Germany had begun developing jet engine aircraft, and Göring replied, "Too late," and laughed. The Reichsmarschall was witty and genial. Foster wore a .45 pistol in his shoulder holster, but had his captive, an expert pilot, tried to take advantage of their close quarters to seize control of the aircraft, Foster would not have been able to free a hand from the instruments to defend himself. He and the world's most famous prisoner of war were defenseless against one another.

After they landed Foster asked Göring to autograph a blank flight report. Spending an hour so intimately with Göring had unsettled him. "I could see that he was like one of our officers if [one of them] had been picked up," he recalled decades later. "I wouldn't say it changed my view of the war, but it showed me that there are. . . . " He let the sentence fade away unfinished. "Well," he resumed, "I questioned all that we knew about these vicious people."

Emmy and Edda Göring, the Reichsmarschall's wife and five-year-old daughter, were moved to Veldenstein Castle, a residence that the family owned in Franconia.

At Augsburg, Göring's privileges were taken away. His wardens took possession of his prized Reichsmarschall baton, a five-pound ivory shaft, embossed with gold eagles and platinum crosses and embedded with 640 diamonds, which Hitler had given him in 1940. However, he still consumed food and liquor in the officers' mess (perhaps to make him more cooperative during interrogations), basked in the awed regard of the American soldiers, and enjoyed attention from the international press. For the last time, he spoke with his anti-Nazi younger brother Albert, who had assisted Czech resisters during the war and frequently aided persecuted Jews. To Albert, Göring hinted that he knew he would probably remain in custody for a long time. "You will soon be free," he supposedly told Albert. "So take care of my wife and my child. Farewell."

Eisenhower continued to ignore Göring's requests for a "man to man" meeting, and soon the prisoner learned that he should prepare for another move, on May 20. Permitted to bring along one aide, Göring chose his longtime servant, Robert Kropp.

Göring's destination was Mondorf-les-Bains, Luxembourg, where the Americans had established an interrogation center code-named Ashcan. (With the same irreverence, the British had named one of their enemy detention centers Dustbin.) Göring may have cheered up when he learned of his destination, because Mondorf, an ancient spa town wedged between Luxembourg's borders with France and Germany, was famous for its vineyards, parks, fields of flowers, and fine hotels. Before his arrival, however, US soldiers preparing for transports of Nazi captives had emptied the ornate but declining Palace Hotel of its furnishings, leaving the guest rooms bare except for folding beds with straw mattresses. Away went the chandeliers, as well as the window panes affording charming views of the town, to be replaced by metal bars and shatterproof sheets of Plexiglas. The soldiers also built a stockade around the hotel, with four watchtowers armed with machine guns, and they would soon install floodlights, fifteen-foot-high, electrified barbed-wire fencing, and additional machine gun posts.

With such decorative touches, it was difficult for the new commandant of Ashcan, US Army Colonel Burton C. Andrus, to keep secret the purpose of the former hotel. But he tried, even as other notable Nazis moved in. Among the first to arrive were Grand Admiral Karl Dönitz, Nazi Germany's final head of state (whom Hitler had designated as his successor in a last fit of pique against Göring); armed forces commander Wilhelm Keitel and his deputy, Alfred Jodl; Robert Ley, a mentally unstable Nazi director of labor who expressed no interest in his food and drink as a prisoner, but urgently requested female company; Hans Frank, the former Reich governor of Poland, already a veteran of two suicide attempts in captivity; the writer of Nazi philosophy Alfred Rosenberg, recovering from a sprained ankle sustained after a drinking binge as the war ended; Hjalmar Schacht, the director of the German central bank, who had opposed Hitler during the war and ended up in a concentration camp; and Julius Streicher, publisher of the notorious anti-Semitic newspaper *Der Stürmer* (*The Stormtrooper*), who had spent his final days of freedom in the Bavarian Alps posing as a landscape painter. Eventually Andrus took charge of fifty-two high-ranking German army officers and government officials at Mondorf. He recalled that he feared attacks on his German prisoners from the outside, "either by fanatical Nazis trying to rescue the inmates, or by the citizens of Luxembourg, who hated not only Nazis but all Germans, after the ruthless treatment they had been subjected to [during the war]." A group of 176 Luxembourgers, recuperating in Mondorf after surviving the horrors of the Dachau concentration camp, were among those who could not be blamed for wanting to lynch the Nazi leaders.

Andrus took his job seriously. The epitome of soldierly crispness, with his glossily lacquered helmet, metal-framed glasses, clipped way of speaking, and rigid bearing, he insisted that his Nazi prisoners treat him deferentially, as their commanding officer. Although *Time* magazine described him as a "plump little figure, looking like an inflated pouter pigeon," the colonel was a lean water-polo enthusiast, born in Washington State, who stood five feet ten and weighed 160 pounds. He had earned distinction as a cavalry officer during World War I and also served as warden of a military detention center at Fort Oglethorpe, Georgia. Before his arrival at the fort, prison discipline had been a disaster. Escapes were frequent, and convicted murderers enforced their own rules through what Andrus called a "kangaroo court." To initiate Andrus, the Georgia convicts had rioted and vandalized the cell block. He forced the leaders of the mayhem to clean up the mess, built solitary confinement cells, and wrote new rules of conduct.

Then he ordered guards to shoot any prisoner attempting to escape. Discipline was excellent after that.

At the end of World War I Andrus was assigned to the Presidio of Monterey, California, where he served as a prison and intelligence officer. During the 1920s he commanded a cavalry troop in the Philippines. His colleagues saw him as formal, heavily starched, imperious, and intolerant of deviations from the rules. The US Army believed those qualities were perfect for the warden of the highest-ranking Nazis at the conclusion of World War II.

Göring arrived at Ashcan disgruntled by the disrespect he had encountered from the gum-chewing American guards who drove him from the airfield. Still wearing his Luftwaffe uniform and sweating profusely, Göring reported to Andrus's office. Andrus disliked him from the moment they met. "With the blubber of high living wobbling under his jacket he presented a massive figure," Andrus observed, adding that he regarded Göring as a "simpering slob." Göring smoldered under the commandant's judgmental gaze.

Along with his footman, Kropp, Göring had brought along a dozen monogrammed suitcases and a large red hatbox. The prison staff spent an entire afternoon searching their contents for contraband and rummaging through such items as jewel-encrusted military medals; diamond and ruby rings; swastika-emblazoned jewelry; cuff links adorned with semiprecious stones; Göring's Iron Cross from World War I; silk underwear; four military uniforms; bedroom slippers; a hot-water bottle; four pairs of glasses; two cigar cutters; and a multitude of watches, stick pins, and cigarette cases. Göring had also provisioned himself with cash amounting to 81,268 Reichsmarks (equivalent in purchasing power to about $1 million today). He bragged that one of the rings was inset with the largest emerald he had ever seen in his long experience as a gem collector. The stone was an inch long and a half-inch wide. Many of these possessions had been stolen from occupied nations, the glittering spoils of war.

Concealed in a can of coffee and in the seams of Göring's clothing, a set of brass vials housed small glass capsules of a clear liquid with a white precipitate: deadly potassium cyanide. Many top Nazis—including Interior Minister and Chief of German Police Heinrich Himmler and possibly Propaganda Minister Joseph Goebbels—had already committed suicide using similar capsules or would soon do so. Göring confided to his aide Kropp that he had managed to hide at least one cyanide capsule in his cell.

The commandant sent Göring to his cell, formerly a luxuriously furnished room that probably had papered walls and a window with a view, now empty except for a flimsy table, chair, and bed with no pillow. Göring, Andrus related, splintered the chair the first time he sat on it. "Had he sat on his table it would have immediately collapsed," Andrus noted, "for it was built to do so to avoid being used by a prisoner to stand on to hang himself." Concerns about suicide attempts also prompted Andrus to issue the prisoners four-inch-long shoelaces, too short for self-strangulation or shoe tightening.

An initial medical check confirmed that Göring was very overweight. His pulse was eighty-four with an irregular heartbeat, his respiration was rapid and shallow, his hands shook, and he appeared "in very poor physical condition," the examining doctor noted. Göring said he had a history of heart attacks.

Initially rude to guards and angry about being detained as a criminal suspect—he often imbued his rising to attention, saluting, and clicking heels in the presence of prison staff with sarcastic overtones—Göring kept protesting to Eisenhower. At Mondorf, he complained, he was receiving treatment "which shook me, as the top-ranking German officer and marshal, deeply." He complained that his room had no light or doorknob; nearly all of his personal belongings had been taken away from him; the confiscation of his medals and marshal's baton was humiliating; lower-ranking Allied officers denigrated him; and perhaps most upsetting, he had lost the services of his personal attendant, Kropp, whom Allied authorities assigned to manual labor elsewhere as a prisoner of war (POW). (Just before Kropp's departure from Mondorf, which nearly brought Göring to tears, the footman performed one last task for his master: stealing a pillow, which the

Americans almost immediately took back.) Göring asked Eisenhower to fly him out of Mondorf to visit his family and to restore Kropp or bring in another German serviceman as his valet. The Allied commander did not respond. Andrus was furious, however, and scolded the prisoners:

> Whereas I do not desire to stand in the way of your writing letters concerning alleged theft of property or other violations of human rights, writing letters about the inconveniences or lack of convenience or about your opinions as to any indignity or deference due you is fruitless and apt to only disgust those in authority. . . . The commandant, his superiors, the Allied governments, and the public of the nations of the world are not unmindful of the atrocities committed by the German government, its soldiers, and its civil officials. Appeals for added comfort by the perpetrators and parties to these conditions will tend only to accentuate any contempt in which they are already held.

Despite that rebuke, Göring became a wearisome critic of the prison, finding fault with everything, especially the food. Andrus insisted that the fare compared favorably with the meals of the prison guards. The jail's schedule called for Göring and the other prisoners to awaken early and assemble at 7:30 a.m. in the dining hall, a dark chamber with arched entries, for a breakfast of soup, cereal, and coffee. Their lunch typically consisted of pea soup, beef hash, and spinach, and they ended the day with powdered eggs, potatoes, and tea for dinner. Each prisoner used a single spoon and rolled his own cigarettes. Andrus dictated where the prisoners would sit for meals, sometimes making neighbors out of captives who intensely disliked each other. The commandant told a story of Göring receiving dinner and lamenting to a German POW server, "This food isn't as good as [what] I fed to my dogs." The POW answered, "Well, if that's the case, you fed your dogs better than you fed any of us who served under you in the Luftwaffe."

This anecdote, possibly apocryphal, captures the animosity Andrus felt for Göring. Like many of this Nazi's adversaries, past and present, Andrus may have mistaken Göring for a stock movie character, the sort of crude manipulator whom British Nuremberg investigator Airey Neave described as "the fat man in endless screenplays who leads the gang of killers from his expensive dinner table." As Neave discovered, however, Göring "was far more shrewd and dangerous than any celluloid character."

● • ●

Hermann Göring, age fifty-two at the time of his capture, was the son of a judge and colonial official in the German colony of South-West Africa (now Namibia). A former flying ace who was once shot down and was credited with destroying twenty-two enemy planes for Germany during World War I, Göring achieved legendary status by flying the unit of planes he commanded into Germany at the end of the war and refusing to surrender to the Allies. He accepted the Pour le Mérite, then his nation's highest military award, for his exploits.

By the early 1920s Göring was a student at the University of Munich, where he first heard Adolf Hitler on a speakers' soapbox. "You've got to have bayonets to back up your threats," he remembered from Hitler's message. "Well, *that* was what I wanted to hear. He wanted to build up a party that would make Germany strong and smash the Treaty of Versailles. 'Well,' I said to myself, 'that's the party for me! Down with the Treaty of Versailles, goddammit! That's my meat!'" Uncertain of his career direction and bitter over the dismantling of Germany's armed forces, Göring devoured Hitler's mix of nationalism, anti-Semitism, and anti-Communism. He supported the National Socialist movement—then small and open to new members, who could quickly rise to leadership positions—to express his hatred of the Weimar Republic that had arisen in Germany, help destroy it, and assume a position of power in a successor government. The Nazi Party was young, but "that meant I could soon be a big man in it," Göring later said. His plan, stoked by opportunism and his desire for personal power, ultimately was realized. "Hermann will either be a great man or a great criminal!" his mother had predicted.

While forming his nascent Nazi movement, Hitler recognized the usefulness of Göring's allegiance and war-hero background. He tapped Göring to lead the paramilitary Brown Shirts of the Sturmabteilung (SA), the first of a staggering number of positions and accolades Göring would accumulate as a National Socialist leader. "For Hitler, Göring was a warrior of superior middleclass origins who could gain the respect of business people and former Army officers and was, above all, a man of unswerving fidelity," the historian Eugene Davidson has observed. Under pressure from Weimar officials, Göring then left Germany and lived in Italy and Sweden for several years, watching the growth of the Nazi Party from afar.

In 1927 Hitler welcomed Göring back to a stronger Nazi organization on the verge of electing members to the Reichstag. After the Nazis' rise to governing power in 1932, Göring, now a top party organizer, planned or played prominent roles in some of the regime's most notorious acts: the Roehm Putsch of 1934, which eliminated the rival SA leadership as a threat to Hitler; the establishment of the Gestapo (secret police); the creation of the first concentration camps for enemies of Nazism; and the persecution of political opponents on whom Hitler blamed the Reichstag fire of 1933. During the remainder of the 1930s, Göring was a key player in the framing of numerous Nazis and military men whose behavior appeared threatening to Hitler and Göring; the Nuremberg Laws, restricting the civil rights of German Jews; decisions that legalized the extermination of Jews; and, in intimate partnership with Hitler, the planning of Germany's preparations for war, among many other deeds. This deep involvement in so many of Nazi Germany's worst crimes later inspired US Nuremberg prosecutor Robert Jackson to declare, "The podgy finger of Göring was in every pie." Göring exploded with laughter when court translators labored to repeat Jackson's phrase in German.

By World War II Göring's titles—surpassed in number among Nazis only by Hitler's own lengthy honorifics—included President of the Reichstag, Hitler's deputy, Prime Minister of Prussia, Reich Minister of Aviation and Commander in Chief of the Luftwaffe, Minister of Economics, member of the Secret Cabinet Council, director of the massive Hermann Göring Works manufacturing combine, field marshal, chairman of the Reich Council for National Defense, and Reich Forestry and Hunting Master. The most precious of Göring's honorifics was the title Reichsmarschall—a rank similar to a six-star general—held only once before, some two hundred years earlier, by Prince Eugene of Savoy.

Second in authority only to Hitler, Göring officially became the Führer's successor-designate in 1935. He put enormous amounts of energy into his duties, making him exceedingly valuable to the Nazi government. At the same time, his vast wealth increased through theft and graft. Unlike many others in the Nazi regime, Göring projected a jocularity that won the affection of soldiers and pilots during the early years of the war. He loved pageantry, costumes, and medals, and once, in an era of formal wear for diplomatic conferences, met US President Herbert Hoover wearing a red silk shirt adorned with a neckerchief fastened with an emerald pin. In Carinhall—his grand countryside playhouse in Prussia, named after his first wife—he gathered tame lions, appeared before guests with spear and helmet as a sixteenth-century warrior, operated a lavishly designed toy railroad, watched cowboy and Indian movies, and displayed works of art stolen from museums and collectors throughout Europe.

As the war turned against Germany and the Luftwaffe collapsed, Göring's hijinks lost their appeal. His influence over Hitler diminished, and his value as an advisor weakened as others, primarily Heinrich Himmler, Joseph Goebbels, Albert Speer, and Martin Bormann, took his place. He grew reclusive; kept far from the lines of battle; and spent more time hunting, appropriating art, and dallying with his toys. At Germany's surrender, just one of his titles, Reichsmarschall, remained. Only Gestapo chief Ernst Kaltenbrunner's reluctance to carry out Hitler's execution order without written confirmation saved Göring's life.

❖ • ❖

The guards searching Göring's luggage discovered gigantic quantities of small tablets made from unknown ingredients. Soon after Göring's arrival, a guard showed Andrus an expensive leather traveling case and said, "I felt you should see this, sir." Andrus opened the case, stared at what he called "the biggest collection of pills I had ever seen in my life"—on detailed inspection about twenty thousand tablets—and immediately summoned

Göring to his office. Göring explained that it was his custom to take forty of the pills a day to treat his heart condition. But these tablets were not part of any normal treatment for heart disease. At the war's end, Göring had hoarded a much bigger stash of pills than the one that dismayed Andrus; he had flushed many tablets down the toilet, believing it would be dishonorable to have so many pills in his possession when he was captured.

Andrus would not take Göring's word for the ingredients or efficacy of the pills, so he shipped a sample to FBI Director J. Edgar Hoover in Washington. Hoover passed it on to Nathan B. Eddy, PhD, a pioneer in the study of drug addiction at the Bureau of Narcotics Research of the US Public Health Department. Eddy's analysis confirmed that the tablets contained not heart medicine but paracodeine, an effective painkiller and "a relatively rare narcotic, not used in the United States," Hoover noted. The FBI deemed paracodeine's addictive potential similar to that of morphine and warned Mondorf prison officials not to abruptly withdraw Göring from it. Hoover asked to be kept apprised of the Nazi's recovery. (Göring was surely unaware of the FBI's analysis, but he grasped Hoover's interest in him when two FBI agents later came to Mondorf seeking a souvenir for the agency's museum in Washington. "Imagine my being featured in the famous FBI museum with the gun of John Dillinger and the mask of Baby-Face Nelson," Göring exclaimed. "It's a fantastic idea!" He suddenly stopped, however, when he understood the implications of this request. "Aha, I'm already indicted. A notorious criminal. American children in the future will shudder when they see a souvenir of the vicious Reichsmarschall in the FBI collection." Eventually the agents persuaded Göring to contribute one of his military epaulets.)

Göring's hoard of pills amounted to nearly the world's entire supply of the synthetic drug, which he had requisitioned from German manufacturers. Developed by German pharmaceutical firms four decades earlier, paracodeine is a depressant with an active ingredient chemically related to the one in opium. "Paracodeine fills a gap between the codeine and morphine groups [of drugs]," noted a German pharmaceutical journal of the early twentieth century. "When paracodeine is given, like codeine, in small doses, it often acts with more intensity than codeine. Compared with codeine, the remedy has a greater sedative power."

Göring was addicted, and to satisfy his need he had pharmacists formulate low-dosage tablets especially for his use. Each tablet contained ten milligrams of the drug, with five tablets delivering the narcotic effect of sixty-five milligrams of morphine, more than enough to anesthetize an average person. At the war's conclusion, Göring often punctuated work and meetings with breaks so he could pop these pills.

Andrus would not tolerate his prison housing an addict. On May 26, Göring's sixth day at Mondorf, Andrus ordered the prison's medical staff—a German doctor named Ludwig Pflücker and the American physician William "Clint" Miller—to wean the prisoner off paracodeine. They began by reducing Göring's daily allotment of pills to thirty-eight, then to eighteen on May 29. An anxious Göring began counting the pills he received and "showed he was disgusted and otherwise showed no effects," Andrus wrote in prison records. Two days later, however, Göring came down with bronchitis, and the Mondorf staff temporarily stopped the withdrawal process. "In my opinion, further reduction in the size of the dosage, or complete withdrawal of the medicine would produce an extremely serious mental and physical reaction in this individual," Miller reported to Andrus. Several weeks would pass before anyone had the resolve to continue Göring's recovery.

● • ●

With Göring's withdrawal still unfinished, a new staff member arrived at Mondorf in early August. He had been ordered to Mondorf from the US Army's 130th General Hospital of the European Theater of Operations, where he worked as a consulting psychiatrist and was in charge of psychiatric services provided to thousands of US soldiers.

Boyish in appearance, solidly built, and ruggedly handsome, with brown, wavy hair, the new arrival was Captain Douglas McGlashan Kelley, a California-born physician. He was near the end of three years in the medical service of the US Army. His responsibility at Mondorf, as Andrus soon explained to him, was to maintain the mental fitness of Göring and the other Nazi inmates until their disposition was determined.

After settling in, Kelley spent time with all the high-ranking Nazis at Mondorf, but he met with Göring first to make a medical examination. Göring must have noticed that this new psychiatrist did not have the distant and scholarly demeanor that he was perhaps expecting. Kelley spoke loudly and directly, and he often moved his bushy eyebrows up and down for emphasis. He began his initial examinations gently, first probing the Nazi's medical history. Kelley did not know what to expect from his infamous patient. He had heard Göring called everything "from a Machiavellian villain to a fat, harmless eunuch, the general tendency having been to identify him as a mere satellite of Hitler, who spent his days seeking medals, glory, and riches," Kelley later wrote.

One Mondorf staff member who already knew the prison's most infamous inmate was John Dolibois, an honest-faced and amiable Luxembourg native and US citizen and Army officer working in intelligence. As a boy he had visited the Grand Hotel during its glory years, before his family emigrated to Akron, Ohio. Working at the prison since May 1945, he tried to protect his relatives in Germany by telling the detainees that his name was John Gillen. Dolibois cultivated a reputation as something of a "soft touch" among the prisoners, and he assumed the duties of a welfare officer—helping with their problems and needs and often lending a sympathetic ear to their complaints—in pursuit of valuable information to pass to the military interrogators who regularly interviewed the captives. Many of the Nazis spoke quite freely, believing they would never face trial for their crimes. "We didn't have to use artificial devices to get our prisoners to talk," Dolibois remembered. "We sometimes had trouble getting them to shut up. Almost all of the men in Ashcan were eager to talk. They felt neglected if they hadn't been interrogated by someone for several days." Dolibois's fluency in German as well as his degree in psychology from Miami University made him an ideal translator for Kelley, who had only a weak knowledge of the language.

A gregarious man, Göring was starved of social stimulation. He welcomed the physician's attention and in one of their first encounters boasted to Kelley that he paid close attention to his own body. The Reichsmarschall, in fact, declared that he had the most admirable physique in all of Germany. He described "in minute detail every scar and blemish on his skin," wrote Kelley, who began sketching a medical history:

> 12 lbs at birth. Not fat—slender as a child—started to gain in 1923.
>
> 1916—16 Nov. Shot down—bullet in rt flank—metal splinters and upholstery. Hosp. to Jan. 1917—16 cm scar. . . .
>
> Was shot in upper thigh—in 1923 at Munich—9th Nov. '23 to March '24.
>
> At that time given morph. self. by injections. After he left hospital took injection and by mouth for ½ to 3/years.

Kelley grew curious about the mountain of possessions that arrived at Ashcan with Göring. The prisoner's collection of toiletries and accessories impressed the psychiatrist, who noted lotion and body powder among the supplies, but not makeup, as had been rumored. What really drew Kelley's attention were the three rings among the Nazi's treasures. They were "truly massive baubles," Kelley wrote, one crowned by a huge ruby, another set with a blue diamond, and the third carrying an emerald. Until his captivity, Göring "always carried these rings so as to be able to select each day the color which best suited his mood," he told Kelley. The psychiatrist also took special note of the massive emerald stored among Göring's belongings.

Göring spoke proudly to Kelley about his well-being, strength, and prowess as a sportsman. "I have always been athletic," Göring told Kelley as they sat side by side on the prisoner's cot, "and until the last years of the war I spent much time skiing, hunting, and mountain climbing." Göring seemed to believe that real danger could never threaten him. On one occasion in his youth, he had stood and watched an avalanche sweep around

him in the Austrian Alps as his companions scurried to safety, and on another he had berated his friends for panicking when their rowboat drifted
near the precipice of a waterfall. "If we go over, we die, and there's nothing
we can do about it, so why get excited?" Göring remembered shouting to
his friends.

Kelley asked Göring about his personal habits, and Göring replied that
he ate with gusto, drank alcohol in moderation, and sometimes smoked
cigars. "He claims to have a normal sexual life and states that it has not
changed since his gain in weight during the 1920s," Kelley wrote.

The psychiatrist next turned to Göring's drug addiction. As Göring explained to Kelley, twenty-five years earlier he had taken part in Hitler's
notorious Munich "Beer Hall" Putsch, a failed attempt by Nazi Party members to seize control of the government of the German state of Bavaria.
Göring, already one of Hitler's chief aides, helped plan the revolt; organized the Nazi storm troopers, who intimidated citizens and took over
government buildings; and spurred on a mob that occupied a Munich
beer hall in which a high-ranking Bavarian official, Gustav von Kahr, was
giving a speech. After twenty-four hours of hostage taking and confusion,
the Nazis and members of the Bavarian State Police fought in the streets
of Munich and exchanged gunfire, leaving twenty people dead and many
wounded. Hitler and his supporters were routed, and Göring took a bullet
in the thigh. A resulting infection left him hospitalized for many months,
during which the drug dependency took root. While doctors had cared for
his leg, Göring had received repeated doses of morphine to dampen his
pain. Gradually his wound healed, but his need for morphine persisted.
When doctors discontinued the shots, Göring went to the black market to
obtain morphine tablets. Exiled from Germany for his role in the putsch,
he was looking for work as an aviation consultant when he and his first
wife, Carin, moved to Sweden in 1924.

He took his addiction with him. He complained that the pain in his leg
had grown unbearable, and the idleness of being unemployed left him feeling purposeless. He upped his daily intake of morphine. The drug made
him at times delusional, untrustworthy, talkative, manic, grandiose, and

insomniac. It lit his emotions like fireworks, igniting fits of rage and violence. He threw furniture around his apartment. Morphine overstimulated his hormonal secretions and his weight ballooned, to nearly three hundred pounds. The svelte, dashing aviation hero of World War I had enlarged grotesquely.

Göring made life miserable for Carin. Doctors told her he was a danger to himself and to others. She committed him to Aspudden Hospital, where, in accordance with the addiction treatment practices of the time, Swedish physicians abruptly reduced his access to morphine. Göring entered the hospital willingly, but he did not foresee the agonies that lay ahead. Physicians refused his requests for more morphine and told him to endure his withdrawal like a man. Enraged by pain, craving, and frustration, he assaulted a nurse, tried to break into the hospital's stores of drugs, and threatened to kill himself. Göring had to submit to a straitjacket before his transfer to a much rougher institution: the Langbro Asylum for the Insane.

He remembered only a jumble of frightful images from the next three months at Langbro. Attendants tied him up in a padded room to prevent him from hurting himself and left him there for days. He was cut off from morphine and endured the full brunt of the harrowing symptoms of cold-turkey withdrawal. Released to his wife's care, Göring relapsed into addiction and was soon back again at Langbro for another round of withdrawal. He repeated the treatment in Germany in 1927, and he told Kelley that he took a final dose of morphine during the winter of 1928–1929 to treat a sore throat. Göring's drug use then ended for several years, even through Carin's death in 1930 and the Nazis' subsequent ascent to power in Germany.

Despite his occasional and controlled use of diet and sleeping pills, Göring seemed to have kicked the drug habit. A change occurred in 1937, however, when a toothache pushed him back to dependency. His dentist believed that nervousness and anxiety were causing the pain, and he gave Göring a bottle of paracodeine with instructions to take two tablets every two hours until the pain diminished. Five days later, when the pain and pills were gone, Göring, anxious to fight off his rising craving for morphine, demanded more. The dentist warned him about the potential for dependency and refused to comply, but Göring had no trouble finding a supply. He was soon taking ten tablets a day.

Göring should have listened to the dentist's warnings about physical and psychological dependence. Although paracodeine did not give him a sense of euphoria, he relied on it to heighten his optimism, alertness, and charm. It also swung his mood between elation and depression and seemed to exaggerate his tendencies toward egocentricity, bombast, and flamboyance in dress and appearance. He stored the tablets in his house in antique Venetian glass bowls, giving him convenient access to the narcotic whenever he felt the craving.

The Reichsmarschall told Kelley that he had taken paracodeine at a relatively low dose until 1940, when wartime stresses multiplied and he began consuming up to 160 pills a day. He reduced that alarming rate of consumption later in the war, but it edged up again as Germany's defeat loomed. "When he was captured, he states he was taking about 100 tablets per day," Kelley wrote in his examination notes—about three times the recommended maximum daily dose. This amount, Kelley observed, was "not an unusually large dose. It was not enough to have affected his mental processes at any time."

Kelley appealed to Göring's pride in his physical strength and prowess to speed up the withdrawal. He realized how easy it was to suggest to the prisoner that he was a mightier man than others and could quit quickly. Göring responded to Kelley's flattery with enthusiasm, concealing his leg pains and other withdrawal symptoms he felt unless specifically asked about them. Kelley gently reduced Göring's intake of paracodeine, and by August 12 the prisoner was free from the drug.

The physician was learning how to manipulate Göring psychologically. But he did not see how the Nazi was influencing his own thinking. By withholding information about his withdrawal discomfort, Göring had managed to convince Kelley that his paracodeine addiction was slight, hardly an addiction at all. Kelley decided that it was more of a "habit." "It was the need to do something with his hands and mouth, to perform an act he was accustomed to, and liked, doing," he wrote. "Just as smokers are careful to have a supply of cigarettes and tobacco on their desks each morning, so Göring would place on his desk a bottle containing a hundred of his little pills. Then, during conferences or discussions, he would reach out, open the bottle, shake out a few tablets into his hand and, popping them into his mouth, chew them leisurely while carrying on his conversation." Kelley added: "I can testify that his addiction was not very severe."

Others at Mondorf heard differently from Göring. He told Commandant Andrus during his withdrawal that his head hurt and he couldn't sleep. He wanted his old dosage of paracodeine restored. The unsympathetic Andrus noted that "he had whined and complained like a spoiled child throughout the weaning."

Göring's long history of dependence on opium derivatives and his unsuccessful attempts to limit his paracodeine use during stressful times of the war made Kelley's claims about Göring's weak addiction ring hollow. A buildup of anxiety, not leg pain, had caused Göring to increase his intake to tens of thousands of paracodeine tablets during the 1930s and 1940s. Today the US Drug Enforcement Administration ranks paracodeine as a Schedule II substance, meaning that its use can lead to dependency and is restricted by law. William Lee, the junkie in William Burroughs's novel *Naked Lunch*, mentions paracodeine as one of his favorite recreational drugs.

The Reichsmarschall played on Kelley's professional pride, flattering him as he submitted to the physician's direction. Kelley was pleased with the way he led Göring through the process, but it is unclear who was leading whom. In the early weeks of their relationship, Kelley had no real appreciation of Göring's successful history of concealment, manipulation, and clever discernment of the motives of the people around him, skills that Göring had honed during his rise in Hitler's Germany. He was no ordinary addict.

While overcoming his paracodeine habit, Göring also accepted Kelley's help in losing weight. During a fat-shedding program that lasted five months, Göring dropped sixty pounds. Protecting Göring's heart motivated Kelley to accomplish this reduction, but the doctor gave his patient a different rationale: losing weight made Göring look better. "He fancied looking like the hero of the Luftwaffe again," Dolibois observed, "the highly decorated ace of the famous Richthofen squadron of World War I." Göring agreed to the weight loss program and ate less. He also requested alterations to his prison garb and uniform. The waist of his pants needed to be taken in six inches. "This concession was granted," Kelley acknowledged, "not because we were interested in Göring's appearance but because, without refitting, he would have been unable to keep his trousers up."

Now in much better health, Göring lost some of his animosity toward his captors, and his disposition improved. He remained anxious, however, sometimes accusing guards of plotting to murder him. He disliked solitude, and one night the violence of a passing thunderstorm, which Göring experienced in the solitude of his cell, set off what at first seemed a heart attack. A doctor called it just a palpitation. Gradually he climbed back into the skin of Hermann Göring, the confident and shrewd player of power politics who had dominated wide stretches of Europe before his capture. He became more comfortable, loquacious, and fascinating to the reassuringly intense psychiatrist who sat and patiently absorbed his every word.

3
THE PSYCHIATRIST

$\mathcal{W}$hen Douglas Kelley stepped into the drama of Ashcan, he had no experience with war criminals and little expertise in treating the withdrawal of addicts from drug dependency. The assignment had come up unexpectedly on August 4, 1945, when he received new orders from the US Army's executive command. "You are to contact Captain Miller . . . [at] Palace Hotel at Mondorf Lesbains, a small town approximately 10 miles south of Luxembourg City," it read. "Captain Miller will give you specific instructions as to your mission." Kelley did not know that these orders would catapult his life in a new direction.

During the previous two months a swarm of psychiatrists and other physicians had applied for permission to come to Mondorf to examine and try to find the reasons for the behavior of the top Nazi captives. One, the American psychoanalyst John Millet, hoped to "add to our information concerning the character and habitual desires of the German people." Others who sought to interview the Nazis wanted far more than their time. "Some went as far as to propose dissecting the brains of the . . . perpetrators: this would involve executing the men by a shot to the chest so as not to damage brain tissue," writes medical historian Daniel Pick. The US military turned them all down in favor of one of its own who had not even requested the honor.

It was a plum assignment, a rendezvous with the men widely regarded as the worst criminals of the century. Kelley's period as the supervisor of several psychiatric hospitals had taught him that aberrant behavior often had mysterious and fascinating sources, and he set his own goals for his stint in this holding pen. He arrived eager to probe the prisoners for signs of a flaw common to Nazi leaders: the willingness to commit evil acts. Did they share a mental disorder or a psychiatric cause for their behavior? Was there a "Nazi personality" that accounted for their heinous misdeeds? Kelley intended to find out. "The devastation of Europe, the deaths of millions, the near-destruction of modern culture will have gone for naught if we do not draw the right conclusions about the forces which produced such chaos," Kelley later wrote. "We must learn the why of the Nazi success so we can take steps to prevent the recurrence of such evil."

Kelley had formed immediate impressions of Göring. From his meetings with the other Nazi prisoners, he recognized that Göring "was undoubtedly the most outstanding personality in the jail because he was intelligent," as Kelley wrote in his medical notes. "He was well developed mentally—well rounded—a huge, powerful sort of body when he was covered up with his cape and you couldn't see the fat jiggle as he walked, a good looking individual from a distance, a very powerful dynamic individual." But having also lightly touched on politics, the war, and the rise of Nazism during their initial cell-bound conversations, Kelley was not blind to Göring's dark side. The ex-Reichsmarschall displayed ruthlessness, narcissism, and a coldhearted disregard for anyone beyond his close circle of family and friends. That very combination of characteristics present in Göring—the admirable and the sinister—heightened Kelley's interest in him. Only such an attractive, capable, and smart man, who had smashed and snuffed out the lives of so many people, could point Kelley toward the regions of the human soul that he urgently wanted to explore.

◆ • ◆

Outsized ambitions ran in Kelley's family. The McGlashans, the family of Kelley's mother, June, were one of California's most precocious and eccentric clans. Kelley was proud of their extravagant saga. They were larger than life, an obsessive assortment of achievers, collectors, and builders of edifices, especially monuments to themselves. The patriarch was Charles Fayette McGlashan, who had arrived in California at age seven from Wisconsin and grew up to become an energetic criminal defense lawyer, newspaper publisher, lover of nature, inventor and holder of patents, and amateur historian.

In the early years of the twentieth century Charles McGlashan's house crowned a hill overlooking Truckee, a rough Northern California town crouched in the Sierra Nevada above the blue jewel of Lake Tahoe. Surrounded by poppies, bachelor buttons, and lilac bushes and perched on a tall stone foundation that sparkled with mica, the house was a startling, two-story structure with white Grecian columns and tall, arched windows that flashed in the sun. Truckee residents long remembered the magical view of this bizarre dwelling, its windows illuminated by twinkling lightbulbs, that rose from the moonlit snow. Every room held treasures that told stories: Persian rugs, cases crammed with Edison music recordings, sculptures and mementoes, furniture chosen with great deliberation.

"Our house sang out from the hill, conspicuous as a wedding cake," remembered one of Kelley's cousins. In the rotunda Charles McGlashan often planted himself in his favorite seat, a black, padded-leather chair that faced a view of a spectacular mountain peak. A footbridge connected the house to a similarly designed circular tower atop one of the region's natural oddities: the Rocking Stone, a sixteen-ton, delicately balanced boulder famous for tipping back and forth at the slightest push. In decades past members of the Washoe Indian tribe had stored food at the base of the boulder, whose motion frightened scavenging animals.

The tower sheltered McGlashan's extensive collection of twenty thousand butterflies, Indian curios, and artifacts from one of the nation's most infamous tragedies. During the winter of 1845–1846, several families migrating west got stuck in a blizzard and had to spend months in the freezing mountains near Truckee. Many in this group, known as the Donner Party, died, and before the rest were rescued, the starving survivors resorted to eating the corpses of their family members. McGlashan spent years collecting remnants from the group's campsites in the nearby mountains and built his house just three miles east of Donner Lake, the scene of the worst months of the tragedy. The museum tower on the Rocking Stone housed many gruesome artifacts, such as the little toe bone of one of the casualties, scavenged from one of the party's fire pits. Nothing like this incongruous pair of buildings existed anywhere else in the Sierra Nevada.

For years McGlashan, an imposing figure with a nobly receding hairline and an aggressive stare, had roamed the region on horseback, stopping to chase butterflies for his collection. "Give me a mountain meadow and you can have the metropolises of the world," he once told a friend. "I would rather chase butterflies on the Truckee meadows than compete for position and fees and fame in any city. Big frog in a little pond? That suits me."

However, Charles McGlashan couldn't help seeking fame and controversy. As a reporter he traveled to Utah to follow up the threads of the much-disputed Mormon Mountain Meadows massacre of 1857. Two decades later he met James F. Breen, a Donner Party survivor, and that encounter set him upon an obsessive, lifelong pursuit of the story of the tragedy, which many in the region considered better forgotten. Lewis Keseberg, the villain of Donner Party lore who had allegedly hastened the deaths of other members of the group, especially intrigued him. Was this man as evil as many people believed? McGlashan tracked down Keseberg in Sacramento, interviewed him, and became convinced of his innocence.

McGlashan took responsibility for locating the rotted cabins of the Donner Party families. At age thirty-one he wrote *History of the Donner Party*, an authoritative work based on scores of interviews with the survivors, which remains in print to this day. In the decades that followed, he took charge of an enormous and ultimately successful effort to build a large monument to the Donner victims at the site of one of the cabins. Others may have seen the Donner tragedy as a horror story that leant no distinction to the Sierra region, but to McGlashan it was something more personally important. To him, restoring the sad events of the migrants to contemporary memory brought distinction to himself and his family, and he took ownership of that calamitous winter. He came to view his research on the events of the Donner Party not just as a groundbreaking interpretation of a human disaster, but as proof of his own worth and achievement. And McGlashan's descendants accepted this view. Their family's distinction was wrapped up in the grisly facts of the human catastrophe that had happened so close to their land. The McGlashans ensured that the Donner Party would never be forgotten. In turn, the Donner Party became a foundational element of the McGlashan family identity. It was a powerful, strange, mutual dependence.

This all-consuming project took a toll on McGlashan's family. His wife, Nona, disliked his frequent absences and his attachment to his work, which made him distant and tense even when he was home. He hiked out to the Donner cabins on the slightest pretext, content to sit among the ruined foundations and tree stumps while imagining that horrific winter decades before. He collected splinters of wood from Donner Party cabin logs, which he later encased in vials and sold for a dollar each to fund his Donner monument. When McGlashan was absent from the meals that Nona prepared for their family, "his empty plate enlarged before her eyes until it filled the whole table," one of their daughters wrote. "If you want to know the truth," Nona said late in life, "I was the chief sufferer of the Donner Party."

McGlashan's polymath interests led him in many directions, including politics (he was elected a California assemblyman in 1884 and chairman of the notorious Anti-Chinese League soon after, as well as being nominated for the state's governorship by the Labor Party) and biology (with Kelley's mother, June, he discovered a butterfly species that became known as *Melataea macglashani*). To others unfamiliar with his workaholism, McGlashan seemed attentive, polite, sharply intelligent, and sensitive. He had a hypnotic gaze, white hair, and a mustache that gave him authority, and complete ease before an audience. If California could boast of imperial families in the years before Hollywood showbizdom, Charles McGlashan headed one of them.

His daughter June followed him into law and was one of the first women admitted to the California bar. They practiced together for several years, and courtroom observers noticed that June had inherited her father's fire as a speaker and persuader. McGlashan taught June, a fellow introvert, that it was pointless to try to make others understand one's own motivations. He told her to simply do what she thought was best without bothering to explain why and see if others would follow. It was a haughty approach that belied the value of differing opinions and the importance of forming connections with other people.

Charles McGlashan had won many plaudits for his work in law, government, history, and science—he was a great man in the minds of most people around him—and he fed on public praise. When publicly challenged, such as when the committee controlling the erection of the Donner Party monument changed his wording of the stone inscription, he would quickly withdraw his support and become bitter. June shared her father's dark and brooding qualities, which lay hidden behind the public sparkle. She bottled up her anger and tried to contain her tension. Before arguing a case in court, she often clenched her fists so tightly she drew blood. And like her father, June would hole up to restore her energy when she felt drained.

In 1909 June married George "Doc" Kelley, a Truckee dentist who practiced law part time, and she left her father's office. Doc was famously affable, a man of simple enthusiasms who immersed himself in the civic life of the town, and who had originally courted June's sister. For a few years June continued working, as the county deputy district attorney, a job that sometimes pitted her against her defense attorney father in court. "The ring of steel and clash of swords brought juries and witnesses to the edge of their seats," a McGlashan family member recalled. "They insulted each other in sophisticated, polished displays of a high intense disdain that drew on the dramatic instincts of both to the fullest."

In August 1912 June gave birth to a son, Douglas McGlashan Kelley. The family moved from Truckee to San Francisco in 1919, and Doc set up a dentistry office at Ninth and Irving, where he worked for more than fifty years. Young Douglas felt the intense love and protection of June, which contrasted with the easygoing companionship of Doc. To her, the boy was the embodiment of the McGlashan line; he was not an amiable nonentity, as June increasingly came to find her husband. As a student, Douglas immersed himself in brainy activities: helping build dioramas for local science exhibits, selling cards that described the constellations, hunting wildflowers, collecting stamps, and reading hungrily and widely. In research notes he took around this time describing the attributes of people born under his astrological sign, Leo (and surely ascribing them to himself), Douglas listed: "Super-vitality, courage, brusque, waste no time in politeness, men of action, energy, enterprise, never listless, stubborn . . . very touchy, passionate . . . perhaps genius . . . generally rise to top of whatever position they choose."

This precocious boy—increasingly certain in his intellectual judgments and commanding in his confidence—soon came to the attention of Lewis Terman, a Stanford University psychologist who was starting a study of the lives of highly intelligent California children. Keenly aware of her son's intellectual distinction, June took him to Terman's numerous examinations and appraisal sessions. Douglas's measured IQ was lofty enough, above 135, to qualify him for inclusion in the study, and he and Terman regularly corresponded for the next four decades as part of the psychologist's drive to find out if exceptionally bright children grew into exceptionally bright adults. Terman kept close tabs on all of his subjects as they grew into adulthood, but he came to regard Kelley as one of the most intriguing and puzzling of the 1,444 children in the study.

By the time Douglas was fifteen he had amassed collections of wildflowers, fungi, and lichens; was a leader of his Boy Scout troop (and would soon become an Eagle Scout); joined his high school's debating society and served as the president of its botany club; and earned money on a lumber crew and as a worker in the school cafeteria. The boy was ardent in his intellectual pursuits, something of a brain beast. He was driven to succeed, to amass and classify knowledge, and to dominate all his challenges.

Years later, even Douglas's young children perceived his need to master everything he tried and make sure others recognized his mastery. Sometime in his teens he took up the hobby of stage magic, a pastime well suited for a boy intent upon impressing others. Whether performing with cards, tricks, or other illusions, the stage magician controls where his audience looks and what it perceives. From simple tricks learned from magazines and manuals, Douglas advanced to more complicated illusions. His interest in magic intensified as a premedical student at the University of California's Berkeley campus. The school's newspaper published amused accounts of magic stunts he promoted and staged for as many of his fellow students as would come watch. These feats included driving a car around campus while he was blindfolded and hooded, a stunt that Berkeley's police chief apparently approved of, but found dangerous enough to comment "on the dangers both to Kelley and passing traffic in downtown districts." Kelley emulated Harry Houdini in public demonstrations by escaping from hand-cuffs while encased in a mail sack and an ironclad sea chest, performed magic at club events and dinners, and printed business cards promoting his skills at sleight of hand. Later he served as president of the San Francisco Society of Magicians. As Kelley himself noted later, working as a magician strengthens the performer's self-confidence and gives him a feeling of su-periority over his audience. He soon learned that well-educated people— those trained to accept suggestions from others, surrender their attention, and arrive at conclusions from observation—were the most astounded folks in the audience at a magic show when a trick defied their expecta-tions. He also glimpsed the downside of the illusion: the audience enjoyed the marvel, but the magician carried the knowledge that it was no more than a trick, a clever deceit.

As Douglas matured, he drew ever closer to his mother's command-ing personality and fell out of his father's orbit. Doc rarely asked young Douglas about his reading or the scientific experiments and Boy Scout ac-tivities that occupied his time. Intellectually, Douglas was a cross between a sponge and a rampaging bull, but Doc didn't seem to understand his son's passions. In addition, measured against the McGlashan clan, Doc was an underachiever, a man content to ply his trade and display his cheerful disposition, itself proof that he lacked the brooding and furious drive of a great man. Douglas observed his father's straightforwardness and good nature and believed they made him appear weak. McGlashans never felt satisfied to drift along in life; they were driven to rise to the top, master their situations, and assert their superiority. They controlled their realms. Douglas absorbed that approach to living from June, and he never strayed from it.

Charles McGlashan died on January 6, 1931—at the very end, he longed to see June, who was herself bedridden with illness—and Nona followed him to the grave three years later. Within another few years the spectacular McGlashan house in Truckee burned down, and the Rocking Stone tower, spared by the flames, was razed. Worst of all, the stone itself had stopped rocking. Guardians of the property had filled the rocking space to prevent the tippy boulder from crushing visitors. The magic of the estate had completely gone.

Douglas Kelley went on to medical school at UC Berkeley and graduated at the age of twenty-four. Now five feet eight and a half inches tall, ruddy, and solidly built, he had wanted to be a brain surgeon, but he believed his hands were too small to conquer that specialty. So he turned instead to psychiatry, perhaps, as family legend maintained, because he knew the McGlashans were a pack of loons. He excelled in the discipline and earned a yearlong postgraduate Rockefeller Institute Fellowship at Columbia University, which led to his doctor of medical sciences degree from Columbia's College of Physicians and Surgeons in 1941. There he spent hours at the New York Psychiatric Hospital. His research in New York opened Kelley to much new thinking on the workings of the mind and covered a wide range of territory, and he collaborated with colleagues to discover a skin test for sensitivity to alcohol consumption, much like tests already in use to measure reactions to allergens. He also dabbled in arcane and strange studies on such topics as the effect of the full moon on the behavior of mental patients, which he reported in *The Psychoanalytic Review*.

More influential on his career was his exposure to the relatively new Rorschach inkblot test, which offered insights into the psychiatric state of patients by allowing trained clinicians to interpret their responses to a standardized set of ten cards showing symmetrical, abstract patterns of ink, some in shades of gray and some in color. In themselves, the inkblots showed nothing. Whatever subjects saw in them, therefore, were projections of their inner personalities.

"The average individual gives from two to five responses to each inkblot," noted a magazine article of the era. "Ten or more indicate ambition—a hard driving toward success, a resolve to succeed by quantity in case sheer quality isn't enough. Fewer than two responses, especially if these are vague and ill-defined, denote the individual who was bound up in himself, lacking ideas and imagination. But when a small number of responses is clean cut, clearly seen and accurately reported, it reveals the skilled and confident individual. He knows what he wants and goes after it." During a test period of about an hour, evaluators typically recorded exactly what a subject said about the inkblots, scrutinizing not only the content of the responses, but whether the subject focused on the whole inkblot image or only part of it, and the number of animals, humans, fantasy figures, and other images discerned in the picture. Cheating was impossible, Kelley believed; the subject's personality came through in any response, no matter how much that person tried to disguise or distort it.

Introduced in 1921 by the Swiss psychiatrist Hermann Rorschach, the inkblot test had gained considerable influence in psychiatry, and later in psychology, as a tool for the investigation of individual personality. (It retains its high status in psychology to this day.) Until the 1960s, when standardized methods of interpreting Rorschach data gained traction, the value of the test depended on the skill and experience of the interpreter in drawing conclusions from the results. Kelley met and grew professionally close to Bruno Klopfer, a leader in championing the Rorschach test in the United States, and by all accounts Kelley was supremely talented as an interpreter. "The method must always be considered an aid to diagnosis and not complete in itself," he wrote. "It is a technique, which when properly used, adds to the armamentarium of the psychiatrist by giving him an additional objective method of diagnosis." He sometimes likened gathering Rorschach results to slicing a thin piece of pie. "And as any pie eater knows, one thin slice gives a good idea of what the whole pie is like," he said.

Use of the Rorschach eventually spread beyond the diagnosis of psychiatric disorders to applications by the government, the military, companies, and anyone interested in determining the personality type of a prospective employee, a person seeking security clearance, or someone in search of a good career fit. But the Rorschach was only approaching wide use during the 1930s and early 1940s, when Kelley took a leading role in advancing it. In 1942 he and Klopfer published *The Rorschach Technique*, a detailed guide to administering and interpreting the test. Kelley's contribution to the book focused on the use of the Rorschach in clinical settings.

Equally fascinating to Kelley was the emerging study of general semantics, a field developed in 1933 by an eccentric engineer, physicist, and former Polish count named Alfred Korzybski. Bald, possessed of a searching gaze and the hands of a wrestler, and frequently fingering a cigarette in a long holder, the imposing Korzybski proposed a method of thinking that he believed would end stupidity and promote sanity, especially in people's relationships with one another. He placed high importance on the principle of "time-binding," the ability of our species to pass along collective knowledge from one generation to the next. Emotional and irrational thinking makes time-binding difficult or impossible, stunting human progress. Korzybski formalized these ideas in his influential book, *Science and Sanity: An Introduction to Non-Aristotelian Systems and General Semantics*, much of which he wrote in his home study with two pet monkeys sitting on his lap.

Eager to apply these ideas to psychiatry, Kelley became a devotee of Korzybski and his new science. Kelley saw general semantics as the study of the communication and preservation of higher ideas. "This communication must be free and mutual, or persons and nations will lead themselves to self destruction by regression to an animal status," he explained.

"Maintenance and progress of higher ideas are the main distinction be-tween human beings and animals." He explored many applications of gen-eral semantics to clinical psychiatry. Unlike animals, who react to stimuli but cannot think of rational explanations for them, humans have the abil-ity to change their behavior by understanding causes, circumstances, and solutions. A soldier may grow conditioned to battlefield danger by becom-ing cripplingly anxious whenever he hears loud noises, but the therapeutic use of general semantics in his case would persuade him that those sounds are perilous only in certain environments and from specific sources. Ra-tional thinking can often overcome the harmful results of emotional reac-tions. Similarly, a skilled debater can persuade an opponent, not by arguing aggressively, but by listening carefully, pinpointing the opponent's emo-tional thinking, and determining what compels the adversary to behave as he does. Solving differences, Kelley maintained, is much easier when one understands the signals that drive others.

● • ●

Kelley's passion for magic intensified. By the mid-1930s he had become an officer in the august Society of American Magicians and had authored several instructional articles in *GENII*, a magazine for conjurers. One de-scribed how to use false shuffling to make an audience member unknow-ingly pick four aces out of a deck of cards, and he introduced readers to such other stunts as "The Kelley Gamble-Trophy Trick" (another card trick), the "City Desk Trick" (a feat of mentalism), and "Let Him Guess" (a prop trick). "Long before the name psychology was on everybody's tongue," Kelley wrote, "magicians employed its principles under the term misdirection."

He sparked Korzybski's interest in magic, which the Pole often invoked when trying to explain the principles of general semantics. Magic tricks, Korzybski said, no longer deceive us when we understand their workings. The shell-and-pea game loses its magic when we see how the pea is con-cealed inside the shell. "A matter of structure," Korzybski said. "And as you know, all of science is a search for structure. When we understand the structure of something then we avoid deception and self-deception. That is one reason why I work to explain the structure of common experiences—war included—and language. But it is not obvious to the naked eye."

Douglas Kelley studied for three years in New York and wrote his Columbia dissertation on using the Rorschach test to assess alcoholics. He took a series of personality and vocational tests during this time. In one vocational appraisal, he scored poorly in the categories that measured fitness for such occupations as psychologist, architect, and engineer, and best matched the test's parameters for real estate salesman and such solitary pursuits as farmer, printer, musician, and author. Kelley's self-confidence allowed him to ignore the profile's suggestions when he made his next career move in 1941, to manage the psychiatric ward at the San Francisco Psychopathic Hospital, an institution affiliated with the University of California Medical School, where he also accepted an instructorship in psychiatry.

Back in the Bay Area, near his family and closest friends, Kelley drew attention by trailblazing a type of occupational therapy that was perhaps unique in American psychiatry. He taught patients how to perform magic tricks, an activity he claimed was more effective in rehabilitating the mentally ill than many other forms of therapy. In an article for the journal *Occupational Therapy and Rehabilitation* in 1940, he noted the importance of the conjurer's intelligence and imagination in entertaining his audience, described how the mind—not the eye—is deceived, and laid out the qualities of stage magic that most attracted him: "No other type of entertainment can be so effectively presented with so little practice. After a single lesson, one can deftly perform easy mechanical effects. Yet the feeling of success engendered by a clever act, so readily learned, stimulates the student to attempt more difficult presentations. He thus gradually develops the true skill and finesse of the finished artist of magic."

Well suited as occupational therapy for depressed, schizophrenic, and neurotic patients, magic could restore their self-esteem, distinguish them in a social group, and prevent them from feeling ignored, Kelley believed.

(For the same reasons, he found it inappropriate for those suffering from paranoia, delusions, and overinflated egos.) "Magic gives the patient a feeling of superiority every time he fools an audience," he told a newspaper reporter. "As a result, it will also promote a mild trend toward exhibitionism. This is a factor of great value in shy and reserved personalities." As a therapy, magic was adaptable, cheap, and safe even for suicidal patients. He spent hours teaching his ailing charges how to perfect the shell-and-pea illusion, make thimbles disappear, rejoin cords that had previously been cut, and perform other parlor tricks; stunts, he declared, that "require no brains and can't go wrong." Kelley took particular pride in the magic-aided treatment of a salesman debilitated by a fear of talking to others. "After mastering three tricks to perform for other patients, the salesman recovered and returned to work," a reporter wrote.

This therapy achieved another kind of magic: bringing Kelley to the attention of the press, which churned out numerous articles on his unexpected use of legerdemain. In San Francisco he evolved into a go-to spokesman on a range of issues in psychiatry. He was quoted on topics as varied as the growing epidemic of mental illness and the lack of facilities and money available to treat psychiatric patients, the high number of military enlistees rejected for mental reasons, and the struggle to provide psychiatric services to the swarms of veterans who had needed them since World War I.

In addition, newspapers gave ample coverage to Kelley's efforts in San Francisco to uncover ways to diagnose patients who refused to take the Rorschach test or accept other investigative attention. One involuntary diagnostic method that Kelley especially favored was the careful use of sodium amytal, a so-called truth serum, to batter down patients' resistance. Kelley valued the drug, routinely used as an anesthetic and sedative, for its effect in smaller doses of leaving patients intoxicated and cooperative. In such a state, often reinforced by a second injection of the sodium amytal, they would willingly answer questions and undergo the rigors of Rorschach examination.

Meanwhile Kelley had met and courted Alice Vivienne Hill, the wickedly smart daughter of a wealthy and conservative family in Chattanooga, Tennessee. Nicknamed Dukie (for "Little Dukie-Do," an endearing acknowledgment of her cutely dignified blond presence), she had emerged from the Girls' Preparatory School in Chattanooga and Ward-Belmont College in Nashville, a prestigious finishing school, where she was president of the senior class and graduated with honors.

Dukie had relatives in Northern California and would often come to visit them. During one visit a cousin arranged for her to meet Kelley at an Eagle Scouts rally in San Francisco, where assistant scoutmaster Kelley had the spotlighted responsibility of lighting the conclave's massive bonfire. As they fell into conversation, Kelley's booming voice—a barreling gale that could overpower a band's playing, pierce through a crowd, and penetrate to the back of almost any room—made music with Dukie's soft Tennessee counterpoint. Dukie felt a rush from dating the young psychiatrist. She found him handsomely beefy, funny, and bursting with ideas, and his teasing about her solemnity made her feel special. In a love note from the late 1930s, Kelley chided her: "Life isn't half so serious . . . and . . . we'll probably arrive—so why worry too much over details along the way?" She was strong, a good match for Kelley's formidable personality. Her family had—in a legendary account—helped establish Connecticut; his, California. They married in October 1940, with Dukie attending her wedding reception, as the Chattanooga papers described for society-page readers, in a lynx-trimmed, Venetian blue wool ensemble, a matching turban, black gloves, and an orchid corsage.

Their time together as man and wife was brief. Within six months of America's entry into World War II, less than eighteen months after their wedding, Kelley joined the US Army as a captain and was shipped off to Europe the following month. With his departure imminent, Dukie gave him an ornately calligraphed and sarcastically faux military order, sealed with wax, that directed the new officer to stay connected with his bride. Kelley was commanded to send her letters containing "a panacea for worry and loneliness," to occupy himself as much as possible with thoughts of her, to dream pleasantly of her, and to remember her "eternal love + devotion + impatient waiting." The document mandated that these orders applied until the end of the war and Kelley's return to "the embrace of the reiteratively aforementioned and everlasting Mrs. Kelley." It was a breezy, witty, affectionate note from a young wife who could have had little idea of the wartime experiences on which her husband was about to embark.

● • ●

On the battlefields of World War I, soldiers had suffered horrendous psychological injuries that neurologists, psychiatrists, medics, nurses, and others had struggled to comprehend and treat. That war left mentally traumatized yet physically uninjured fighters—some of whom hadn't come close to combat—paralyzed, blind, catatonic, dizzy, forgetful, terror stricken, hallucinatory, and awash in nightmares. Just among the Allies of World War I, more than 1.6 million soldiers were laid low by wounds to the psyche. Psychoanalysts speculated that old conflicts in the unconscious, sometimes reaching back to childhood, accounted for this newly recognized war neurosis. Others suspected malingering. Caregivers subjected the affected troops to bed rest, solitary confinement, disciplinary punishment, electric shocks, and character-building talks in attempts to return them to health. Practitioners more familiar with recent advances in psychiatry used talk therapy, hypnotism, and reeducation. Were these patients insane, cowardly, weak willed, or something else?

World War II presented fighters with equally fearsome horrors. Far greater numbers of Americans experienced psychological trauma than in the previous war, and anyone who could relieve the troops' tortures and, better still, send them back to duty, would be a hero to the military. Between Pearl Harbor and the end of the war, the US military was overwhelmed by 1.1 million disabling, psychiatric traumas. Fear and stress were most often responsible. Kelley, serving as an army psychiatrist, called the problem "combat neurosis" and "combat exhaustion."

Under the command of Lloyd J. Thompson, the army's highest-ranking psychiatrist in the European theater, Kelley established the neuropsychiatric ward of the 30th General Hospital, one of the Allies' first medical institutions devoted to combat exhaustion cases and to the training of doctors to manage battle stress successfully. With an abundance of psychologically distressed soldiers at his disposal, Kelley set aside ninety beds in his English hospital for the most treatment-resistant cases of battle neurosis. He trained other doctors in battle psychiatry by staging shows that portrayed techniques of treatment using physicians and actual patients as actors. (Kelley could not resist introducing the hospital staff and patients to Oscar the Duck, a mechanical bird he used to pick cards in some of his favorite magic tricks. He put Oscar to work in the rehabilitation of patients, as he had previously done in San Francisco.) The hospital later relocated to a former school building in Ciney, Belgium, closer to the fighting.

There Kelley and his colleagues had to determine whether they could heal traumatized soldiers for return to combat or to noncombatant duty, or if patients had to go back to the United States for further treatment. (A substantial number, he found, should never have been admitted into the military because they were psychopaths, mentally defective, or psychotic.) Being close to the front allowed Kelley to treat mentally wounded soldiers—who he insisted were not insane—as soon as possible, with the chance of healing them within three weeks. After resting them with a hot shower, a good hot meal, and a deep, long sleep provoked by a high dose of insulin, he put them on a treatment regimen that initially included lengthy individual psychotherapy. That proved impractical when the patients piled up, however, and he turned to a new course of treatment starting in January 1944. Frequently following a round of narco-hypnosis—the use of such drugs as sodium pentathol or sodium amytal to induce a mental intoxication in which the patients relaxed their inhibitions and their recollection of the painful events of their traumas—Kelley placed soldiers in condensed sessions of group psychotherapy that he designed to allow them conscious insight into their problems. In meetings lasting four to five hours, groups of ten to twenty combat-exhausted soldiers heard lectures from Kelley and others on the hospital staff familiar with the clinical application of general semantics. They gave the patients medical explanations for their symptoms and prepared the soldiers for symptoms of combat neurosis that they might develop. The group sessions always closed with discussions of the patients' questions and their personal responses to the shocks of war. This was one of the first uses anywhere of group psychotherapy, and Kelley attributed its success to his Korzybskian method of giving "the patient some understandable, acceptable reasons for the development of his symptoms and [offering] him for the first time some techniques to overcome them. Basically, the techniques taken from Korzybski's methodology represent a way to break up an acute conditioned reaction." In an approach typical of the clinical application of general semantics, patients could replace their embarrassing neurotic symptoms with a rational, scientific explanation of their illness.

Kelley's treatment of traumatized and shell-shocked servicemen filled a need for psychiatric treatment that had haunted the Allied armies. Seventy-five percent of casualties in 1943 at the Kasserine Pass in North Africa had been psychiatric cases without any visible wounds. Throughout the North African campaign of the early years of the war, only 2 percent of the victims of combat exhaustion could regain their health enough to return to duty. Sixteen months later, during the D-Day invasion at Normandy, more than 95 percent of the soldiers with combat neurosis returned to duty, and the training Kelley gave US military physicians undoubtedly contributed to that figure. Some of the improvement was due to nothing more than confidence. By giving soldiers traumatized by battle an explanation for their distress, Kelley helped them manage their emotions. It helped that Kelley radiated self-confidence in his methodology and won the trust of his patients through his boyish—and at times mischievous—exuberance.

His friends in the military appreciated his boisterous animation even if they didn't always believe in Kelley's methodology, unsure if he was a highly specialized medical man or a whiz kid with a fine array of tricks.

One army buddy, Howard Fabing, who worked with Kelley in the wartime hospitals, recognized that "there was so much pure larceny in his heart. . . . He loved cons and grifters and wires and heels, and he was one of the few people who was always good for a laugh through the long months of periodic boredom which occurred in our war." On one memorable day in August 1944 Kelley gutsily assisted a US Marine Corps flight surgeon in a scientific experiment. Aboard a flight originating at Ridgewell, Essex, England, aloft between twenty-three thousand and twenty-six thousand feet, he agreed to remove his oxygen mask for forty-five minutes to study the effects. Although he exhibited the bluish skin symptomatic of a lack of oxygen, as well as euphoria, fatigue, and slurred speech, "Kelley's tolerance to decreased barometric pressures is greater than any that I have observed," the surgeon reported. The former Eagle Scout was remarkably tough.

Promoted to the rank of major in May 1944, Kelley took on steadily increasing responsibilities. During the remainder of the war he supervised all research for the development of new methods to treat combat exhaustion, took charge of the treatment of all psychiatric army cases in Europe, organized the army's psychological clinics, and won appointment as European theater consultant in clinical psychology in March 1945. By then, as Germany's surrender drew near, Kelley's work was tailing off. "I suspect in the not too far future he and others of the organization may find themselves deployed home," a fellow officer wrote to Dukie in May 1945. It wasn't to be.

● • ●

By midsummer 1945 the Hermann Göring familiar to his Nazi peers had returned to health in prison. Confident and charismatic, he ached to again challenge the world. He became a feisty leader of a group of several fellow prisoners who had found their way, unwillingly, to Mondorf. Like Göring, Karl Dönitz had sent messages to General Eisenhower protesting that his treatment was not in accordance with the Geneva Convention standards for prisoners of his rank captured in war. Eisenhower refused to order any changes in Dönitz's treatment, noting in a public statement his displeasure with the almost luxurious conditions of captivity in which some Nazis lived in the days immediately after their surrender. He declared that "senior Germans will be given only minimum essential accommodations which will not be elaborately furnished and that all prisoners will be fed strictly upon the ration that has been authorised for German prisoners of that particular category."

After two months the presence of Göring and other top Nazis in Mondorf was no longer a secret. Reporters spread word of the prisoners idling away their hours in a luxury hotel, and Radio Moscow gave its listeners a weird and fantastical description of Nazis confined to a palace in which they were served rich cuisine and vintage drinks on silver platters, grew fat and sassy, and were chauffeured around the prison grounds in luxury automobiles. Alarmed by these fabrications, Colonel Andrus declared an open house for the press on July 16 and issued subsequent invitations for reporters to examine the prison. He used these opportunities to show that no Nazis were being pampered on his watch. Reporters arrived and wrote about the ordinary food, the condition of captives' underwear, the tidiness (or lack thereof) of their cells, and the fences and guns that surrounded the prison.

Andrus's discipline, reporters learned, was no sham. He enforced behavior that grated against many of the inmates. The Nazis were required to rise to their feet upon the arrival of visiting Allied officials, for example, and on one occasion Dönitz—like Göring, upset over treatment he thought unbefitting a former head of state—failed to do so. "Get up, that man!" Andrus shouted, and Dönitz reluctantly rose from his chair. The early press reports, however, had already swayed public opinion. Allied officials wanted Göring and the other high-ranking Nazis moved to a real prison.

●　•　●

Göring, among others, still considered himself a captured chief of state and reiterated that he was puzzled by his continued incarceration. Unable to imagine a forthcoming trial—there was little precedent for trying heads of state—he expected eventual release from prison. Others had more prescience; Franz von Papen, a former vice chancellor of Germany from the early years of the Nazi regime, felt dread when guards moved him to a cell closer to Göring's. Few of the prisoners, however, realized exactly what the Allies had in store for them. Over in the British detention center, Dustbin, where prisoners could listen to the radio, former Nazi munitions head Albert Speer heard about a planned war crimes trial. He hinted to other prisoners that he wanted a cyanide capsule similar to those Göring possessed, but none came his way.

William "Wild Bill" Donovan, director of America's Office of Strategic Services and a future founder of the Central Intelligence Agency (CIA), worked on the nascent prosecution of the upcoming war crimes trial and frequently visited Mondorf. On August 8 the four Allied powers at last agreed on a charter for the tribunal. Although France, Great Britain, the United States, and the USSR would cooperatively prosecute and judge the Nazi defendants, the United States took the leading role in administering the International Tribunal, and one of America's Supreme Court judges, Robert Jackson, agreed to head the prosecution. Jackson's team targeted Göring as the top-ranking Nazi in Hitler's absence and devoted much of its energy to obtaining his conviction.

Three months after Göring had arrived at Mondorf, he and a select group of top Nazis learned that they had another move ahead. They did not know where or when. Perhaps in preparation for this transfer, on August 6 Kelley wrote up a detailed physical, neurological, and psychiatric evaluation of Göring. He judged his patient alert, perfectly adjusted to his prison surroundings, and cooperative. Göring's environment barely affected his emotions; instead, "strong and labile," his emotions "are generated primarily from within." At the same time, Kelley observed, Göring showed no interest in the affairs of others. Because of his military training and self-discipline, Göring claimed the sufferings of others did not bother him. Kelley consequently declared him "an aggressive narcissistic individual," fixated upon himself.

To help Göring sleep after his withdrawal from paracodeine, Kelley had prescribed the barbiturate phenobarbital. He concluded in the psychiatric report: "Internee is sane and responsible and demonstrates no evidence of any type of psychopathic deviation." This appraisal of Göring's fundamental sanity would not change in the months ahead.

In the early morning of August 12, a convoy of US Army ambulances and other vehicles appeared on the front drive of the Palace Hotel, and fifteen prisoners bearing satchels filed into them. The detainees, soon to be defendants, were deprived of belts, ties, and shoelaces. (The remaining Nazi detainees traveled separately.) Three armed guards rode in each vehicle, and Andrus jumped into a lead car. Without escorts, sirens, or any sign of the importance of its passengers, the convoy quietly passed through Mondorf and proceeded to Luxembourg City, where a pair of C-47 transport planes awaited its arrival at an airfield.

Göring, carrying his red hatbox and yanking up his roomy trousers with his free hand, was among the first out of the ambulances. Ignorant of the cargo they were about to carry, the pilots watched with astonishment as the Nazis boarded. The captives took seats on benches running lengthwise through the planes, which were furnished with little else except a toilet bucket and urinal.

Two guards, one carrying a .45-caliber pistol and the other a billy club fashioned from a mop handle, climbed in. An armed guard kept watch over the prisoners from the rear of each plane. As each aircraft took off and banked to the southeast, most of the prisoners kept quiet, including Julius Streicher, who was airsick. The exception was Göring. "Take a good look at it," he told his companions as they flew over the Rhine River. "That's the last you may ever see of it." Göring later asked to inspect the controls up front. Colonel Andrus denied the request. The city of Nuremberg lay ahead.

Kelley followed the Nazis to the Nuremberg jail. His new orders were to evaluate the mental fitness of the top twenty-two men to face justice in the trial to come. His experiences with the Nazis at Mondorf, and with Göring in particular, continued to send his thoughts soaring beyond the concerns of his official duties. Was there a mental flaw common to these prisoners? Did they share a psychiatric disorder that caused them to participate in the monstrous deeds of the Third Reich? Working among these Germans made Kelley wonder whether he could answer the pressing questions that occupied his mind. Perhaps his scientific study of these men's minds could identify a telling factor that would be useful in the prevention of the rise of a future Nazi-like regime.

The need was urgent. Without official sanction, Kelley was developing a plan to explore the psychological recesses of the brains of the captive Nazi leaders.

4

AMONG THE RUINS

*F*or years the German city of Nuremberg hosted enormous Nazi Party congresses. Its name was used on a set of laws that denied basic human rights to German Jews, and the town stood for the principles of European fascism. But by mid-1945 it barely stood at all. Heavy shelling and forty air raids had pulverized the city. A single British air attack in January 1945 had flattened the center of Nuremberg and killed eighteen hundred people. Residents had worked around the clock for a month to find and bury the dead. More than half of Nuremberg's homes lay in rubble—90 percent in the old part of town—and hundreds of thousands of Germans had fled the area. Many of those who remained lived in damp cellars.

Colonel Andrus and his procession of German prisoners motored through a city filled with eerie scenes of people huddled around outdoor cooking fires, families occupying apartments with walls sheared off and rooms exposed to view, and hungry Nurembergers emerging from underground hovels to wander among heaps of bricks that still entombed their neighbors. Staircases led to empty air. Lacking money, patrons of the black market used cigarettes as currency. The water was undrinkable. Residents of the city remained angry and dangerous. The place smelled of death, dust, and disinfectant.

Although few of the people in Nuremberg understood it—residents, occupiers, and prisoners alike—this battered city would soon host an event more momentous than the Nazi rallies that had filled newsreel frames around the world a decade before.

The US Army requisitioned the Grand Hotel, a social center of the city that had previously housed guests at Nazi Party rallies. It was one of the first large buildings in Nuremberg to undergo repair; a bomb had gutted one part of the hotel from roof to street. Previously the neighborhood had been a risky location for Allied soldiers, a place of frequent assaults and robberies by Nurembergers. In its new function, the hotel housed military and civilian men working on the future war crimes proceedings. (Women lived in another hotel a few blocks away, nicknamed "Girls' Town.") For a long time it was the only large structure in town with electric lights; at night it blazed amid the surrounding darkness. "To arrive at my room on the fourth floor, I had to walk a temporary gangplank strung over still another cavernous hole caused by a second Allied bomb," one Allied occupier wrote. "The gangplank had a flimsy railing on one side and the whole contraption wobbled when one walked over it." Here the tribunal staff lived and drank and danced in a crowded American-style restaurant called the Marble Room, which was closed to German civilians. (Similarly, Americans in Nuremberg were not allowed to patronize most German bars and restaurants.) The bar was well stocked. Dinner, served by waiters in tailcoats, cost the equivalent of 60 cents. From the hotel's doorways and windows floated the music of the victors, a sound that one visitor remembered as "cheap and potent." The Russian occupiers sometimes broke out of their isolation to party and drink prodigiously here.

The Palace of Justice was one of a few sizable buildings in Nuremberg that escaped destruction, although an air raid had damaged the roof, gutted its upper floors with fire, and collapsed the clock tower. In the last days of the war the building sheltered Nazi SS divisions making a final stand before Allied forces overcame them in May 1945, and months later defeat still colored its six hundred rooms and endless corridors. Fleeing Germans and occupying Allied soldiers had left the Palace of Justice's main court-room a mess, with shattered windows, upended chairs, and Coca-Cola cases stacked on tables beneath the still-intact chandelier and baroque clock. Here in wartime a special court under the eye of the notorious Nazi judge Oswald Rothaug had delivered verdicts against the Nazi regime's political and racial opponents. The Americans were collecting construction materials from hundreds of miles around in a $5 million effort to repair the building and enlarge the courtroom for a judiciary purpose that few outsiders yet comprehended. German workers cleared broken glass and rubbish from the high-ceilinged rooms. One day during reconstruction, as a reminder of how unsafe any standing building in Nuremberg remained, the courtroom noisily collapsed into its own basement. Meanwhile, tanks, armed soldiers, and antiaircraft guns protected the building from an SS uprising or other rumored possible attacks by Nazi partisans or victims of the fallen regime.

Colonel Andrus's procession of top Nazis was headed for an adjoining three-tiered prison complex built in the nineteenth century. Kelley thought the shape of the prison evoked a gigantic left hand. Three wings extended like fingers at the top, another wing formed the pinky at the west, and a final corridor, the future home of Göring and the other prominent Nazis, took the thumb's place at the east. Part of the prison held German civilian criminals under a different commander, but the area that Andrus directed confined some 250 men and women in three wings, many of them witnesses and possible defendants for future war crimes trials. The building was badly damaged, requiring timbers to prop up walls and workers to rebuild the outer prison walls, which had holes in them big enough to steer a truck through. German prisoners of war, many still wearing SS uniforms, made the repairs. At night some of those same POWs retired to cells in the prison, where only one guard looked after every fifty captives. "There was nothing to stop them from overlooking into our prison yard," Andrus observed, "hardly any obstacle to their choosing a moment and then shooting in themselves. . . . If some fanatical gang had taken it into their heads to lead a truck with high explosives and send it speeding through the wall to the jail itself, we should have all been blown skywards." The facility was dangerously understaffed by Americans, and Andrus considered his security contingent unwilling castoffs and poor performers. He fumed over the security mess he and the top Nazis were entering, and he thought they had arrived at Nuremberg too early.

The colonel soon went to work fortifying the prison with more guards. He declared it Nuremberg's "dark secret" that his security staff were "bottom of the barrel," inexperienced in prison work, and obsessed by returning home. Some amused themselves by scrawling graffiti on the prisoners' cell walls; others didn't know how to use a gun. There weren't enough men to check on the possibly suicidal prisoners in their cells more often than every half minute. Although he eventually beefed up his guard staff, Andrus never succeeded in acquiring top-quality men for the prison's security work and suffered a turnover rate of 600 percent during the next eighteen months.

Kelley, who had now been on war duty in Europe so long that Dukie was calling herself a war widow, had a new official job. In addition to doctoring the top Nazi prisoners, as he had at Mondorf, he was now tasked with assessing the sanity of the prisoners—who ranged in age from Baldur von Schirach at thirty-eight to Konstantin von Neurath at seventy-two—and judging whether they were mentally fit for a future trial. While he accepted his official duties with all seriousness, he set them within the demands of his personal ambition. He came to understand his purpose in Nuremberg "to be not only to guard the health of men facing trial for war crimes but also to study them as a researcher in a laboratory," he wrote. If Nazism was an illness that could infect people anywhere, even growing to epidemic proportions around the world, then the men he visited in their Nuremberg cells represented isolated concentrates of the disease that could yield a protective inoculation. Although the cause of prisoners' behavior lay outside his official purview, Kelley had to dig more deeply to satisfy his personal ambitions. He set for himself a thrilling, officially unsanctioned, and time-limited quest. "I took it upon myself to examine the personality patterns of these men and, to a degree, the techniques they employed to win and hold power," he wrote. His self-appointed mission was to understand the Nazi mind. "Of course we were not interested in whether they were guilty or not," Kelley later spoke of this time. "Nor were we steering towards therapeutic care. We just wanted to find out as much as possible about them."

He toured the prison soon after his arrival in Nuremberg. The top Nazi prisoners occupied solitary confinement cells on the ground floor of the east-running corridor, an area called the War Criminals Wing. "Cells lay on both sides of the corridor, and at either end circular stairways led to the two upper tiers of cells," Kelley observed. The cells, nine by thirteen feet, were austere and stripped of anything a prisoner could use to commit suicide. Bolts fixed the beds to the walls. The mattresses were stuffed with straw. Damp plaster fell from the walls. Flimsy tables that could not support a man's weight held the prisoner's smallest personal items, and the rest had to sit in piles on the floor. One prisoner, the former economics minister Hjalmar Schacht, described the tables as "unsteady wooden erections of thin lathe with a thin sheet of cardboard nailed on top. Writing at this table was sheer torment for it wobbled continually."

A single barred window admitted some light. Chairs, by regulation allowed no closer than four feet from a wall, were removed at nightfall. That left the inmates little to do but sleep and pace the rough, stone floors. The entrance doors had foot-square observation windows, never closed or blocked, that also admitted meals. A single lightbulb attached to the outside of the door glowed during the day. "A guy could go nuts sitting in a little cell with what some of these boys have got on their minds," Andrus noted.

Colonel Andrus demanded silence in the cell block. Even the guards kept quiet except to give orders to prisoners or point out infractions of the rules. Like every prison, however, the Nuremberg jailhouse echoed with the sounds of forced confinement. Doors slammed and heels thudded on hard floors. Keys jangled. "The very *air* feels imprisoned," Andrus observed with satisfaction. Wire netting enclosed the spiral stairways and covered drops through which a prisoner could attempt suicide. Guards lined the hallways, initially one for every four prisoners, checking the inmates through the door windows that gave a view of the entire cells except for the lavatory area in a corner by the cell door. But even when they occupied this small sanctuary of privacy, using a toilet that lacked a cover and seat, the inmates' feet could be observed. The sentinels spied upon the prisoners day and night. Kelley observed that the top Nazis found this confinement humiliating and undignified, forcing them to taste "the bitter gall of their own boastful words." Compared with Mondorf, this place was tough.

Other rules regulated the behavior of the prisoners. Andrus made no allowance for the former rank of his captives. They could keep in their cells only a minimum of personal articles: family photos, books from the prison library (which required the purging of Nazi texts), toiletries, cigarettes, and writing materials. Inmates' heads and hands had to remain visible to guards while they slept, no matter how much the cold made them want to bury themselves in their blankets, and the sentries aimed blinding flashlights into the cells at night to enforce this rule. Prisoners were not allowed to turn away. Their letter-writing was limited and monitored, and they could receive few parcels. Supervised hot showers were limited to one per week. In a fortified inner courtyard the prisoners, two at a time, could walk and exercise for fifteen to thirty minutes each day among the undernourished trees. The exercising prisoners had to walk at least ten yards from one an-other or on different sides of a dividing wall. Armed sentries watched from encircling guard towers.

At unpredictable intervals, guards told the prisoners to strip and stand in a corner of their cells while staff searched for contraband: anything that could be used for suicide or escape, forbidden food, and unauthorized reading material. Kelley noticed that "these shakedowns were so thorough that prisoners needed some four hours to restore their cells to order." If any prisoner attempted escape, Andrus reached back to his iron rule at Fort Oglethorpe to decree the guards' response: "If time permits they will call 'HALT' before they fire. The Commandant will back them fully in their actions."

Suddenly fallen from privilege and power, looking and feeling shabby in their mismatched wardrobes, many of the prisoners directed their resent-ment against Andrus. They found the commandant high-handed, prickly, comically formal, and disrespectful. He said to their faces that he could not care less about their status or their fate. Göring belittled him as "the fire brigade colonel"; Schacht complained that Andrus's breath smelled of booze. Several felt personally humiliated by having to clean their own cells, and the enforced silence infuriated others. Joachim von Ribbentrop was notorious for performing his cleaning chores poorly, while Keitel shone with military thoroughness.

On occasion, though, Andrus showed a surprising kindness. When former propaganda minister Hans Fritzsche arrived at the prison late at night from Russian detention, the colonel apologized because the closed kitchen could not cook up a hot meal for the prisoner at that late hour, and he sent a piece of cake to the hungry man's cell. On another occasion Andrus rescinded his ban on shoelaces, at least for the older prisoners, acknowledging that their use provided an ease of walking that outweighed their possible danger as an aid to suicide. The commandant also had a corny though predictable sense of humor, sometimes repeating his favorite jokes endlessly.

Colonel Andrus, who viewed his prisoners as "a group of men who could probably be counted as among the worst the Lord has let live on this earth," enforced a stifling daily routine. After rising early, the prisoners were given washing water by POW workers. Breakfast, often cereal, biscuits, and coffee, arrived in metal containers without handles. Attendants tracked every spoon; knives and forks were not allowed. Lunch usually consisted of bread, soup, meat, and vegetables. Most of the prisoners ate heartily. The 6:00 p.m. dinner marked the day's final illuminated activities. There wasn't much difference between the dull sleepwalking of their daytime existence and the slumber they began at their 9:30 p.m. bedtime.

Kelley was one of a small number of prison staff members with unrestricted access to the War Criminals Wing. Another was Ludwig Pflücker, the kindly German physician, himself a POW, who attended to the prisoners' daily health needs in the Nuremberg jail as he had at Mondorf. Pflücker maintained a surgery room where he measured blood pressure and treated such disorders as former field marshal Wilhelm Keitel's flat feet and former governor-general Hans Frank's hand paralysis. Lutheran chaplain Henry F. Gerecke and Roman Catholic priest Sixtus O'Connor, fluent speakers of

German, held weekly religious services in the prison's makeshift chapel, which contained an altar and organ. Although Allied interrogators working for intelligence units and the tribunal's prosecution could not speak with prisoners in their cells, they frequently pulled the top Nazis out of the prison for question-and-answer sessions. Welfare officer John Dolibois was now working elsewhere in military intelligence, so others filled in to help Kelley with translation.

Thus confined, silenced, and restricted, the highest-ranking prisoners hungered for company. The captives "were quite glad to talk to anybody, even a psychiatrist," Kelly discovered. And when they talked, the prisoners often spoke freely, torrentially, and without prompting—far more openly than they ever confided in the Allies' official interrogators—making these psychiatric interviews some of the easiest Kelley had ever conducted. "Every man was an authority on his neighbor," the psychiatrist said. "If you wanted to know about A, you talked to B about him, and you may be sure that B brought out the worst features in A. Göring talked about Ribbentrop, . . . Streicher about Frick, and so on. The only time they talked about themselves was when they wished to glorify their own position and emphasize their cleverness or innocence."

Loneliness and isolation increased the flow of their talk, but Kelley's skills as an examiner also made the Nazis drop their barriers. He based his interviews on an unspoken yet tangible respect between patient and doctor. The prisoners realized that Kelley wanted to understand their thinking and motivations without casting them as monsters or characters from a nightmare. His background in general semantics made him sensitive to their words, able to find significance in the cadences of their talk and the movements of their bodies, and he gleaned much without them being aware of it. He was the one person in Nuremberg who persuaded this collection of scared men with oversized egos that he wasn't merely interested in finding out what their misdeeds were—he wanted to understand *them*.

Every day Kelley spent hours with the top Nazis. He listened to them, scrutinized them, and recorded their thoughts, giving all of them the first mental examinations of their lives. For Kelley, the German language sometimes got in the way, but many of the prisoners spoke decent English. (Göring, for example, understood English well, something many Americans learned when they saw his facial expressions during translated conversations.) In any case, at all times he met the prisoners with an interpreter, whose ability Kelley checked by rotating from one interpreter to another to compare their translations. Aware that the captives might say anything to make a favorable impression, Kelley also read their letters, found transcripts of their speeches, plowed through often execrable books they had published, and watched Nazi newsreels. He interviewed their acquaintances and any colleagues he could track down.

● • ●

Colonel Andrus believed that danger lurked everywhere for the Nazi prisoners in Nuremberg jail. POWs and criminals were a risk for taking potshots at his prize captives, for example, as they walked the few hundred meters between the prison and the Palace of Justice. His fears were realized one day when an escort was taking Göring from the prison to the adjoining building. The armed guard, following Göring by the mandated six steps, suddenly heard something whiz through the air, followed by a sickening thump. Embedded in the wooden planking behind Göring was an eight-inch SS combat knife. The sentry looked up, but was unable to determine who had thrown it or whether he or Göring was the intended target. "And if Göring himself had died who could prove that an American did not do it?" worried Andrus, who kept the dagger as a souvenir. The commandant wasted no time in erecting a covered and walled walkway between these sections of the justice complex to prevent assassination and escape.

After the prisoners had settled in, US military security experts devised what they hoped were escape-proof procedures to control movement between the prison and the adjoining Palace of Justice. Starting in the court area, they set up obstacles, barriers, bells, sentries armed with firepower and billy clubs, peepholes, searches, square-grilled windows, all-business bureaucrats, warning signs, locked doors, permit requirements, and metal-clad surfaces confronting anyone trying to pass between the two sections of the complex.

Thinner and broken of his addiction to paracodeine, Hermann Göring was among the best adjusted to life as a prisoner. "The sudden change of environment from a situation wherein his slightest wish was immediately granted to incarceration in a tiny cell containing only a bed, a table, a chair, and a toilet, must have been profoundly shocking," Kelley observed, "and yet Göring probably complained less and accepted prison routine with more grace than almost any other of the group." Even so, he confessed to Kelley that he sometimes felt depressed. "Psychologically, I feel because of the environment right now very subdued," Göring stated in a note he sent to the psychiatrist. "Physically, besides repeated heart palpitations, not too bad."

Visitors to cell no. 5 often found him reading a book while sucking on a large, handcrafted pipe. One such caller observed that Göring looked theatrically well, with a brown tint to his skin "like that of a veteran star inured to make-up and costume." It seemed as if incarceration had made him healthier, although he retained an air of corruption, like a once-distinguished man fallen into debauchery.

With his gray uniform hanging in folds from his shrunken frame—a look that *New Yorker* correspondent Rebecca West said lent him "an air of pregnancy"—he still conjured up energy and enthusiasm. "Each day when I came to his cell on my rounds," Kelley wrote, "he would jump up from his chair, greet me with a broad smile and outstretched hand, escort me to his cot and pat its middle with his great paw. 'Good morning, Doctor. I am so glad you have come to see me. Please sit down, Doctor. Sit here.'" This was a practiced manipulator at work, and Kelley's skills and insights as a psychiatrist did not prevent his feeling attracted to Göring's charm. These encounters between the dank, plastered walls of Göring's cell, in fact, pitted one highly confident egotist against another.

Göring's social ease and assumed leadership extended to his former colleagues. When he and his fellow captives managed to converse in the exercise yard, Göring tried to lift the spirits of the others. He fancied himself the most esteemed living Nazi, and he predicted honors that would accrue to the Nuremberg prisoners in the future, such as the marble tombs that he was certain loving Germans would eventually build as the resting places of members of the Nazi regime. Göring, Kelley was learning, determinedly lived in the present. A realist, he adapted magnificently to change. He focused on responsibilities and pursuits that led to his goals, and he awoke each morning convinced that the day offered "the rosy dawn of an always better future," Kelley observed.

With that optimism, Göring discovered humor in imprisonment and became the cell block's champion jokester. Kelley rarely found his jokes funny, but Göring, eyes sparkling in his role as prison comic, enjoyed them if nobody else did. Kelley was fascinated "not by the tale, but by the teller," as when Göring delivered this routine:

> If you have one German, you have a fine man; if you have two Germans, you have a Bund; three Germans together result in a war. On the other hand, if you have one Englishman, you have an idiot; two Englishmen immediately form a club; and when three Englishmen get together you have an Empire. One Italian is always a tenor; two Italians make a duet; when you get three Italians, then you have a retreat. One Japanese is a mystery; two Japanese are a mystery. But three Japanese? They are a mystery, too!"

Heaving with laughter, Göring could barely get out the punch lines. He also enjoyed quoting from a notebook he kept of German "underground" jokes that poked fun at his foibles and those of Hitler and other Nazi leaders.

He tended to his personal life, however, with absolute seriousness. On the table in his cell he kept framed photos of his wife, Emmy, and their young daughter, Edda. His devotion to them impressed Kelley. Andrus acknowledged Göring as the most prolific letter-writer among the captives, and the only inconvenience of prison life that the Reichsmarschall complained about was the difficulty he found in communicating with his wife.

During the 1920s Göring had married a glamorous blond singer, Carin von Kantzow. She helped him survive his bouts of narcotic addiction, and together they traveled extensively. Emmy Sonnemann, a well-known actress, had first encountered the powerful couple in 1931 when she was driving in an open-top automobile to give a private performance for dignitaries in the city of Kochberg. The Görings' entourage passed the car at great speed, spraying Emmy and her party with mud and rocks. She formally met Göring after the show. Later in 1931 Carin went to Sweden, where she died of tuberculosis, but Göring stayed in Germany to advance the Nazi cause with Hitler. "When her final illness came he was under the sway of newer enthusiasms," Kelley observed drily.

In 1934 Göring moved Carin's body from Sweden to his magnificent estate in the Schorfheide forest, now christened Carinhall. He kept up the hunting grounds, ballrooms, and ostentatious pageantry of Carinhall as a shrine to his late wife. "Thus did Göring try to appease his conscience with a display of pomp and ceremony," Kelley noted. "He must always have had some deep guilt feelings about his treatment of this first wife. After all, she had left her husband to marry him, and he had then become too embroiled in politics even to be at her side in death. The story of his inattention to his wife had spread through all Germany."

Göring married Emmy in 1935. He continued referring to his favorite retreat as Carinhall, but he christened another hunting lodge Emmyhall. When Emmy gave birth to daughter Edda three years into their marriage, Göring ordered five hundred planes of the Luftwaffe to race across the skies of Berlin in celebration (though he said he would have doubled the number if Emmy had given birth to a boy). Although fellow Nuremberg inmate and publisher Julius Streicher had insinuated in print that Göring was gay and the pregnancy had resulted from artificial insemination, "I am quite convinced that the daughter his wife bore in 1938 is Göring's own," Kelley wrote. Seeing Göring's dedication to writing to Emmy, Kelley was convinced their marriage was a happy love match, not a political arrangement.

As the supportive wife of a top Nazi official, Emmy Göring shared in the regime's responsibilities for its unsurpassed wrongdoings. And she suffered her own trials after her husband's capture, when she lived at Valdenstein Castle. An American soldier once brought her the false news that a US military court had already acquitted Göring of all crimes and that his return to her was imminent, and Emmy rewarded him with an emerald ring. Not long after, another soldier malevolently or mistakenly informed her that Göring had been shot. Throughout it all, Emmy maintained the bearing of a Reichsmarschall's wife. Edda resembled her father and made a good impression as a well-mannered and cheerful child.

Kelley was experienced enough in psychiatry to treat Göring and his other Nuremberg charges as he would patients in civilian life, without showing his opinions about their horrendous acts. Without being judgmental, he encouraged Göring and his Nazi colleagues to respond freely to questions about their government and their role in it. Göring, starved for attention, was glad to have an intelligent person to talk with.

In several of their conversations, Göring discussed his emotional attachment to animals. Like many hunters, he loved his prey and had redrafted Nazi Germany's hunting and forestry regulations to give animals enlightened treatment. In addition, he advanced a remarkably compassionate and progressive antivivisection law. Violators landed in concentration camps. As a physician, Kelley did not approve of the effects of German antivivisection legislation on the protection of public health and the development of life-saving vaccines. "Germany has more diphtheria per square inch than any country in the world," he observed, "thanks to Hermann Göring's forbidding the production of anti-toxin for diphtheria."

Kelley struggled to reconcile Göring's empathy with other species with his cruelty to vast numbers of fellow humans. This man put his weight behind legislation to protect stray dogs and cats, but led gory purges of his enemies, declared his right to execute opponents without due process, and as Luftwaffe chief authorized the aerial bombardment of civilians in the heart of Rotterdam during the Nazis' 1940 invasion of the Netherlands, an assault that killed a thousand noncombatants and left eighty-five thousand people homeless. "For . . . his friends, for his family, nothing was too good. Beyond this circle his interest in any other living thing amounted to almost total disregard," the psychiatrist observed.

Slowly Kelley assembled a picture of his highest-ranking patient. Göring's efforts to be a model prisoner and present himself in the most flattering light were working. Their time together showed Kelley the charm, persuasiveness, and "excellent intelligence bordering on the highest level" of Göring. The Nazi was funny, charismatic, well mannered, and cultured. These admirable qualities did not blind the psychiatrist to Göring's inherent wickedness, however. Kelley was intrigued by Göring's "ability to carry out policy no matter how brutal."

The Reichsmarschall clearly enjoyed their frequent talks on topics ranging from military tactics to the coming Cold War. Göring interested Kelley, and the prisoner took note of that attention. He favored the quick-minded Kelley over the other staff members of the prison; the psychiatrist was perhaps the only person Göring thought he could trust within the confines of the jail. On one occasion Kelley asked Göring whether he subscribed to the Nazi Party's position on the racial inferiority of non-Aryans. "Nobody believes that rot," Göring stated. "When I pointed out that it had brought about the deaths of nearly 6 million human beings," Kelley recalled, "he added, 'Well, it was good political propaganda.'" From that exchange Kelley concluded that the prisoner showed a "complete lack of moral value."

Göring wanted to reward Kelley for his attention. During one meeting in his cell, he offered to bequeath Kelley the spectacular emerald ring he had in his possession when captured, which the Reichsmarschall valued at about $500,000. Kelley pointed out that he could not accept such a valuable gift—and besides, Göring's wartime booty was no longer his to give away. Göring looked pained, "not the action of a man suddenly realizing he's a pauper, but rather the reaction of a small boy who was prevented from doing something he plans," Kelley later said. The prisoner quickly rallied. "Well, here is something just as good," Göring replied and inscribed to Kelley an eight-by-ten-inch photograph of himself dressed in full military regalia.

Despite Kelley's interest in and affinity with Göring, he made time for all of the prisoners in his charge, and he found things in each that fascinated him. They in turn reacted variously to Kelley's constant presence. Most treated him with respect, regarded him highly as a physician, and viewed him as a professional doing his job, not as an enemy tapping them for incriminating information. Held nearly incommunicado, they saw the doctor as one of their few contacts with the outside world and welcomed his visits as breaks in their usual solitude and dull existence. Only a few, like Schacht, who dismissively referred to Kelley's profession as "a dreary calling indeed," disliked his frequent visits to their cells.

Hobbled by joint pain, the humorless Alfred Rosenberg, a writer and indoctrinator of Nazi Party culture and philosophy, had lurched into Allied custody after a tipsy fall while drinking, which landed him in a hospital. Few Nazis read more of his tedious writing than absolutely necessary, although some were awed by the physical heft of such works as *The Myth of the Twentieth Century*, which one American psychiatrist had called an "immensely paranoid version of history, religion, and the importance of Germany in both spheres." A native Estonian schooled in Germany, Rosenberg had joined the German Worker's Party, a precursor of the Nazi Party, even before Hitler. Although his academic background was in engineering and architecture, his writing focused on the racial primacy of Nordic people such as the Germans, the ascendancy of the National Socialist movement over Christianity as the driving inspirational force of Europe, and the plots of Marxist and capitalist Jews to seize economic and political control of the region. These ideas had taken root in Hitler's *Mein Kampf*. A mediocre political organizer, Rosenberg was most valuable to the Nazis as a scholarly personification of the aims and social theories of the party. When asked about his Jewish-sounding surname, he always said it was a Gentile name that came from his claimed Icelandic ancestry.

He held a variety of posts in the Nazi government, including bearing the unwieldy title Deputy of the Führer for the Supervision of the Entire Ideological Training and Safeguarding of the National Socialist Philosophy for the Party and State, but never rose to the job he wanted most, foreign minister. His actual influence as a Nazi government official peaked in 1941, when Hitler made him Reich Minister for the Occupied Eastern Territories after Germany's invasion of the USSR. On his watch, millions of civilians were deported and murdered. He failed as an administrator—subordinates tended to ignore his directives—and he stole art and furnishings for Göring and German institutions.

Sitting in a Nuremberg prison cell was a spectacular comedown for Rosenberg, who eight years earlier had received from Hitler the first German National Art and Science Award—a Nazi version of the Nobel Prize—in the same city. Compared with Göring's mountain of possessions, Rosenberg had arrived at prison with an impoverished assortment of items: a hat, an overcoat, a handkerchief, keys, a rubber stamp, and a nightshirt. As the only government-sanctioned philosopher Kelley had ever met, Rosenberg was a fascinating subject. He struck Kelley as "a tall, slender, flaccid, womanish creature whose appearance belied his fanaticism and cruelty." The psychiatrist marveled at Rosenberg's one-track mind, which could turn a conversation on any topic into a discourse on racial purity. "I was more than casually interested as a psychiatrist to find in Rosenberg an individual who had developed a system of thought differing greatly from known fact, who absolutely refused to amend his theories, and who, moreover, firmly believed in the magic of the words in which he had expressed them." Yet despite the supposed wizardry of his language, Rosenberg often could not complete his sentences or track his own thoughts.

Rosenberg never considered the possibility that he was guilty of any crimes. Kelley soon concluded that the prisoner's dullness and mental confusion deprived him, more than most of his fellow captives, of an awareness of the limitations and fallacies of his own thinking. He was, in

Kelley's opinion, an intellectual bumbler, a purveyor of hazy and nonsensical philosophy.

Bearing fewer intellectual credentials was Julius Streicher, publisher of the anti-Semitic newspaper *Der Stürmer* and a high-level Nazi party official, governor-general of Franconia, the German province that included Nuremberg, until he made foolish insinuations about Göring's virility in 1940. He stood out among his fellow prisoners as a pariah. When Kelley met with Streicher in his cell, he couldn't believe that the man could possibly have been effective as a hawker of hateful ideology. Streicher was "lounging on his cot, a bald, paunchy, loose-skinned man in cast-off GI work clothes," a thoroughly unimposing figure.

Even more than Hitler—of whom Streicher was among the earliest followers—the husky, long-winded, and uncouth publisher believed that Jews were evil and subhuman, and anti-Semitism formed the foundation of all his political beliefs. Despite fractious personal relationships with other Nazis, Streicher, who had often carried a riding crop, never wavered as one of his Führer's strongest and most vocal supporters. In articles, crude cartoons, and editorials, his newspaper cheered the burning of synagogues, the destruction of Jewish property, and physical attacks on Jews. In the guise of journalism, he spread specious stories about Jesus's Aryan background, Jewish laws that permitted pedophilia and prohibited giving gifts to Christians, and the Jewish belief that Jesus's mother was a prostitute. This anti-Judaism was no fringe conviction in Germany; in less crude form it fired the political, military, and economic aims of the Nazi regime, and nearly every Nazi official subscribed to it.

Yet Streicher's fellow prisoners had refused to speak to or eat with him at Mondorf—Admiral Karl Dönitz even presented a petition to Andrus requesting Streicher's banishment from the common table at mealtimes—partly because of his reputation as a sadist, rapist, and collector of pornography. (Newspapers described his pornography stash as "the largest library of its kind the world has ever known.") Many who crossed paths with him in Nuremberg quickly judged him loathsome. "He was a dirty old man of the sort that gives trouble in parks," wrote *New Yorker* correspondent Rebecca West, "and a sane Germany would have sent him to an asylum long before." He refused to take responsibility for furthering the anti-Jewish hatred that led to mass murder and the Holocaust. Streicher was no stranger to the Nuremberg jail, having visited it in the past to administer whippings to convicts.

Streicher often dropped crude allusions to his sexual vigor, kept a clean cell, and practiced morning calisthenics in the nude before pouring a bucket of water over his head to conclude the exercise session. He fancied himself a martyr to his cause and could not talk on any subject for longer than a few minutes without descending into a soliloquy on "the Jewish problem," the psychiatrist learned. "Twenty-four hours a day, his every thought, his every action bore some reference to his beliefs," Kelley wrote. Even his vast and infamous collection of pornography, Streicher maintained, held keys to understanding Jewish thinking, because Jews were always the origin of obscene literature. "The enthusiasm with which he described these volumes led me to suspect more than interest in their alleged source," Kelley noted.

The only prisoner who could tolerate closeness with Streicher was Robert Ley, the former director of the German Labor Front that had replaced the country's trade unions and managed the Nazis' workforce, including slave laborers. Ley had donned Tyrolean clothing after the war while trying to hide in a shed in the mountains near the Nazi stronghold of Berchtesgaden. After his capture, Ley attempted suicide three times.

Kelley found Ley almost identical to Streicher in appearance: squat, bald, and paunchy, garbed in an ill-fitting, discarded GI uniform. A veteran of the German Air Force during World War I, he had been seriously wounded when his plane was shot down in 1917. Kelley took detailed interview notes on this accident: "Fell 2900 meters, pilot killed. Ley thrown against cowling—unconscious 2–3 hours, struck forehead—no fracture. Was unable to speak for half a day—speech slowly improved. Still stutters slightly." Ley's stammer was most pronounced when he grew excited—which occurred often after 1924, when he became an enthusiastic follower of Hitler. He always claimed that a couple of jolts of American whiskey helped him overcome his speech impediment, and he frequently indulged.

Working as a chemist, Ley lost his job after political disputes with his employer and went into politics full time. He developed into one of the Nazi Party's busiest spokesmen. "An inner voice drove me forward like hunted game," he told Kelley. "Though my mind told me differently and my wife and family repeatedly told me to stop my activities and return to a civil and normal life, the voice inside me commanded, 'You must, you must,' and I obeyed that irresistible force, fate. Call it mystic, call it God." Ley never gave up his fervent support of Hitler, even in defeat. "He gave the impression of being intellectually gifted, vital, tough," a translator recalled. "But he really was just a bullshitter of the highest order."

Kelley detected something psychologically amiss in Ley. Chatting with him was impossible, a descent into verbal chaos. "Often when I talked with him in his cell, he would begin an ordinary conversation and, as he became interested, he would stand, then pace the floor, throw out his arms, gesticulate more and more violently, and begin to shout," Kelley wrote. In addition, Kelley had discovered that as Labor Front leader, Ley had proposed utterly irrational programs to benefit Germany's workers, including the building of one hundred ships to take workers on pleasure cruises, the construction of grand residences to improve the nation's housing shortage, and the provision of new cars for laborers. He so deeply idolized Hitler that he wrote a book overly dripping in praise, which even Hitler could not tolerate, ordering the destruction of the print run.

Clearly the prisoner lacked sound judgment and ran on unchecked emotions. What exactly was wrong with Ley? To learn more, Kelley arranged to interview the Labor Front leader's former secretary. She described him as an idealist "who always saw the world through rose-colored glasses, who was always drunk and who, therefore, always saw people better than they really were. . . . [Ley] lived in a world removed from reality." To Kelley,

Ley's lack of verbal control, his bad judgment, and his general lack of inhibitions pointed to a diagnosis of brain damage.

Several other prisoners piqued Kelley's curiosity. Joachim von Ribbentrop, Rosenberg's rival in the sphere of Nazi foreign relations and Hitler's foreign minister from 1938 through the war's end, occupied cell no. 7 in a shaky state. He told Allied interrogators that as a legitimate government official, his arrest had shocked him. With only an elementary school education and a background in the liquor business that had given him little political experience, Ribbentrop was sensitive to any suggestion of shortcomings, including the whispers of fellow diplomats that he was just a "champagne salesman." (Another nickname, "the movie actor," stuck because of his theatrical expressions and gestures.) His notions of his inferiority led to a strong personal attachment to Hitler. Kelley believed that Ribbentrop had long seen Hitler as a father figure, and the Führer's suicide left the foreign minister feeling abandoned. The disorder of his prison chamber seemed to mirror his mental disorganization, and he often peppered Kelley with such questions as, "Doctor, what shall I do? What shall I do?" Kelley noted, "He walks up and down his cell muttering to himself. He is like a little boy whose parents are taken away from him, and he is suddenly told to shift for himself. He doesn't know what to do."

Ernst Kaltenbrunner, the top-ranking Gestapo leader in captivity, was a former lawyer. He was the tallest of the prisoners, and the many scars on his face lent him a sinister appearance. His unfortunate victims had often guessed that the terror chief's web of scar tissue came from dueling, but it actually resulted from his being propelled through an automobile window during a traffic accident. Kelley pegged him as a cowardly man despite his intimidating appearance, "a typical bully, tough and arrogant when in power, a cheap craven in defeat, unable to even stand the pressures of prison life."

As Kelley deepened his knowledge of the prisoners, the International Military Tribunal in which the top Nazis would face judgment haltingly moved forward. Enormous quantities of official Nazi documents were making their way to Allied investigators and prosecutors. Representatives of the United States, Great Britain, France, and the USSR, after rejecting the possibility of quick executions without trial, negotiated how a war crimes tribunal could be conducted and who would first face judgment. Such an international court had never before come together. Although the Soviets made plain their wish that any trial would automatically end in death-penalty verdicts, and the British more quietly agreed, the arrival in Nuremberg of more than a hundred American legal staff members signified that the United States would lead the other countries in organizing the proceedings and setting the standards of justice. The Office of Strategic Services (OSS), the American wartime intelligence agency, was officially handling the investigation of the suspects. Its former head, William "Wild Bill" Donovan, collaborated with chief prosecutor Robert Jackson to assemble evidence against the Nazis. Damning evidence was found of SS death vans that murdered Jews, the gas chambers of Auschwitz, and other horrors of the Holocaust, in addition to proof of war crimes and violations of international law.

Kelley began to see more clearly the social and political hierarchy of his charges. They reminded him of the directors of a business, all under the leadership of the late CEO, Adolf Hitler. One clique—which included Göring and Rosenberg—he called the "brain group," the men who had shaped Nazi ideology and policy. There were also salesmen—Baldur von Schirach, Franz von Papen, Konstantin von Neurath, and Ribbentrop— who sold Hitler's ideas to the world. Military and domestic enforcers, including Kaltenbrunner, Wilhelm Keitel, Alfred Jodl, Erich Raeder, and Karl Dönitz, mobilized armies and weapons to enforce transactions. Finally, Third Reich, Inc., employed lawyers and bureaucrats who "tagged along." Altogether the captive Nazi leaders constituted a "board of directors" of their defeated regime, a ruling group that had run a nation but frequently had little contact with one another.

Yet unlike any corporate board of directors, this one had unleashed six years of war upon the world, cynically disregarded treaties and international agreements, wiped out countless communities of innocent people, enslaved millions, concentrated additional millions in camps designed to murder them efficiently, and legalized racism and terror. What made these men criminals? Did they grasp at opportunities that could tempt many of us? Were they born with evil tendencies? Did they share psychiatric disorders—a type of "Nazi mind"—that could account for their behavior? Kelley understood that his access to this collection of many of the century's most notorious criminals could lead him to answers and renown.

The prison authorities, not to mention the prosecutors for the future trial, were uninterested in the questions that excited Kelley's curiosity. Nobody in Nuremberg wanted to know what made these human beings in high Nazi positions commit such nefarious acts.

● • ●

In seeking to isolate the workings of the Nazi mind, Kelley was venturing into a controversial field of study, the intersection of psychiatry and criminology. Sociologists had long speculated on the causes of criminal behavior and studied the social forces that produce crime. But psychiatrists had less successfully looked within criminals, using their expertise on emotional states, subconscious motivations, and diseases of the mind. For decades, going back to the pioneering psychiatric work of the eminent nineteenth-century American physician Benjamin Rush, doctors had searched for flaws in some people that caused deviant behavior. These early investigators had thought of the elusive flaws as biological—something wrong or evolutionarily backward in the body. But what if the defect was not in the organism, but in the mind? The pioneering nineteenth-century criminologist Cesare Lombroso had speculated that criminals act in accordance with their nature: they are born bad. He began searching for the innate physical and mental characteristics of criminals. Much of Lombroso's work has long been discredited as inaccurate, racist, and a form of social Darwinism, but in attempting to measure the psychological states of his criminal subjects, he pulled criminology into the realm of psychiatry. He pegged criminals as impulsive, immature, deprived of affection, and lacking in restraint, all qualities that later studies bore out. This inspired others to wonder whether, if the seeds of criminality were psychological, a clever investigator could make his name by identifying one or more measurable and diagnosable mental disorders that led to such behavior.

In court, where psychiatrists were increasingly testifying on the sanity of accused criminals, the mind experts simply addressed whether the accused person could distinguish right from wrong, not how he might fit some psychological profile of criminally insane perpetrators. Through the early years of the twentieth century, scientists of many types honed in on various mental defects supposedly shared by convicts. In Britain in 1913, Charles Buckman Goring (no relation to Hermann Göring) found that weak intelligence was the only shared quality among convicts he studied. Later studies tagged certain psychoses and neuroses as better identifiers of criminals than low intelligence. By the 1930s an enormous study of the psychiatry of crime in the prisons of New York State was beginning to indicate that personality disorders were the sparks of much criminal behavior. These disorders included antisocial behavior, narcissism, and paranoia.

Consequently people who worked with criminals increasingly viewed crime as a medical problem. Throughout the American justice system, police officers, social workers, lawyers, and judges were accepting the important role of psychological factors in criminal behavior. Hundreds of psychiatrists applied their skills in prisons.

In 1943, in the middle of World War II, the American psychiatrist Richard Brickner published *Is Germany Incurable?*, a book that Kelley owned. Brickner tried to view the crimes of the German government as he would examine the behaviors of a patient. He declared that although many individual Germans were mentally healthy, their nation's actions "have been typical of what the psychiatrist finds in certain highly alarming types of individual behavior." He discovered evidence of German mental disorder in news dispatches that the journalist William L. Shirer sent back to the United States during the early months of the war. In one, Shirer described an audience's mass salute of Hitler at the Berlin Opera, "their faces now contorted with hysteria, their mouths wide open, shouting, shouting, their eyes burning with fanaticism, glued on the new god, the Messiah." In addition, Shirer wrote about Germans outraged over the British bombing of civilians in Freiburg while they took joy in their military's own destruction of buildings and cities in Belgium and the Netherlands, and Brickner noted Göring's wartime announcement that Germany was prepared to drive all of Europe into starvation to get enough food for its own needs. These incidents illustrated a peculiar sense of justice, "one rule for me, another for the rest of the world," Brickner wrote.

Specifically, Brickner determined that the German nation, including the Nazi regime, suffered from paranoia, "the only mental condition that frightens the psychiatrist himself—because, unless checked, it may end in murder. . . . Murder is the logical denouement of its special outlook on the world." Paranoiac people suffer from megalomania, a need to dominate others, feelings of persecution, and a compulsion to falsify the past to fit their view of the world. Fascism, aggression, and anti-Semitism, then, were only symptoms of what ailed Nazi Germany. "Instead we are confronted with a group who employ whatever power they may have under whatever system of government in a strangely intense and terrifying manner." Brickner believed that many Germans were either paranoid themselves or highly susceptible to paranoid influences from others.

Brickner took pains to keep from tarring all Germans as mentally disordered evildoers, and he acknowledged that paranoiac behavior at times blossomed in many other countries, including in the American Ku Klux Klan movement. His point, though, was to show how paranoia had infiltrated Germany's mainstream culture, which suggested ways for other countries to respond to it, as a psychiatrist might treat it in a patient. He proposed placing Germany after the war under "mental reconstruction": supporting clear-minded Germans while demonstrating to the rest that healthy behavior had benefits and that their paranoiac values had damaged their country. Brickner maintained, however, that holding the Nazis responsible for their crimes before an international tribunal would be futile. A trial of German leaders would only strengthen German paranoiac delusions that their people were persecuted martyrs.

Diagnosing a group-held disorder that may cause aggression among the citizens of a warring nation is not the same, however, as searching for psychological traits that a collection of notorious war criminals might share. Kelley had no idea whether men like Göring could be cured of criminal tendencies, and he never tried to treat his Nuremberg patients in that way. Instead, he began to study them as subjects, as a biologist might scrutinize animals confined in laboratory cages. And he could do more than observe them—he could measure their psyches using such examination tools as the Rorschach inkblot test, which had interested him for so many years.

Kelley faced an ethical dilemma: Whom did he serve, the prisoners or the tribunal that would prosecute and punish them? When he met with prisoners to discuss and diagnose their problems, was he an agent of the prison or an advocate for the prisoners' health? He met these questions as a strong authoritarian (as his children would later discover) who respected authority. His job as a Nuremberg physician was to maintain—not to treat or improve—the health of his prisoners. He would perform his duties diligently and thoroughly. To the prisoners he would do no harm. There was massive pressure to bring the Nazis to justice, and Kelley would gladly do his part in that effort—as long as he could satisfy his own professional curiosity about the Nazi warlords. The Nuremberg prison, he knew, was a psychiatrist's playground.

5
INKBLOTS

Somehow, in a turn of events that would have flummoxed military administrators of the other Allied occupying forces, Kelley had become essential to the operations of Nuremberg prison. British military representative Airey Neave called the psychiatric and psychological scrutiny of the captives "essential to the American way of life at Nuremberg." The language of psychiatric evaluation was foreign to the other armies, but Kelley turned its novelty even in the American context into an advantage, emerging as an authority figure many of the Nazis felt comfortable confiding in or at least engaging in unofficial conversation. To him they said things that remained untold during sessions with the prosecution-minded official interrogators. Through his presence, responses, and open ear, he sensitively orchestrated humane moments in the prison as he pursued his goal to illuminate Nazi behavior.

Because of Kelley's limited knowledge of German, good translators were crucial to his work. After an absence of several weeks, welfare officer John Dolibois was back, much to Kelley's relief. Dolibois suspected that Kelley overestimated the knowledge of psychology he had gained from his college courses, but in any case the men worked well together.

Some weeks later, at the end of September 1945, another valuable translator arrived, US Army Sergeant Howard Triest. A German native born in Munich and a veteran of the D-Day landing at Omaha Beach, Triest had blond hair and blue eyes. He concealed his Jewishness from the

Nuremberg inmates and believed they spoke more freely to him as a result. Even sitting in the same room with them demanded steely nerves and great self-control, because much of Triest's family had perished in Auschwitz. "I had too much personal history to be charmed by any of them," he says, "and I knew that whatever they'd say to charm would be a damned lie." He remembers getting along well with Kelley. "He didn't seem to me a fellow who would be shaken up by a lot of things. . . . [He] never really came open with his private life or with his history. I had no idea where he came from, what he did [before the war], or what his family was like."

◆ • ◆

Kelley later claimed he had devoted at least eighty hours to each of the twenty-two defendants—probably an exaggeration, because it would have left him with no time to do anything else at Mondorf and Nuremberg—but out of scientific obligation and by preference he spent the most time with Göring. Amid the scant furnishings of Göring's cell—with letters, packets of K-ration sugar, and a deck of American Legion playing cards on his table and sometimes bundles of laundry on the bed—they built a rapport and courted each other with a mutual fascination, which is not exactly the same as feeling sympathy or respect for one another. Each understood what the other said and how he felt, realized he could more or less be himself when they were together, and enjoyed the other's company. Göring wanted attention to improve his mood, the open ear of an intelligent conversational partner who could help establish his historical legacy, and an occasional favor. Kelley was drawn in by this spectacularly intriguing and rewarding psychological subject who was a captive source of information: a prisoner facing damning evidence of his criminal behavior, whose emotional responses could be appraised.

As Kelley could see, in embracing Nazism, Göring had sought to satisfy his personal designs and craving for power. His loyalty to the party was not about Hitler, not about Germany, and least of all about the preservation of a supposed Aryan race. His aim was to advance Hermann Göring, and he had joined the Nazis to lead a rising party. His self-interest was notable even compared with other narcissists. Göring possessed the most undiluted self-centeredness Kelley had ever experienced.

The psychiatrist understood the tragedy of Göring's fate, at least as the Reichsmarschall saw it. As Hitler's official successor until the confusion and treacheries of the final days of the war, Göring had nearly attained his dream of ascending to the supreme leadership of Germany, to become the second Führer, when Hitler committed suicide. By then, however, the cause was lost. "He reached his goal too late," Kelley acknowledged. "At Nuremberg he was a Führer without a country, a marshal without an army, a prisoner accused of waging aggressive war against peaceful peoples and of the deliberate murder of millions."

On the other hand, Göring wanted Kelley to know that he was not Hitler's stooge. He claimed that increasingly as the war went on, he had seen Hitler's miscalculations and faulty judgments, and he was one of the few Nazi leaders who had called them to the Führer's attention. Alone among the prisoners at Nuremberg, Göring said, he had argued with Hitler. Mischievously, Kelley replied that Americans generally regarded all top Nazis, Göring included, as Hitler's yes-men. "That may well be," Göring said, "but please show me a 'no-man' in Germany who is not six feet underground today."

The prisoner usually was warm and friendly in conversation. "In fact, when Göring chose to do so, he always tried to persuade us with his charm and relaxed conversation," recalled Dolibois. "Even when he challenged what to expect in court, he did so with a smile and often friendly sarcasm. Of course . . . Göring did not flash his good side unless he expected the visitor to be receptive."

If Kelley had been familiar with the work of Hervey Cleckley, an American psychiatrist who had introduced the concept of the psychopath in *The Mask of Sanity* four years before, he might have applied that label to Göring. But there is no evidence that Kelley had yet read Cleckley's book. *The Mask of Sanity* characterized psychopaths as people who carry on normally in public, making a pretense of conforming to social norms while they conceal savage impulses and a dearth of empathy, which appears only in private. Kelley never used the term *psychopath* to characterize Göring or any of the other Nazi prisoners, but his notes of their conversations described classic psychopathic behavior.

During one talk, for example, while chronicling his early years in the Nazi Party Göring mentioned his collaboration in the 1920s with Ernst Roehm in establishing the SA, the organization's army of brownshirted storm troopers. Kelley saw that this difficult work, vital to the survival of the Nazi Party, had bonded Göring and Roehm in friendship. Then, without making much of it, Göring related how he and Roehm later started competing for Hitler's attention. The competition ended tidily when Göring ordered Roehm murdered during the bloody party purge of 1934, the Night of the Long Knives. Story over: Göring made it plain to Kelley that he was ready to move on to a new topic.

"But how could you bring yourself to order your old friend killed?" Kelley blurted out. Göring sat silent and fixed his eyes on the American. The look expressed bewilderment, impatience, and pity. It was as if Göring were thinking, "Dr. Kelley, I must have underestimated you. Are you an idiot?" Years later, Kelley had not forgotten what Göring did next: "Then he shrugged his great shoulders, turned up his palms and said slowly, in simple, one-syllable words: 'But he was in my way. . . . '"

The shrug signified his release from the responsibility of considering his comrade's welfare and interests. What else could a man like Göring do? He had other concerns. Kelley sometimes let pass this sociopathic thinking, which seemed to belong to someone neither sane nor insane, but in a twilight region of social and cultural derangement. Psychopaths as we now know them, with their lack of interest in others and focus on advancing their own narcissistic goals, were not on Kelley's radar.

At other times, however, Kelley argued with Göring. When the Reichsmarschall once declared that obeying orders, even illegal ones, was justifiable to preserve social order and military discipline, Kelley countered, "To hell with military discipline. With civilization hanging in the balance, we've got to put an end to militarism once and for all, and expend every effort to avoid another war, for the next one will spell the doom of mankind." The former chief of the Luftwaffe took that in stride. "Yes, that's what I thought after the last war," he said. "But as long as every nation has its selfish interests, you have to be practical. Anyway, I'm convinced that there is a higher power which pushes men around in spite of all their efforts to control their destiny." The exchange inspired Kelley to take note of Göring's cynicism and "mystic fatalism."

In similar fashion, Göring eventually shook off his personal discomfort in prison, informing Kelley that he felt relatively well in confinement because of the quiet environment. He also quoted biblical scripture, a passage from Psalms 78:26 ("He caused an east wind to blow in the heaven, and by his power he brought in the south wind"), in which God miraculously provides food for the wandering Israelites. He wanted the psychiatrist to know that he was a survivor who would always get by.

There was a purpose to Göring's acceptance of his present condition. He had work to do. Although he strenuously denied the Allies had any right to try him and his colleagues as war criminals, he accepted the inevitability of the victors exacting punishment on the vanquished and saw it as an opportunity. With the world watching, he could mount a defense of Nazi policies and a resurrection of his own reputation. Those ends reduced all his personal complaints and inconveniences as a prisoner to insignificance. "He spends all his time trying to discredit all the other party men, even Hitler, so that the history books will remember only him," Kelley told an interviewer a few months later.

> Like the rest, he shies away from any involvement with the atrocities—he is completely innocent, according to him, even though it has been proven that atrocities did take place in the early days of the concentration camps from 1933 to 1935, when Göring was in command of them. Of course, the wholesale slaughter and murder did not develop until later, under Himmler.

Göring only complained to Kelley and the other Nuremberg jail staff when he found fault with the treatment of his family. He told Kelley that when he had surrendered to the Americans, the only consideration he had asked for was good care for Emmy and Edda. Göring devoted much of his epistolary energies to his wife and daughter, and he asked Kelley and translator Dolibois to track them down and deliver his letters to them. (Prisoner Fritz Sauckel, who spent three years with the Nazi government as a high-ranking administrator of slave labor, also asked Kelley for assistance contacting his family. He had lost touch with his wife and ten children, and one soldier son had not been heard from since two months before the war's end.)

The Reichsmarschall unleashed his frustrations and expressed his confidence in Kelley in a letter to Emmy in the first weeks of October 1945:

> For three months I have been writing to you without receiving an answer. . . . Today I can send you a letter direct: Major Kelley, the doctor who is treating me and who has my fullest confidence, is bringing it to you. You can also talk to him freely. The greatest torment of my soul was and is the fact that, up until now, I have not known where all of you were and how you were getting along. You can send me an answer through Major Kelley, and you will understand how I long for it. . . . I don't need to tell you what I am going through here. The hard fate of our fatherland and the tormenting worry about you and your future are the most difficult burdens for my soul. My dearest wife, I am so sincerely thankful to you, for all the happiness that you always gave to me, for your love and for everything. How is little Edda taking it all? . . . Give Eddalein a kiss from her Pappi and greet everyone for me. You are embraced and kissed in sincerest love and longing by your Hermann.

Although Emmy Göring avoided contact with most Americans, she readily agreed to see Kelley. When she accepted the letter from Kelley, she feared reading what she thought would be her husband's final farewell. She passed the correspondence unread to her niece, who confirmed that it contained better news. Then she read it. When she finished, she spoke with Kelley, whom she judged "an honest and very humane man." She asked, "How is my husband?" Kelley replied, "He's behaving like a rock in a stormy sea."

On the spot Emmy wrote out a response that Kelley carried back to her husband:

> Finally, finally a letter from you. I can't tell you how happy I am. My love and my thoughts are with you every second. We are fine, we have food to eat and we have wood. . . . My only thought, my prayer every night is that you may be with us once more. Stay in good health. Thank God, Edda is still too young to share our worries. . . . Hermann, I love you above all, keep faith and God will lead us together again. Everybody sends his love and we all embrace you. I send you all the kisses which I have given you in the past and which I want to give you in the years to come. I love you, always yours, Emmy

To which her daughter added a line: "My dearest daddy, come back to me soon. I am longing for you so much. Many thousand kisses, your Edda."

Göring received Emmy's letter with joy, but he also expressed stoicism and regret:

> You can well imagine how inexpressibly happy I was over your dear letter. It was the first ray of light in this dark period. . . . You will already know from the newspapers that my trial as so-called war criminal will begin on 20 November. We must be prepared for the worst. Nevertheless I hope by the Almighty that we can still meet again. I pray everyday that I may keep the strength to uphold our dignity—for it would be better to come to the end with dignity than to live on without honor. I think only of you and only the worry over your welfare tortures me now. I have always known and felt how much I love you, but now the true depth of our love has been revealed to me for the first time I thank you eternally for the

great happiness that your love gave me. You must know how great
my longing and homesickness is for you and Edda. Sometimes I
actually think I will die of it. Why did it have to turn out this way? If
we had even suspected this development, we would certainly have
gone another way. Now we leave everything to God's will. . . .

    Never let Edda away from you.

On the back of this letter Göring added a postscript: "Major Dr. Kelley,
who is bringing this letter to you, is really an extraordinary gentleman. First
Lieutenant [Dolibois], who accompanies him, is very warm and human
and I have known both gentlemen for several months. You can trust them
completely."

Göring later wrote again to Emmy: "To see [Edda's] beloved handwriting, to know that your dear hands have rested on this very paper—all that
and the contents itself has moved me most deeply, and yet made me most
happy. . . . Sometimes I think that my heart will break with love and longing
for you. That would be a beautiful death."

"It is my opinion that Frau Göring reciprocated to the fullest her husband's feeling and remained throughout completely loyal to him," Kelley
later wrote. Nobody knows, however, whether Emmy Göring would have
approved of a startling plan her husband was formulating for Edda. He
asked Kelley to take care of young Edda in the United States if both mother
and father died. Kelley told his wife about this entreaty when he returned
home months later; it is unknown how Dukie responded to the prospect
of adopting and rearing a Nazi's daughter. This astonishing request—a sign
of Göring's respect for Kelley—moved the psychiatrist, who knew how
much Edda meant to her father. Though he never recorded how he replied
to Göring's appeal, Kelley surely rejected it on professional grounds.

● • ●

On October 8 two army jeeps full of security officers escorted a fast-moving
ambulance into the Nuremberg prison grounds. A scrawny man with cater-
pillar brows over tense eyes, wearing a gray Luftwaffe suit, old overcoat, and

rumpled hat, emerged from the back of the medical vehicle and blinked at his surroundings. His garb lacked any military insignia, but the spectacular boots he wore—made from soft black leather, rising high on his legs, each with a pair of serpentine zippers—gave him a distinctive military deportment. For the first time in four years, Rudolf Hess was back on German soil.

On May 10, 1941, in accordance with a suggestion from his astrologer, Hess—then age forty-six, healthy, powerful as Germany's Deputy Führer and the third-highest-ranking Nazi after Hitler and Göring, somewhat lucid, and wearing those aviator's boots—had climbed alone into a Messerschmitt fighter plane in Bavaria and flown it over the North Sea to the green fields of Scotland, where he bailed out. Kelley later asked Hess why he had abandoned the aircraft in midair: "I had never flown that type of plane before and wasn't sure I could land it," Hess said. "Then, too, I was uncertain of the location of the English fields. I did a good job, though, and struck the ground thirteen feet from where I planned."

The British Home Guard detained and interrogated him. He was on a mission of peace, he explained as he hobbled on an ankle injured during his parachute jump, and he wanted to speak with Douglas Douglas-Hamilton, the thirteenth Duke of Hamilton, a conservative politician who had previously met Hess at the 1936 Olympic Games in Berlin. Hess probably believed that the duke was sympathetic to the German cause. Douglas-Hamilton was summoned and listened in astonishment to the Nazi's wish to meet with King George VI, get Winston Churchill sacked, and negotiate a truce with Britain allowing the two nations to collaborate in the military defeat of the Soviet Union. Britain would retain control over its own empire, Germany would be free to dominate the rest of Europe, and the two powers could coexist, with the Bolshevik menace removed. Hitler had not approved of Hess's mission, and he angrily condemned it in public when he learned of it, even calling Hess insane.

Hess's surprise arrival disrupted Churchill's viewing of a Marx Brothers movie. The prime minister decided that a meeting between Hess and the king was out of the question. "I was taken to a prison somewhere in England where all they did was ask me military questions," Hess later told

Kelley. "I denied any knowledge of military events and demanded my rights as an emissary. The English would then ask me, 'Do you have anything to show that you are an emissary?' I would reply, 'Of course not. I am the Führer's deputy.' They would then ask, 'Did the Führer send you?' I would reply, 'He knows nothing about my mission.' So the English would say, 'Then you are a captured aviator, a prisoner of war. Tell us about the disposition of your troops.'"

During his four years as a British POW, held captive for a time in the Tower of London, Hess saw few people other than military interrogators, low-level government officials, and psychiatrists. The interrogators already knew his background. Hess was born in Alexandria, Egypt, the son of German merchant parents. He was a fellow soldier with Hitler in the 16th Bavarian Regiment during World War I (although the two did not become acquainted until after the war) and trained as a pilot. He had been influenced by antidemocracy agitators while he studied at the University of Munich and became an early member of Hitler's Nazi movement and a co-convict with the future Führer in Landsberg Prison after the failed Munich putsch, where he transcribed Hitler's *Mein Kampf*. As the Nazis gained political power, he devoted all of his energy and attention to the glorification and rise of his leader. Nazi insiders knew him as Hitler's most unwavering supporter.

Hitler made Hess his private secretary and gave him administrative control over much of the party's political apparatus, and he named him Deputy Führer in 1933. A story circulated that Hitler chose Göring as his successor rather than Hess during this period partly because he disapproved of Hess's drab taste in home furnishings. During the mid-1930s Hess's influence grew as he collaborated in many of his government's most repressive actions, including the murder of Nazi Party undesirables during the Night of the Long Knives, the passage of the Nuremberg Laws and other anti-Jewish legislation, the formation of pro-German bunds in other countries, and the persecution of minority groups that led to the Holocaust. Inventing the slogan "Guns before butter" to spur rearmament, Hess often spoke at party rallies, introduced Hitler to massive crowds, and urged the public to support Germany's path toward war. Colorless and devoid of braggadocio, he lacked charisma. Hess so passively deferred to Hitler's judgment that it was rumored that Hitler had even selected Hess's wife for him.

In an examination of Hess soon after his capture, Dr. N. P. Dicks speculated that Hitler had been Hess's father figure until the outbreak of war showed Hess the cruelty and ruthlessness of his Führer. Thereafter Hess transferred his filial feelings to King George VI and hatched his peace plan. Hess's primary psychiatrist in England, J. R. Rees, agreed with this assessment and supervised Hess's care. For sixteen months starting in October 1943, Hess claimed he had no memory of past events, even of his childhood. British doctors subjected him to narco-hypnosis using the anesthesia drug evipan—a procedure intended to make him remember through outside suggestion—but the attempts failed, and Hess refused to submit to similar treatments in the future. Then, starting in February 1945, he said his previous amnesia had been faked. (Kelley later observed that "such fallacious claims are typical" of personalities like Hess's.) Then Hess flipped again and reported that his amnesia had returned in July 1945. He announced to his captors that Jews were hypnotically controlling people around the world, including his own psychiatrists.

Angry and frustrated over the failure of his peace mission, Hess imagined that his British keepers were plotting to kill him. Always a hypochondriac and a longtime believer in the value of natural food, he grew suspicious of all the meals served to him and sometimes switched plates with his jailers to avoid being poisoned. His physicians even sampled his medications while he watched. Nevertheless Hess remained convinced that his life was in danger. He saved food samples, wrapped tightly in paper packets, that he insisted were tainted. His paranoia expanded into delusions of persecution by Russians, Jews, and other enemies.

Twice while in British hands Hess tried to kill himself. In the first attempt in 1941, he called a psychiatrist to his cell, shoved the doctor aside, and bolted through the open door for the stairs. He plunged over the bannister and made a clumsy landing on the surface below, breaking his left thigh in three places. Then in 1945 he jabbed a bread knife into his chest and told his guard, "Look! I have stuck myself in the heart." The dull weapon caused a wound that required only two stitches. Hess said that Jews had left the knife nearby to tempt him. His thinking seemed so disordered that Churchill considered repatriating him to Germany rather than turning him over as an accused war criminal to the International Tribunal in Nuremberg. The Russians, however, insisted on bringing him to trial. A British doctor judged him paranoid and delusional immediately before his departure for Nuremberg.

Colonel Andrus escorted Hess into Nuremberg prison, and within minutes they encountered Göring in a hallway (the meeting was not planned). "Hess immediately recognized Göring, stopped, and threw up his arm in the Nazi salute," Andrus remembered. "Göring looked surprised but did not return the salute, which had been banned in the prison. I told Hess: 'Do not salute like that again! It will not be tolerated. In this prison it is a vulgar gesture.' He stared back at me with his deep-set, black eyes. 'The Nazi salute,' he said evenly, 'is not vulgar.'"

As Andrus explained to the former Deputy Führer the other regulations of the prison, Hess did not respond, stood without expression, and "fixed me with a cold, glassy-eyed stare." At last Hess began speaking with intensity of the efforts of the British to poison his food. Along with everything else in his possession—his personal articles included a pocket watch, key, Luftwaffe watch, and silver wax seal—Hess surrendered the packets of allegedly tainted sugar, chocolate, and crackers, sealed up with red wax, that he had been saving from his British confinement. Andrus immediately decided that the prisoner's mental imbalance was fraudulent. "He was—as I expressed at the time in verbal and written reports—a total fake."

Later meeting with Kelley, Hess complained of cramping stomachaches that had troubled him for years. Yet he refused medicines and said he preferred treatment with herbal and homeopathic remedies and vitamins. (In Germany, Hess had founded an alternative-medicine hospital that bore his name, "where the only requirement was that men practicing there could not be medical doctors," Kelley reported.)

Hess made a strong impression on Kelley during one of their earliest encounters in his cell. He still wore the Luftwaffe uniform and leather flight boots he had donned for his mission to Scotland. Hess said he could remember nothing of his past, not even his birthday or place of birth, but he expressed concern about the disposition of his packets of purportedly poisoned food. (Kelley later took possession of some of these packets and brought them home with him to the United States.) "While his demeanor was strictly formal, polite, he still spooked me.... The faraway look on his face set him apart as someone not quite normal," remembered Dolibois, who accompanied Kelley as translator, although Hess spoke English fluently and understood it perfectly. From what Dolibois had already heard of Hess—his hypochondria, paranoia, affinity for astrologers and quack healers, and supposed inability to remember his Nazi past—he dismissed the prisoner as "a flaky jerk. . . . I thought he was putting on one helluva good act."

The former Deputy Führer's behavior often puzzled others on the jail staff. On one occasion a guard who had collected several Nazi signatures on a US dollar bill approached Hess in his cell to ask for his contribution. "Hess smiled, agreed to sign, took the bill, and went to the back of the cell," Kelley reported. "He then faced the soldier, smiled again, bowed, and proceeded to tear the bill into little fragments which he threw out the window. Hess smiled again to the soldier and said: 'Our German signatures are precious.'"

Kelley worried that Hess, though currently sane and free of psychosis, was "a profound neurotic of the hysterical type" who could suffer a breakdown as the trial drew close. "All through my life I've felt people might kill me," Hess had told the psychiatrist. He might even again attempt suicide, "and it is extremely likely that he will produce some hysterical gestures before he is fully disposed of."

The psychiatrist wrote that it was possible Hess had been faking amnesia so long, he had come to believe in it. He concluded that Hess's amnesia resulted from a tangled combination of hysterical autosuggestion and conscious malingering. As for Hess's overall mental health, Kelley noted that "if one considers the street as sanity and the sidewalk as insanity, then Hess spent the greater part of his time on the curb."

Kelley thought the best course with Hess was to resume the British treatment of narco-hypnosis to restore the prisoner's memory. Instead of evipan, however, Kelley hoped to use one of the pharmaceuticals with which he had successfully treated combat-exhausted soldiers, sodium amytal or sodium pentothal. "We could have found out in two days how much of his amnesia was real and how much was faked simply by giving him an intravenous injection," Kelley later complained. From his work with battle-shocked soldiers, however, Kelley realized that these drugs carried a slight risk of a fatal reaction, "although in more than 1,000 such cases personally treated, I have never seen one." The potential value of narco-hypnosis outweighed its hazards. If Hess's amnesia was genuine, Kelley predicted a full recovery. If Hess was shamming, the absence of recovery would reveal that as well. Kelley asked Andrus to approve the treatment.

Colonel Andrus was wary of drugging Hess. "Hess believes or has pretended that the British attempted to poison him," he wrote to the chief American prosecutor for the upcoming trial, US Supreme Court Justice Robert Jackson. "Treatment with drugs might call forth the same suspicion or allegation against us by him. Undo alarm might be injurious to the patient," not to mention to the prosecution. Jackson, who admitted that he would agree to the treatment for an amnesiac member of his own family if he had one, rejected using it in Hess's case if there was even the smallest possibility it could harm him. Before learning of Jackson's decision, Kelley asked Hess to weigh in on the use of narco-hypnosis to overcome his amnesia. Hess seemed open to the idea until Kelley remarked that it "always worked." Hess then declined the treatment and refused to undergo any form of hypnosis. "For a long time he even objected to our taking blood for a Wassermann [syphilis] test, but on this count we were sustained by the higher authorities," Kelley wrote.

Meanwhile, US Army interrogators tried to batter down Hess's amnesiac shield. They brought in his old professor and mentor in geopolitics, Karl Haushofer, who said, "Don't you remember me, Rudolf? How we used to go for walks together and discuss books?" Hess showed no recognition. They presented him with eight of his former secretaries, at whom Hess stared blankly. They even confronted him again with Göring, whose old grudges against his former rival for Hitler's favor spurred him to try to demolish Hess's real or feigned forgetfulness. Their transcribed conversation revealed Göring's vanity more than any of Hess's lost memories:

GÖRING: Don't you know me? You don't recognize me?

HESS: Not personally, but I remember your name.

GÖRING: But we talked a lot together.

HESS: We were together; that must have been the case, must have been so. As the Deputy of the Führer . . . I must have met the other high personalities like you. I cannot remember anyone, to the best of my will.

GÖRING: Listen, Hess, I was the Supreme Commander of the Luftwaffe, and you flew to England in one of my planes. Don't you remember that I was Supreme Commander of the Luftwaffe? First I was a Field Marshal and later a Reichsmarschall, don't you remember that?

HESS: No.

GÖRING: Don't you remember that I was made a Reichsmarschall at a meeting of the Reichstag while you were present? You don't remember that?

HESS: No.

GÖRING: Do you remember that the Führer, at a meeting of the Reichstag, announced . . . that if something happened to him, that I would be his successor, and if something happened to me, you were to be my successor? Don't you remember that?

HESS: No . . .

GÖRING: Do you remember that you moved to the Wilhelmstrasse, into a palace which really belonged to me, as the Prime Minister of Prussia, but I enabled you to live there?

HESS: I don't know.

Göring, who Kelley believed "wanted to preserve the fiction that the Nazi Party was made up of strong men," eventually gave up in disgust, declaring that Hess was "completely crazy." He told Dolibois, "We knew all along that Hess wasn't really normal. His flight to England made that very obvious." Göring claimed to be most disturbed by Hess's inability to remember the glory years of the Nazi regime, but Dolibois suspected that the Reichsmarschall feared going into the upcoming trial without a mentally competent, high-ranking comrade at his side.

● • ●

Down the prison hallway, Streicher had established cordial relations with the incognito Jewish translator Howard Triest, whom he characterized as "the perfect Nordic." Gathering information for the tribunal on crimes against religious groups in Germany, Triest sat calmly in Streicher's cell, taking notes, as the prisoner fulminated against Jews. "I can smell a Jew a mile away," he told Triest. He strongly suspected that Kelley was Jewish. "I can see it in their face, their eyes, their hair, from the way they walk, even the way they sit. And I know you are a pure Aryan." While asserting that he did not dislike individual Jews and even praising a Jewish doctor who had previously treated him, Streicher maintained that his anti-Semitic publishing had improved the world by spreading word of the dangers of allowing races to mix. When he had some papers requiring translation into English and didn't trust Kelley or any other possible Jew to handle them, he gave them to Triest. "Here," Streicher said, "you do the translating. You're a good German."

Alfred Rosenberg remained reserved and distant, rarely straying from unreal theorizing on the rise of Nazism and German anti-Semitism in his discussions with the prison staff. When speaking of these topics, his sleepy face came alive. Rosenberg loved talking about his book *Myth of the Twentieth Century*, which Kelley had examined and judged "unbelievably obscure and hazy." Although the philosopher acknowledged that European people had interbred so much that their racial distinctions had mostly disappeared, he held that Jews—Asiatic and Arabic in origin, he believed—had maintained racial purity because of their religious traditions. As a separate race, they could degrade what homogeneity remained among the Nordic people by marriage with them. Criminalizing intermarriage let Germans take the first step toward shedding their racial impurities. Americans of Nordic stock, Rosenberg argued, could protect their nation from racial contamination only by exiling different racial groups to distant geographical reservations. Germany could have adopted such measures if only outsiders hadn't interfered, leaving the Nazis with extermination as the best option. He told Kelley that his plan to elevate Nordic people by subjecting other groups to slave labor and death could have produced dramatic effects within three or four generations.

On a visit to Rosenberg's cell with interpreter Dolibois, Kelley began questioning the prisoner about one of his published works. Rosenberg, who knew that Dolibois was a Roman Catholic, firmly closed the book in the interpreter's hands and refused to discuss it in Dolibois's presence. "This young officer is working for his country," Rosenberg told Kelley. "He is a good soldier and also a good Catholic, and I do not wish to change his way of life. If he were ever to read this book, he would renounce the Church immediately." (Dolibois later characterized such talks with Rosenberg as "stupid discussions.")

Meanwhile Ribbentrop was failing to support himself even as well as Rosenberg. Prison staffers reported him as self-pitying, withdrawn, passive, frustrated, and depressed. He looked decrepit for a fifty-two-year-old man, slept poorly, was plagued by headaches, and continued to keep a messy cell that many visitors considered symbolic of a distraught mind. Other prisoners weren't surprised. Schacht referred to Ribbentrop's "extraordinary stupidity" and his lack of manners and cordiality. Kelley judged Ribbentrop a suicide risk, although he speculated on "a good possibility, however, that once he is sentenced and the burden of depression removed, his whole arrogance may return. If this occurs, he should face his sentence with considerable fortitude. It is possible, however, that he will break at the end."

As an escape from his troubles, Baldur von Schirach, the former Reich Youth Leader and governor-general of Vienna, had begun writing poetry.

One sample he penned for the psychiatrist's approval, titled *"Dem Tod"* ("To Death"), signaled his apprehensions about the future:

> *Your dark eye I have so often seen,*
> *That you have become like an old friend to me.*
> *When the bullets scourged, you stood at the mark,*
> *And looked at me. To the left and right fell*
> *My neighbor. Yet you turned away.*
> *I greeted each grave later, all alone.*
> *When the bombs burst from the sky,*
> *You drew to me the house's silent guest.*
> *Yet you have not done your work on me.*
> *I know, my friend, that your eye is on me.*

Visitors to Schirach's cell thought he appeared gaunt and haunted, a look perhaps befitting a prison poet. He confided to Kelley something that he did not want to tell anybody else, even lawyers working on his defense. "He had intervened to save several Jews from concentration camp at the risk of his neck, because he had been forbidden to make a single exception," Kelley wrote after an interview with the prisoner on October 27. "But in view of the great mass of murdered victims, he did not want to lower himself to seek clemency because of a few people he had spared, making a pitiful spectacle of defense like some of the others."

Life in Nuremberg prison went on for the captives. They traipsed to the exercise yard wearing a ragtag assortment of clothing that they had brought with them or scrounged from the staff. Göring sported yellow top boots that the guards coveted and offered packs of cigarettes for, Rosenberg walked the grounds in overalls, and Schirach had somehow acquired a military camouflage jacket. Although Streicher was shunned and Schacht avoided his fellow captives, the rest gathered together in small groups to share bits of news, wonder about their families, complain, and speculate on their futures. Göring always tried to keep their hopes high and encouraged them to remember their status as German leaders. All they had done wrong, he assured them, was to be defeated by the Allies. Göring's job as booster was difficult, because, as Kelley believed, nearly all of the Nazi prisoners suffered from depression.

Colonel Andrus wondered what they dreamed about at night. It didn't surprise him that many of the prisoners dreamed of him. "I was to them a symbol of what they were facing," Andrus speculated. "There is always a tendency among people confined in prison to hate their custodians. The custodian is to them the embodiment of the retribution they have to face for the evil they have done." The prison's pastors, however, embodied something more benevolent to the prisoners, at least among those who attended services, which did not include Rosenberg, Streicher, and Hess. Both the Protestant chaplain, Henry Gerecke, and the Catholic priest, Sixtus O'Connor, were popular among the inmates, and they poked fun at each other about the dastardliness of their followers. "At least we Catholics are responsible for only six of these criminals," Father O'Connor told the Reverend Gerecke. "You Lutherans have fifteen chalked up against you." Gerecke declared his conviction that the top Nazis were not "a breed apart." He found them similar to other people, though poisoned by prejudice and greed.

Göring, who often hastened to chapel services to get a good seat, was among the prisoners Gerecke saw most often. Seated near the altar and its simple ornaments, with an organ wheezing nearby, Göring sang hymns louder than anyone else. "He almost drowned out the organ," Andrus remembered. He may have valued chapel only for its social opportunities, though, because he was a lapsed Lutheran, he informed Gerecke.

Hans Frank, the balding and dour former governor of Nazi-occupied Poland who had taken part in the Nazis' "Beer Hall" Putsch of 1923, had become something of a model prisoner under the influence of Father O'Connor, who baptized the Nazi in his cell on October 25. A lawyer, once Hitler's personal attorney, who devolved into a brutal administrator responsible for the deaths of millions of Jews and Poles, Frank had tried to erase Polish and Jewish culture in his region. He now made a point of thanking prison staff for their attention, appeared emotionally composed, and professed finding relief in his Catholic faith after what he described as betrayal by Hitler when the Führer took away many of his political titles at the start of the war. (Frank had left the Church years earlier when he joined the Nazi Party.) "He feels essentially guilty, but since rejoining the Church has developed a serenity of approach as a protection," Kelley observed. "It was obvious that Frank, to himself, was a great tragic figure, a representative of God, who had sold his soul and was but purchasing it back at the cost of his life," Kelley noted, and Frank's sanctimonious attitude—what the doctor called his "beatific tranquility"—left a bad taste in the psychiatrist's mouth.

Kelley formed a more positive impression of Admiral Karl Dönitz, a friendly though somewhat distant figure who often exhibited a sharp sense of humor and showed no trace of depression. With graying hair and mischievous eyes, Dönitz made good-natured jokes about the inconveniences of prison life, from the food to the spartan and seatless toilet in his cell. In a psychiatric report to Andrus, Kelley called Dönitz "one of the most integrated personalities of the whole setup" and a man blessed with "creative capacity, imagination, good inner life." Intent on improving his English, he read poetry and impressed Kelley with his intelligence. "It is my opinion that Hitler used good judgment in selecting Dönitz as his successor. Dönitz is undoubtedly a leader of great stature and a most competent man," the psychiatrist asserted.

Some of the prisoners readied themselves for the war crimes indictments they suspected were coming, while others wrote correspondence and read books. The prison librarian commented on the high level of the reading material the Nazis requested. Many wanted works by Goethe. Hess was one of the most ferocious readers in the months to come, plowing through two books a day. Schacht read through several volumes of Beethoven's letters.

The psychiatrist also spent time in other wings of the Nuremberg jail building, which housed lower-ranking suspected war criminals and people the Allies were holding as possibly useful witnesses in forthcoming trials. There he frequently spoke with Karl Brandt, formerly Hitler's personal physician and director of the Nazi euthanasia program for mentally and physically disabled citizens. Brandt worked under the direction of Leonardo Conti, who headed the medical programs of the Third Reich. In the final days of the war Hitler had ordered Brandt's execution because the doctor had abandoned Berlin, against orders, with his family. In a notebook Kelley kept of his prison interviews, he jotted down about Brandt: "Authorize death of those people who according to human consideration are incurable. . . . 'Existence without living.'" Kelley came home from Nuremberg with a set of X-ray images of Hitler's skull, taken to help treat a sinus infection in 1944, and Brandt may have guided Kelley to them.

● • ●

Kelley was assembling an archive of Nazi psychological profiles. Collecting ran in his blood, especially from his McGlashan ancestors. He surely knew how deeply the acquisitive and categorizing impulses influenced his family. His grandfather McGlashan had collected twenty thousand specimens of butterflies, gassing them and displaying their bodies in cases he had designed and patented. He could watch them at his leisure, stare at them as closely as he wanted. Their mysteries were frozen, no longer impenetrable. Each butterfly contained a world. Decades later, McGlashan's grandson found the specimens of Nuremberg just as engrossing.

He soon received permission from Andrus to begin administering the Rorschach inkblot test to the Nazis. Kelley knew the test would have little value in court, and in fact the International Tribunal never heard the results. He turned to the inkblots because he knew the assessment well and grabbed at the chance it offered to scrutinize this historic collection of men. The Rorschach assessment worked in a way similar to the techniques of general semantics, by using storytelling to enter the minds of subjects and examine their emotions, attitudes, and personality.

Even in the unnatural setting of a prison, the Rorschach opened a door to fundamental areas of the personality that might otherwise resist scrutiny. Kelley called the Rorschach "the most useful single technique in a mental examination." If the Rorschach results of the Nuremberg prisoners showed patterns or similarities, Kelley would be close to discovering essential features of the Nazi mind. Like stage magic, the test depended on the skill and interpretive artistry of the examiner.

Kelley gave the Rorschach tests to the prisoners in their cells, usually with each Nazi sitting on his bed. He preferred to work with an interpreter alongside, even if the prisoner was fluent in English. Kelley had trained both Dolibois and Triest in scoring Rorschach records to avoid errors in translation. Bored with the monotony of their prison lives, most (but not all) of the Nazi inmates cooperated with the testing, and "many of them commented favorably upon the testing program," Kelley wrote. Occasionally Kelley had to return to an inmate to clarify a response, which was made possible by "one of the advantages of having your subject always on hand," a special privilege of the psychiatrist who worked in a prison. He planned to repeat the Rorschach tests about a month later.

The prisoners of course interpreted the cards in various ways. Card VII, which shows an empty white area surrounded by a semicircle of connected gray and black blots, prompted a remarkable variety of responses. Karl Dönitz said, "This is very nice. Faces of two little girls looking at one another. They have the expression of being curious to learn the secrets of life. They may be dancing together, too." Robert Ley looked at the same card and described it as, "Cloud formations. Thunder clouds." Joachim von Ribbentrop gazed at the picture for ten seconds and remained silent.

The Rorschach testing especially intrigued Göring, who carried on an animated dialogue during the examination, laughing, snapping his fingers, commenting on the difficulty of interpreting some of the cards, and thoroughly enjoying the process and attention. Göring "expressed regret that the Luftwaffe had not had available such excellent testing techniques," Kelley wrote in a preliminary report on the examinations. The lack of testing tools was the Nazis' own fault, Kelley observed. "Perhaps if the Nazis had not so whole-heartedly curtailed the function of the intelligentsia of

Germany, these testing techniques which were for a large part developed in Germany would have been readily obtained."

Kelley's interpretation of Göring's results focused on several distinctive features. Most of Göring's responses included what Kelley called "kinesthetic determinants": the frequent use of human or animal movement in his descriptions of the images. To Kelley's surprise, this characteristic revealed Göring's introverted personality, not the extreme extroversion the psychiatrist expected to find. Kelley also noted Göring's fondness for the word "fantastic" in his Rorschach responses, which often described witches, prehistoric animals, ghosts, and whirling dervishes. The psychiatrist found a narcissistic preoccupation with himself in Göring's descriptions of such figures as "a spook with a fat stomach" on Card IX. Just as significantly, Göring accepted the inkblot pictures as whole situations instead of as details of larger scenes. "There is little attempt at critical analysis, either of the details themselves or of their relation to the general concept of which they may be part," Kelley observed. "The situation is dealt with in the grand manner and Göring passes on to the next. . . . [T]his is his natural way of behaving."

All told, Göring's Rorschach results gave Kelley "a picture of a person of considerable intellectual endowment, highly imaginative, given to an expansive, aggressive, phantasy life, with strong ambition and drive to quickly subjugate the world as he finds it to his own pattern of thinking, a pattern which deviates from the common world of experience." Kelley opined that Göring's fantasy-dominated ambition might be running amok, and that the Nazi was "a man [who] still must be reckoned with." A non-psychiatrist might have inferred the same things from Göring's past behavior, and one has to wonder how much Kelley's knowledge of his favorite prisoner's notorious acts influenced his Rorschach interpretation of the Reichsmarschall.

Testing Hess presented special obstacles because the prisoner, despite his outward cooperation, tried to control his responses, "not knowing how revealing even the most banal answer could be," Kelley wrote. Hess sat on the cot in his cell between Kelley and Dolibois. Together they ran through what Kelley called "a very careful Rorschach, recording every remark." Hess frequently reacted to the cards by laughing, shaking his head, and calling them senseless.

To Andrus and the Nuremberg prosecution team, Kelley justified giving the Rorschach examinations by characterizing them as ways to predict whether any of the prisoners might suffer a nervous breakdown during the forthcoming trial and to help determine that all of the examined Nazis were sane, including Ley, Hess, and Streicher, whose mental competence was in doubt. Hess displayed "an introverted, shy, withdrawn personality who, suspicious of everything about him, projected upon his environment concepts developing within himself." Streicher exhibited a paranoid personality. But both Hess and Streicher "showed no evidence of overt psychosis and must be considered legally sane."

All in all, the tests showed that "although many of [the prisoners] were not what we would call ideally normal, none of them were sufficiently [deviant] to require custodial care according to the laws of our country," Kelley wrote. "In most cases they might be considered eccentric or fanatic." This included Ley, whose Rorschach record Kelley found the most interesting by far. The psychiatrist advanced a diagnosis of brain damage in Ley's frontal lobe, even though the inmate's physical exams had turned up no evidence of neurological problems. In the Rorschach testing, however, Ley had misnamed colors, offered confused descriptions, and given responses that lacked context and sense. Kelley speculated that Ley had injured his frontal lobes during the plane crash in World War I that left him unconscious and stuttering.

Kelley had started to think beyond the trial and his eventual return to the United States, to a special disposition he had in mind for his Nazi Rorschach results. These went beyond the medical function Kelley had used to justify the test to the Nuremberg authorities. He wrote in a memo to Andrus that he wanted to submit the test results to Rorschach experts across the globe "to produce the clearest possible picture of these individuals, the [greatest] group of criminals the human race has ever known." Kelley was convinced that the test results had historical value. They offered possible answers to the questions of why German citizens followed these men on a disastrous and destructive course and what motivated unusual but still normal people who knew exactly what they were doing as they ruthlessly ran a regime that persecuted and killed millions.

On October 8 Kelley administered to Göring the Thematic Apperception Test (TAT), a psychological examination designed to shed light on the subject's worldview, self-image, and relationships with other people. Kelley subjected only a few of the prisoners to this evaluation. He showed Göring a set of twenty cards illustrating men and women in simple settings, or showed scenes with no people in them at all. Göring's task was to spend five minutes on each card telling stories that narrated what was happening in the image, what led up to it, what the characters were thinking and feeling, and how the events concluded.

Göring spun this tale from the second TAT card Kelley showed him:

> There is a man, a farmer, deeply devoted to his work and a lover of nature. His fate is revolving around two women, one pregnant woman leaning against a tree, undoubtedly a woman from the country, and the other one, a young girl mentally more alert and from the city. The man is impressed by the younger girl. A conflict arises in the man's mind, but due to the expected child and his devotion to the soil, he will return to his wife, and the young girl will go back to the city and go her own way.

Kelley's interpretation of this story is unknown. A layperson might speculate that Göring was subconsciously speaking of his own two wives and the claims each had made on his loyalty.

After looking at the ninth card, Göring said: "These are men who rest in the grass after hard work. A boy looks on and studies the faces of these men. He thinks that he would not want to lead a life like theirs. He looks at their faces and studies their types so that he never may be forced to lead that kind of hard and monotonous life." Again, an amateur could find this story laden with fear and determination. It expresses a commitment to rejecting an unpleasant fate to which others have ignorantly surrendered. Perhaps it says something of Göring's determination to lead Germany away from what he considered the demeaning course it had followed in the 1920s.

● • ●

On October 6 the Nuremberg prison staff was hit with the news that an inmate being held in one of the other wings had taken his own life despite all of Andrus's measures to prevent suicides. He was Leonardo Conti, MD, one of Hitler's chief medical advisors and Karl Brandt's superior. As state secretary of health and head of national hygiene, his unsavory responsibilities included launching the so-called euthanasia programs designed to kill the aged and disabled and sponsoring experiments on humans in concentration camps. Among the experiments were studies of the effects of poisons, bacteria, and freezing of captives, as well as other horrific tests. Kelley had once interviewed him in his cell, describing the Nazi physician as a "shy little man" who mildly protested that he was forced into euthanasia work.

The Swiss-born Conti, an early Nazi Party member, had asphyxiated himself: he wrapped his neck with a shirt sleeve, tied the other end of the shirt to the bars of his cell window, and dropped from a chair. Kelley rushed to the scene that morning to pronounce Conti dead. The Nazi physician left behind a note detailing the remorse he felt for lying to Allied interrogators, although he declared, "I have never been a coward. I wanted so much to see my family again." Andrus kept Conti's suicide out of the newspapers, ordered all chairs removed from prisoners' cells at night, and scheduled more frequent searches of their belongings.

During the same period Kelley saw a decline in Robert Ley's mental stability. In their interviews Kelley watched Ley swing from excitement to depression, and Ley talked so much, stammering throughout, that "it was a real chore to sit and listen to him for an hour at a time," Kelley said. The psychiatrist attributed some of this behavior to the brain damage he had diagnosed, but Ley's fellow inmates, subjected to his rants and despair during exercise times, could not understand it. They "did not know that the inhibitory centers of his brain had ceased to function—that he quite literally had no judgment but only spontaneous emotional responses—as a vital, tough, excitable, intellectually gifted individual," Kelley noted. "He was generally disliked."

Ley spoke of his anguish over being viewed as a political gangster and facing trial as a criminal. His defense was that he had committed no crimes, declared no wars, planned wondrous social reforms while administering the German Labor Front, and acted only to advance his country. Putting him and his colleagues on trial would only spread Hitler's ideology and cast the Allies as enemies of the new Germany to come.

● • ●

During the third week of October the prosecutors of the International Tribunal completed the indictments against the top twenty-two Nazis. A group that included Kelley, Andrus, British representative Airey Neave, a translator, and a chaplain assembled to present the official documents to the prisoners, who were now formally defendants. The Germans had been charged with a variety of offenses against international law, some of them new to jurisprudence, including membership in such criminal organizations as the SS and the Gestapo, conspiracy to wage aggressive war, crimes against peace through the waging of aggressive war, involvement in war crimes, and committing crimes against humanity. As the group made the rounds of the cells to deliver the indictments to the prisoners, Kelley took notes on their responses.

Göring was first. Through the window in his cell door they saw him sitting on his cot, his clothes hanging loosely, perhaps recently awakened from a nap and not expecting a visit, with a crooked frown on his face. He lurched to his feet when the door opened; his mouth gave a startled twitch. The boot heels of the visitors crunched on the stone floor as the group surged forward, but only Andrus, the translator, and Neave could fit inside the cell. The others peered around them or over their shoulders. Göring's table still held the photos of Emmy and Edda, along with a stack of books. The prisoner did not initially meet the stares of the Allied representatives, but he soon faced Neave and focused his eyes—the beady and shiny eyes that had disconcerted so many of his political opponents—on him.

"Hermann Wilhelm Göring?" Neave said. The Reichsmarschall must have sensed something important was happening. "*Jawohl*," he answered. Neave explained that he was serving on Göring the indictment from the tribunal. Grimacing, Göring accepted the indictment and listened to Neave's explanation of his right to legal counsel. He did not even glance at the documents, but seemed interested in Neave's British service dress uniform. Kelley wrote down Göring's next words: "So it has come." Neave observed that "the words seemed very ordinary, not like the end of twelve years of absolute power. In that featureless cell, they did not sound dramatic. It was as if Göring ignored the presence of an audience and was thinking aloud."

Informed that he could choose his own lawyer or pick one from a list that the tribunal had drawn up, Göring said, "I do not know any lawyers. I have nothing to do with them." It was hardly surprising—he had lived above the law for so long. When Neave recommended finding counsel, Göring expressed skepticism that any lawyer could help him. "It all seems pretty hopeless to me," he said with quiet firmness. "I must read this indictment very carefully, but I do not see how it can have any basis in law." With twenty-one prisoners to go, Andrus began to lose patience. Neave repeated his advice to engage an attorney. "Lawyers!" Göring said. "They will be of no use in this trial. What is required is a good interpreter. I want my own interpreter." Andrus smirked; he remembered Göring's requests for special treatment at Mondorf. The prisoner would have no personal interpreter. Neave bade the prisoner good-bye; Göring bowed. The group backed out of the cell and the door slammed shut.

Hess received the group in his usual manner. He rose as the assembly filled his cell and "stared straight through me with his burning eyes," Neave remembered. "His glance at my British uniform was unfriendly. . . . Then he lifted up one manacled hand in an odd gesture of derision. He bared his teeth in a mischievous grin." Neave began his formal introduction, "Rudolf Hess?"

The prisoner made no response, so Neave placed the indictment in Hess's hand, now free of the manacles. He mentioned the prisoner's right to legal representation. Hess's reply alarmed the group: "Can I defend myself?" Told he could, Hess said, "Then I wish to do so." The prisoner then grimaced with pain as one of his stomach attacks struck him. Hess dropped to his cot and rocked his body until the pain faded. Then he again arose and asked if he would face justice in the company of his Nazi colleagues. When Neave said yes, Hess responded, "I do not like to be tried with Göring." He returned to an Edgar Wallace novel he had been reading, at which point the meeting concluded.

Next was Ribbentrop, and then the rest. Ribbentrop complained that he didn't know any lawyers. News of the indictment shook Rosenberg. Keitel, wearing slippers, tried to click his heels. Jodl fretted over his choice of an attorney. Walther Funk, the former minister of economics who suffered from urinary pain, wept and did not rise from his bed when the group entered his cell. "Be a man, Funk!" Andrus shouted at him. Ley "became violently disturbed, orating and ranting, maintaining his innocence, and swearing that he would never face trial against such charges," Kelley observed. Only Dönitz appeared to expect the indictment, and he calmly offered the name of the lawyer he wanted to defend him.

By the end of October 1945 the start of the trial was only four weeks off. An alteration in the prison's staffing was imminent. At the age of twenty-six, John Dolibois had decided that he'd already spent more than enough time in contact and conversation with Nazis. He wanted a change, and he told Colonel Andrus of his wish to leave the prison and return to his military station in Oberursel, Germany. Andrus consented to relieve him of his duties as welfare officer and assistant to Kelley, and Dolibois gladly served his remaining months in Europe as a motor pool officer. He would return to Nuremberg a few times to attend the trial, only as a spectator. Later, Dolibois regretted leaving Nuremberg. "I could kick myself for not staying longer, getting more involved, making history," he declared.

His replacement was on his way and would arrive during the final week of October. He, like Kelley, had a plan to advance himself professionally by exploiting his time at the prison, and he already had a scheme to transform the position into something completely new: a job as prison psychologist. He knew little about Kelley and his work at Nuremberg, and he hadn't the slightest foreboding that his presence in the prison would put him in conflict with the senior-ranking psychiatrist.

6

INTERLOPER

On October 20, the day the Allied prosecutors delivered to the tribunal its indictments against the prisoners, a stocky man with wire-framed glasses and a demeanor of persistent seriousness arrived at the Nuremberg jail along with a new shipment of Nazi prisoners intended for later interrogation and trial. He was Gustave Mark Gilbert, age thirty-four, a native of New York State whose parents, both Jewish immigrants from Austria, had made sure he grew up bilingual in German and English. He had earned a PhD in psychology from Columbia in 1939 and had served as a first lieutenant during the war, treating what he called "misfit soldiers." After Germany's surrender he worked as a military intelligence officer. "I had seen the collapse of the Nazi war machine and the evidence of Nazi barbarism in places like Dachau concentration camp before V-E Day," he wrote. Gilbert's professional interests in Nuremberg were similar to Kelley's: "I had naturally been interested in finding out what made human beings join the Nazi movement and do the things they did."

So far his pursuit of that interest had yielded little of value. When asked why they had committed criminal acts as Nazis, the Germans of low military rank and civilian status whom he had previously interrogated spoke only of following orders and having no power to make a difference. Gilbert hoped that their military and political leaders held captive in Nuremberg could provide more illuminating information. When he arrived at the jail as Dolibois's replacement as morale officer and interpreter, he reported to

Colonel Andrus and immediately asked for more responsibility. He hoped to take advantage of this opportunity to become what he called a "participant observer," to study and judge the prisoners as a human being, not as a detached spectator, a role he viewed as consistent with his responsibilities as a psychologist. "Psychology, above all, is applying human understanding in a scientific manner. . . . The only profession I have ever encountered which separates the role of a human being from his professional activity," he declared, "was the role of the SS man." Gilbert rarely mentioned that his academic study had been in social psychology, and he knew little of the field's clinical applications. Still, why waste his training on duties limited to translation and other mundane affairs?

He inquired of Andrus whether a psychologist might be useful in the Nuremberg prison. The commandant seemed not to have been aware of Gilbert's academic training; in Dolobois's words, "with all due respect, Andrus would not have known a psychologist from a bootmaker." Nevertheless he soon approved Gilbert's request. Gilbert went to work as prison psychologist—an appointment that was never made official—under Kelley's nominal direction, although the two served in different administrative units, and Kelley's authority was due to rank only. They shared an office.

Gilbert met Dolibois in the officers' mess in the prison, where Dolibois noticed that the newcomer "could hardly wait to get to work on the Nazis." And Gilbert already knew what he wanted to do with his Nazi research. "Right from the beginning, he made no secret of the fact that he would write a book," Dolibois recalled. "His actions toward that end became somewhat annoying—the constant search for quotable items and literal 'news.'" Dolibois agreed to remain at the jail for a few days to help Gilbert adjust to his new work, which had no official description or classification, and to show him around. "I suppose I could have identified myself as 'prison psychologist,'" Dolibois said, "by virtue of analyzing what I learned interpreting for Dr. Kelley and snooping around the prison to chat with the inmates." But he didn't regard his role (or Gilbert's) as particularly important.

As Dolibois had, Gilbert bore the difficult responsibility of keeping up the prisoners' morale through visits and conversation. He joined the select club of Kelley, others on the medical staff, and the security staff in having unrestricted access to the top Nazis. To those duties Gilbert added working with Kelley and any visiting experts in examining the minds of the prisoners. And like Kelley, he had to grapple with the conflict between his duties as a psychologist, who might receive confidences from the prisoners, and as a member of the military, with the job of monitoring and reporting on the captives. Right away Gilbert understood that his military responsibilities were paramount. "There was just one limitation on this," he explained years later when he appeared as a witness at the trial of Adolf Eichmann in Israel, "and that was that, as the Nazis ridiculed and cursed each other behind one another's backs, they would sometimes ask me to please not say anything about it to the others until the trial was over. I kept that confidence." Gilbert long denied, however, that he worked to strengthen the cases of the tribunal's prosecution team. He served "neither at the behest of the defense counsel, nor the prosecution. I was on the prison staff and, of course, as objective as it is humanly possible to be in these circumstances," he said.

Gilbert went about his prison business with energy and efficiency. His fluency in German led several of the captives to welcome his conversation. He would not take notes in the defendants' presence, but immediately afterward wrote at length in his personal diary about each of his meetings with the Nazis, including long direct quotations. The prisoners were ignorant of his transcriptions of their conversations. His ultimate aim, like Kelley's, was to augment "the trial itself as a vehicle for examining the Nazi system and the men who made it." Gilbert also admitted that he made notes of his conversations with the prisoners "because some of it was so incredible that I felt I had to have a record of these people because my colleagues would never believe me." He hoped first to become familiar to the prisoners and collect their personal responses to the indictments they had received. After that, Gilbert wanted to give them a new battery of psychological tests that could shed light on their psyches.

He did not immediately disclose to the prisoners that he was Jewish. He wanted to test the claim of Nazi ideologues that they could immediately recognize Jews. "Not a single one could," he said, including Streicher, who now had failed twice—with Gilbert and Triest—and whose faith in the infallibility of his racial instincts also led him to erroneously identify some of the judges selected for the tribunal as Jews. When Gilbert eventually let the Germans know he was Jewish, most professed not to care and responded "that they never had anything against Jews personally, that this was all silly ideological nonsense, and that some of their best friends had been Jews." Only Streicher and Rosenberg showed some nervousness after Gilbert's revelation.

The new arrival, one year older than Kelley, threatened the psychiatrist. Despite the use Kelley had found for Dolibois, who had rudimentary training in psychology, he did not want a PhD psychologist at his side. Kelley had already completed all of the psychological testing of the prisoners that he needed. He thought repeated testing would yield less accurate results than had the initial round and strongly believed his expertise in giving and interpreting the tests exceeded Gilbert's. Kelley also suspected that Gilbert lacked his own professional authority and would have trouble developing rapport with the prisoners. Eventually, however, Kelley accepted Andrus's appointment of the psychologist because he saw in Gilbert "a young man whose career might be helped by being there," Dukie later remembered. "Doug often did this sort of thing."

● • ●

Together Kelley and Gilbert visited Robert Ley in cell no. 11 on October 23. The prisoner was pacing and distraught. He lamented his inability to defend himself against crimes of which he had no knowledge and repeated his claim that he and Hitler had only worked in the best interests of their country. Then Ley stood against the wall and stretched out his arms like a man pinned to a cross. He begged to be shot on the spot rather than face a trial as a common criminal. Kelley wrote an update of Ley's psychiatric condition for Andrus and prosecution team member William Donovan. He described the inmate as excitable, emotionally unstable, and depressed. There were no signs of psychosis, however. Despite the frontal lobe damage that Kelley suspected Ley had suffered, he declared Ley legally competent, sane, and responsible for his own actions. Kelley observed that Ley had busied himself preparing his upcoming court defense and, despite the psychiatrist's earlier fears that Ley might attempt to take his own life, he now "presented no evidence of suicidal intention."

The next evening, at around 8:15 p.m., a guard raised an alarm in the cell corridor. Ley had secretly fashioned a noose from the hem of a towel and the zipper of his jacket, soaked the knots in water to make them tight, and tied the end of this makeshift rope around the pipe of his toilet. He then stuffed his mouth with his own underwear to prevent himself from crying out and lowered himself onto the toilet. Leaning forward, he asphyxiated himself. Since the toilet area was concealed from the guard's view, and Ley was short enough to remain unseen when seated on the commode, it took several minutes for the sentry to notice that anything was amiss. Ley was found unconscious, slumped on the toilet. Dolibois, in his final hours as a prison staffer, was among the first to rush into the cell. "The lifeless body of the onetime leader of the Reichsarbeitdienst sat on the small toilet seat, his legs stretched out rigidly, face beet-red, eyes bulging," he recalled. Dr. Pflücker quickly arrived, but his attempts to revive the prisoner with artificial respiration failed, and fifty-five-year-old Ley was pronounced dead at 8:35 p.m. The prisoners in nearby cells remained asleep or feigned slumber.

"Such a death is both slow and painful," Kelley wrote. "It demonstrated Ley's violent will to die." Some among the Americans found humor in the event. When Drexel Sprecher, a member of the prosecution team, arrived at work the next morning, he encountered a procession of translators marching through the offices in mock solemnity. "They were trying to hum a funeral march and doing a bad job of it," he remembered. In private conversation, Andrus intimated how deeply Ley's suicide had stung him. "What a way to die," he told a member of the prosecution team, "strangled with his own loincloth on his dung heap."

The suicide continued to be a great embarrassment to Andrus and the Americans. Andrus immediately tightened security in the jail. Previously one guard had been assigned to observe every four adjacent cells of the top Nazis, ensuring monitoring of each prisoner at half-minute intervals. Now he set a guard outside each of the cells, around the clock. The guards stood at the peepholes continuously. A suicide like Ley's "could not be allowed to happen again," Andrus observed. In addition, after a package arrived for one of the trial witnesses containing a suicide kit including a vial of cyanide with needles and syringe, the prison stopped accepting all packages of clothing and food intended for the prisoners.

The top Nazi captives received the news of Ley's death individually in their cells on October 29. "It's just as well," Göring told Kelley. "I had my doubts about how he would behave at the trial. He would probably have made a spectacle of himself and would have tried to make a fantastic, bombastic speech. It is a good thing he got himself out of the way."

Kelley's reaction to Ley's death equally lacked empathy. He called the suicide a fortunate turn of events because Ley "could never have successfully been tried. . . . He was too far gone for that. So Robert Ley did the world a favor when he hung [sic] himself—did me personally a particular favor, because his was the one brain that I suspected would have organic damage."

And Kelley was after that brain, which, tongue-in-cheek, the psychiatrist said Ley had "kindly made . . . available for post mortem examination." Hoping that a study of the organ would confirm his Rorschach-inspired diagnosis of organic damage and shed light on Ley's deterioration, Kelley found an army colleague, pathologist Najeeb Klan, who agreed to remove the dead man's brain in the Nuremberg morgue. Kelley then sent it on a strange journey. A GI bearing a square wooden case, labeled "spices," soon appeared at Army Post Office 124. The soldier wanted it shipped registered airmail to the Office of the Surgeon General in Washington, DC. The postal workers thought that a very expensive way to send a box of spices. "Robert Ley's brain," the soldier tersely confided, as quoted in an article published by a US military newspaper, a clip of which Kelley sent to Webb Haymaker, a neuropathologist working at the Army Institute of Pathology.

Haymaker was the recipient of the disguised package. His examination of the brain showed a "long-standing degenerative process of the frontal lobes" in the region that Kelley had predicted was injured, a finding that microscopic study confirmed. The pathologist's report on Ley's brain exhilarated Kelley. "I shall be everlastingly grateful to Robert Ley for giving it to me," he said.

Kelley's rejoicing was premature. In 1947 Haymaker sent specimens of Ley's brain to pathologists at the Langley Porter Clinic in San Francisco for another opinion. The examination there produced no clear findings of organic damage. Haymaker passed the news to Kelley in a letter that December: Ley's brain abnormalities "were of a lesser scope than we had at first believed. Personally, I think maybe we had better let the whole thing lie buried, as the degree of change [in the brain] could be subject to a difference of opinion."

● • ●

Gilbert had learned how to administer the Rorschach test at Columbia but was not much interested in the assessment. He understood its value, however, and introduced the inkblots to the Nazis Kelley had not yet tested and retested others. Gilbert's repeat of the Rorschach test with Göring arrived at a different interpretation than Kelley's. Gilbert determined that Göring's results "betrayed the qualitative mediocrity of his intellect." Although the Reichsmarschall described plenty of human and animal activity in the inkblots, Gilbert found a lack of originality in Göring's responses that "revealed his superficial and pedestrian realism, rather than brilliantly creative intelligence." In other words, Göring was smart and cynical but no genius. Gilbert also labeled Göring depressed and depraved.

Two Rorschach evaluators, two very different interpretations: Why? Kelley read imagination, power, and boldness into Göring's responses, probably because the psychiatrist had formed an unusual bond with him during their months of almost daily contact. In such qualities as self-confidence, stubbornness, dedication to work, and focus on one's self, the two men were alike. They both were high climbers in their fields and adept manipulators of others. Without knowing it, Kelley identified with Göring. Gilbert felt none of that rapport and viewed his subject more coolly.

Gilbert retested Hess with the Rorschach as well, finding a shortage of emotion, empathy, and maturity in Hess's meager responses. The prisoner never saw living creatures of any kind in the blots, described little motion, and perceived "lifeless details" in the images. "All of this bespeaks impotence and lack of vitality in his mental resources," Gilbert concluded, and he noted Hess's "severely constricted personality with a most tenuous grip on reality."

The psychologist embarked on another series of tests of the prisoners using a German translation of the Wechsler-Bellevue Adult IQ tool, a battery of memory, verbal, mathematical, and conceptual examinations. These tests gave the Nazis such tasks as assembling jigsaw puzzles, finding the missing parts of pictures, and swapping numerical digits for symbols. Göring eagerly accepted the challenge, "behaving like a bright and egotistical schoolboy who was anxious to show off before the teacher," Gilbert remembered. When Göring failed to recall a nine-digit series of numbers after sailing through previous memory challenges, he struck his cot with his fist and cried, "Ach, come on, give me another one—I can do it!" When the Reichsmarschall succeeded on the retry, to Gilbert's visible amazement, Göring "could hardly contain himself for pride and joy." Göring praised American psychological examinations as "much better than the stuff our psychologists were fooling around with." (Keitel similarly complained to Gilbert of the "silly nonsense" German military psychologists resorted to during evaluations of Wehrmacht members; he had eliminated their testing after his own son flunked an officer candidate evaluation.) Like Kelley, Gilbert quickly learned that appealing to the prisoner's vanity and craving to impress bought Göring's hard work and enthusiasm.

Using a scoring formula that took account of the gradual failing of brain function that he thought likely came with aging, Gilbert came up with IQ results that placed many of the top Nazis well above average in mental acuity. The banker Schacht topped the group with a score of 143, followed by Artur Seyss-Inquart at 141, Göring and Dönitz at 138, Papen at 134, Frank and Schirach at 130, Ribbentrop at 129, Rosenberg at 127, Hess at about 120, and Streicher trailing the pack at 106. Predictably, Göring was disappointed that he had not emerged on top. Streicher's lackluster performance surprised no one.

Gilbert tried some other psychological assessments, including a test that asked the prisoners to form a coherent comic strip out of images on a series of cards (which none of the Nazis could figure out), the Thematic Apperception Test (to which Hess responded with variations on "I can't tell" and "It only makes me sleepy looking at it"), and exercises in making change for imaginary purchases of postage stamps, which befuddled Streicher and, amazingly, Schacht. "Any financial wizard who is good at arithmetic is probably a swindler," Schacht said, brushing off his blunders. Gilbert ultimately concluded that successful people in any realm of activity—including the management of a fascist regime—were likely to possess above-average intelligence. Although he thought these men were all smart enough to have known better than to authorize war crimes and atrocities, Gilbert also knew that "IQ dictates nothing but the mere intellectual efficiency of the mind, and has nothing to do with character or morals, nor the various other considerations that go into an evaluation of personality." Not impressed by the high IQ scores, Andrus judged the Nazis not even particularly smart: "From what I've seen of them as intellects and characters, I wouldn't let one of these supermen be a buck sergeant in my outfit," he said.

Although Kelley, a major, outranked Gilbert, a lieutenant, the latter roamed the prison, examined the defendants, and managed his tasks largely independently of the psychiatrist. They sometimes did not share their data and appear to have rarely consulted with one another. At some point, however, Kelley broached with Gilbert the possibility of taking advantage of their unique access to the prisoners to collaborate on a book about the workings of the Nazi mind. The prestige associated with introducing the world to this information would be immense, both men believed, and they agreed to share the glory in a single volume. The partnership would not go as they planned.

Differences in personality and approach made some prisoners prefer Gilbert to Kelley and vice versa. Gilbert's Jewishness set some of the Nazis on edge. Others preferred his more demonstrative helpfulness and energetic personality. After his IQ examination with Gilbert, Hans Fritzsche confided to the psychologist his certainty that he would end up on the gallows. "It wouldn't be too bad if one could feel he was dying an honorable death, as a sacrifice to protect Germany's honor," Fritzsche said. "But to die in shame, with the contempt of the whole world on one's head—*pfin teufel!* It's bitter!" Gilbert recorded that he listened without replying, noticing the graying of the Nazi's hair. Franz von Papen, the former German vice chancellor, disliked both Kelley and Gilbert and complained of "gentlemen who called themselves psychiatrists [and psychologists]; . . . few of them gave the impression of having any genuine scientific qualifications."

Göring, on the other hand, greatly preferred Kelley's straightforward professionalism to what he perceived as Gilbert's manipulative hostility. To many of his interrogators and members of the prison staff he expressed his dissatisfaction with the legality and morality of the International Tribunal, although he eventually chose a defense attorney, Otto Stahmer, a former German judge who professed certainty that Göring was completely innocent of all charges. To Kelley, however, Göring confessed other concerns. Five days after Kelley's last letter-carrying mission to her, Göring's wife Emmy had been arrested at her residence in Veldenstein, suspected of complicity in her husband's art thefts. She was confined to a civilian internee camp at Straubling, near Regensburg. His daughter Edda was separated from her mother and relocated with her nanny to a residence in Neuhaus, managed by Catholic nuns, with about ten miles separating them and no contact allowed. Emmy referred to this occurrence as "one of the darkest days of my life. I was forced to be separated from my child without even knowing where she would be sleeping that night." On her way to Straubling, Emmy popped a peppermint candy into her mouth, causing the American officers in charge of her to panic. They thought she had taken poison.

The fracture of the family outraged Göring, who again raised the promise that his family would be well cared for. A separation of mother and daughter was not good care, the Reichsmarschall insisted. Separation from her daughter tormented Emmy, and seven weeks passed before she had any news of Edda. Kelley reported this breaking of promises to Andrus, and his intervention worked. Göring's anxiety over his family was damaging "his mental and physical health," Andrus wrote to the commanding general of the Third US Army, which had detained Emmy. Weeks later, on November 24, the director of Emmy's camp walked into her room and announced, "Edda is here." They shed tears of happiness at their reunion, but Edda was now her mother's cell mate. A former Luftwaffe officer scrounged up a straw mattress for the girl. Göring was grateful and gladdened when he heard the news. He had somehow managed to get one of his letters smuggled out of the Nuremberg prison and into Emmy's hands, secretly passed to her by the inmate worker who brought her meals. However he managed it, it was a sign, entirely missed by his guards, that Nuremberg's prison walls were permeable.

Göring continued to share reminiscences with Kelley, including franker admissions about his relationships with Hitler and the other defendants. When Hitler had named Göring his official successor during the early years of the war, "I was pleased for myself, though it was only what I expected," Göring said. "But I was furious that Hitler should name that nincompoop Hess to be my successor. I told Hitler so, too, and made a big fuss." Göring paused in his story to lean forward on his cot, set his hands on his knees, and face Kelley. "Do you know what Hitler said?" he continued. "He said, 'Now, Hermann, be sensible. Rudolf has always been loyal, a hard worker. I must reward him, so I give him this public recognition. But, Hermann, when you become Führer of the Reich—poof! You can throw Hess out and appoint your own successor.'" Göring's eyes glowed at the end of the anecdote, his excitement about the prospect of exercising power rekindling despite his incarceration.

During another conversation, Göring gave Kelley an account of his decision to join the Nazi Party after the end of World War I. Göring claimed to have carefully examined the numerous right-wing groups then sprouting up in Germany and allied himself with the National Socialists because of their appeal to military veterans who were dissatisfied with the terms of the Treaty of Versailles. With those veterans among its membership, the Nazi Party controlled enough bodies to mount a putsch, which it did in Munich in 1923. The anti-Semitism of the Nazis struck Göring as useful bait for potential adherents with gripes more emotionally rooted than the mere imposition of an offensive peace treaty. "You see, I was right," Göring told Kelley. "The people flocked to us, the old soldiers swore by us—and I became head of the nation." Then the Reichsmarschall seemed to remember that his assumption of the Führership never really happened and nearly cost him his life. "Too late you would say?" he went on. "But perhaps not. Anyway, I made it."

It was a declaration worthy of a McGlashan, and it must have rung in Kelley's ears. Göring appeared to suggest that his rise to the top of the Nazi heap, a promised promotion that he expected to be realized after Hitler's suicide but that never occurred, still might have future value to him despite his certainty that the Allies would eventually sentence him to death. "You know I shall hang. I am ready. But I am determined to go down in German history as a great man. If I cannot convince the court, I shall at least convince the German people that all I did was done for the Greater German Reich. In fifty or sixty years there will be statues of Hermann Göring all over Germany. Little statues, maybe, but one in every German home."

The prospect of death did not trouble him, he explained. As a military commander who ordered countless men to their deaths in battle, he always accepted the possibility of facing the enemy on the field. Now that the Allies were upon him, Göring planned to "dish it out," to do as much damage as he could on his way down. "I do not recognize the trial's legal jurisdiction, but since they have the power to enforce their will, I am prepared," he boasted, "to tell the truth and face anything that may come." His approach, he insisted, was practical, the consequence of his preparation and experience as a soldier and wager of war.

Was it really practical, though, for a man who considered himself a revered leader to make his neck available for the hangman's noose? Göring seemed to feel uncertain about the propriety of his current imprisonment. When he confessed to Kelley his fear that fate could thwart the best planning of men who tried to control their future, Kelley called the admission "the only time I ever saw Goering realize that he alone could not face and perhaps conquer the entire world."

Certainly the Nazi decried his imprisonment and forthcoming trial as an injustice possible only as part of the Allies' spoils of victory, but he was much happier plopped on his cot behind bars than contemplating the prospect of a still-living Hitler occupying a neighboring cell. "It was not cowardly of Hitler to commit suicide," Göring maintained. "After all, he was chief of the German state. It would be absolutely unthinkable to me to have Hitler sitting in a cell like this waiting trial as a war criminal before a foreign tribunal. Though he hated me at the end, he was for me, after all, a symbol of Germany. . . . I would still rather suffer any consequence than to have Hitler alive as a prisoner before a foreign court." Göring already regarded suicide as a logical choice when honor and national dignity came under attack.

Kelley had concluded that Göring's denials that he was a homosexual—a rumor that Streicher's accusations had given new life in 1940—were plausible. "He naturally denied any perversions, and psychiatric observation and independent conversations with other prisoners who had known Göring well seemed to bear him out," Kelley observed. What, then, accounted for the sexual energy that Göring projected, and his absorption in his own appearance, wardrobe, and physique? "He probably sublimated his sex drive into hard work, which gave him his amazing ability to keep going eighteen hours a day," Kelley wrote. "Undoubtedly ambition took precedence over 'amour.' However, his home life was a happy one, and the devotion between Göring and his second wife seemed satisfying to both."

Yet Kelley learned that personal considerations sometimes trumped Göring's loyalty to Hitler and Nazi policy. One day Göring told Kelley and translator Triest about his efforts to assist the family of the Jewish nurse who had helped him recover from his wounds after the Munich putsch of 1923. Years after he had benefited from her healing attention, he pushed ahead the paperwork that enabled her family to move to England and escape Nazi persecution. Göring made it clear that this was an individual decision, one that made no difference in his overall opinion of Jews or their role in German society.

To Kelley, Göring's confidences confirmed that the Nazi leader craved attention and needed it to lift his spirits. He admired Göring's willingness to take responsibility for his actions and the energy with which he defended himself, but Kelley never lost sight of the Reichsmarschall's worst traits. "Göring hasn't changed a bit," he told journalists months later. "He is still the same swaggering, vain, conceited braggart he always was. He has made up his mind he's going to be killed anyway, so he's very anxious to be considered the number one Nazi, a curious kind of compensation."

● • ●

Hess still vacillated between amnesia and lucidity. On October 30, 1945, he claimed not to remember the contents of the food packets he had so carefully conveyed to Nuremberg from England. "He readily admitted that the writing on each package was in his handwriting and identified various documents, but seemed content to merely glance at them, identify his handwriting, and hand them back," Kelley wrote. "His only explanation for the time-consuming wrapping and sealing job which he had performed was: 'It certainly seems a good way to pass the time.'" A couple of weeks later, authorities tried to spark his memory by showing him newsreels of him and his codefendants attending Nazi events and rallies. Handcuffed to two guards and placed in a part of the impromptu prison screening room where lights would reveal the emotions that played across his face, Hess was observed by chief prosecutor Jackson, special assistant Donovan, and interrogator Colonel John Amen, along with Kelley and another American psychiatrist brought in to consult. The movies began with a welling underscore of Wagnerian music. Hess leaned forward and rose as, on the screen, he bellowed a speech and ended it with thunderous *Sieg Heil*s, to the Führer's visible satisfaction. Hess sat and calmed down during clips of Göring, Ley, and Streicher. The lights rose, and Hess let a minute go by before speaking. "I recognize Hitler and Göring," he said. "I recognize the others, but only because I heard their names mentioned and have seen their names on cell blocks in this jail." He said he did not recall attending any of the filmed events. "I must have been there because obviously I was there. But I don't remember."

Kelley had not been watching the screen. He stared at Hess's hands, where the prisoner unconsciously revealed his tension "by a tightening of the hands, readily visible to anyone looking for this symptom," the psychiatrist wrote. "He certainly recognized some of the scenes shown in that picture, although his denial was complete. He realized his inner tension and perhaps recognized its manifestation in the tightening of his fingers."

As the opening of the tribunal neared, the prosecution worried about the damage a disordered Hess could do if he gave testimony that focused attention on the symptoms of his mental problems and was unable to assist in his own defense. To confirm that Hess was fit to stand trial, the Allies convened a pair of experts to review Kelley's psychiatric reports and examine the prisoner for themselves. The experts were Nolan D. C. Lewis, a noted psychoanalyst who directed the New York Psychiatric Institute and edited the *Journal of Nervous and Mental Disease and Psychoanalytic Review*, and Donald Ewen Cameron, a Scottish-born psychiatrist then teaching at McGill University in Montreal and later notorious for performing mind-control and behavior modification research for the CIA.

Lewis and Cameron spent many hours with Hess, bringing in Gilbert as a translator. They took evidence from Kelley, Andrus, and others who had passed time with Hess. In an eight-page report, they agreed with Kelley's determination that Hess was sane and not psychotic. The prisoner's amnesia, they found, was inconsistent. Even when he claimed no memory of meeting certain people or reading particular books, he could recall some events and ideas connected with those people and books, and he inexplicably had access to other memories from the same times and places. The psychiatrists' examination suggested that "a part of the memory loss is simulated and it is probable that the hysterical or unconscious part is rather superficial." Hess's reflexive replies of "I don't know" and "I don't remember" to so many questions were likely "originally developed consciously as a protective measure during a period of stress . . . [and] it has become habitual and has therefore become unconscious in part."

In other words, Hess had pretended to forget past events to make his life easier during his early captivity in England and had continued not remembering them—at times unconsciously and habitually—during his weeks at Nuremberg. Although he initially faked his amnesia, at least some of it might no longer be feigned. And Hess felt no motivation at this moment to bring his memory back. Still unstable and anxious, "he obviously wanted to retain the amnesia," the psychiatrists determined. In interviews with the press, Kelley compared Hess's memory with an atrophied limb that had lost its muscle tone, a body of water dotted with islands of forgetfulness, and an ice-choked ocean in which opening "the right channels [makes] these 'icebergs' melt away."

The doctors continued whacking away at Hess. In all, three Soviet, one French, three English, and one additional American psychiatrist scrutinized the mysterious prisoner. The British team found him sane enough to understand the charges against him and the proceedings of the tribunal. His amnesia, however, was a handicap to working with his attorney and his assembly of a defense. A Russian and French panel concurred, finding Hess "not insane in the strict sense of the word." Kelley continued to insist that Hess was truly amnesiac, but that much of his forgetfulness resulted from "a large voluntary block." He predicted that the amnesia would disappear on its own, during or after the trial. Given the partly intentional aspect of Hess's disability, the tribunal bore the responsibility of determining whether he should stand trial. Kelley believed the best course was to try Hess and then ask for psychiatric opinion on whether a death sentence, if in the offing, was justifiable for someone in Hess's state of mind.

Although Andrus permitted the repeated psychiatric exams of Hess, he did not want the other Nazi defendants to face the same medical scrutiny. In advance of one psychiatrist's arrival to see Hess, Andrus advised that "he not be granted permission to conduct examinations of other prisoners. All other prisoners are in obviously good mental health and special examinations are not desirable as such examinations suggest an undue interest in the prisoner's mental condition, a situation which should be avoided." In his own determination, unapologetically lacking in medical basis, Andrus—who scornfully noted that Hess once forcefully replied, "No," instead of "I don't remember," when asked if he had studied astrology—judged Hess an incorrigible fraud. "I was able to see through him and he knew it," the commandant wrote. "I told him more than once that it wasn't a very manly thing to do." Hess would respond with silence or by shaking his head and repeating that he remembered nothing.

Hess himself took an interest in medical diagnosis, although his approach was unorthodox. One day, out of the blue, he asked Kelley, "Do you know about the studies of the size of the pupil of the eye?" Kelley replied that he was familiar with the pupil's expansion and contraction to admit more or less light into the eye.

"He interrupted me a bit scornfully, since I obviously did not know what he was driving at," Kelley recalled. Hess said, "I mean the science of diagnosis based on the size and shape of the pupil. Haven't you heard of it?" Kelley had not. "It really hasn't been accepted by doctors in Germany, either," Hess continued, "but a scientist—he wasn't a medical man—and I studied it a long time. By the change in the pupil, you can not only tell what is wrong with anyone, you can tell where his illness is."

When Kelley expressed skepticism, Hess's manner immediately chilled. "I quite realize that an American medical man would not believe this," he said, "but it is quite true. Even I can do it a little." Hess then stared into Kelley's eyes like a Nazi Svengali, "and for a moment I was afraid he would label me with some disease," Kelley admitted. "Apparently all he discovered was disbelief, for he indicated that the interview was at an end."

Kelley faced a medical conundrum of a different sort in the face-scarred and square-jawed Ernst Kaltenbrunner, the highest-ranking SS officer in captivity. Kaltenbrunner, whose dangerous persona had crumbled into spells of depression and fits of weeping in prison, was deeply frightened by the prospect of the trial. The psychiatrist regarded him as potentially suicidal, a "crybaby who is convinced that 'everyone picks on me.' . . . The

hardness of character which marked him as an executioner had been replaced by this soft, sobbing personality who eagerly sought reassurance as
to his future." Kelley recognized Kaltenbrunner's reaction to stress as one
common to aggressive people, who show toughness when things go well
but crack under personal setbacks.

On November 17 Kaltenbrunner suddenly complained of a terrible
headache and listlessness. Kelley kept him under observation until the next
day, when the prisoner's symptoms worsened to a stiff neck and pain when
he moved his head. Suspecting spinal meningitis or some other contagious
disease, which would have required a quarantine of all the prisoners and a
delay of the trial, Kelley sent Kaltenbrunner to the hospital, where a spinal puncture revealed that a blood vessel had spontaneously ruptured in
his brain. Blood was seeping into the fluid surrounding the brain and the
spinal column. Although the condition is potentially fatal, Kelley believed
Kaltenbrunner had skirted disaster and only needed several weeks of rest.
His mind was unaffected, although his anxiety over the forthcoming trial
might have caused the hemorrhage by pushing up his blood pressure. As
a result, Kaltenbrunner missed the opening days of the trial. Andrus later
remembered hearing that "Kaltenbrunner, the man who had terrified millions, had nearly died of fright." Kaltenbrunner suffered a second hemorrhage a few days after he returned to prison but quickly recovered from it.
Kelley again found him psychiatrically sound, but warned prison authorities that another attack "may well prove fatal. It is impossible, of course, to
predict if or when such a hemorrhage might occur."

Sometime that autumn, Kelley and translator Howard Triest traveled
together to Erlangen, a town less than ten miles from the prison. They
stopped at a university library and stumbled upon a hoard of books that Allied authorities had seized in denazification sweeps. Many of the books had
been written by the top Nazi prisoners, and Kelley and Triest pulled out
samples for their own collections. After they returned to Nuremberg, their
army truck loaded with Nazi volumes, both men sought the autographs of
the imprisoned authors on the title pages of the volumes and later returned
to America with the books. Kelley never explained why he collected the

Nazi books, but they surely provided a conversation opener when he met with the prisoners, and he likely gained insight into the authors' minds through their response to the requests for autographs. Besides, Kelley remained a collector of exotic species—in his case, Nazis. Speaking sixty-five years later, Triest described his own collection as "a souvenir of my time at Nuremberg and [a] tangible reminder of a difficult personal period. It was something I could show my friends and family when I returned to America to say that I really had been there. I had been with the leaders who had killed my people. For me it was about remembrance—remembrance of Nuremberg. I never thought back then that the trial would attract the interest and have the status that it does today."

From those who trusted Kelley, the psychiatrist gleaned strategic information that he considered important enough to pass along to the tribunal's prosecutors. He sent a series of memos to William Donovan revealing changes in the health of the defendants and their psychiatric states, but probably the most important tidbits for Donovan were the doctor's disclosures about the prisoners' defense strategies. In a memo on November 11, for example, Kelley wrote about Göring's intention to call as a tribunal witness Lord Halifax (E. F. L. Wood), a conservative British politician who had met Göring eight years earlier when the Englishman favored appeasing Germany in its expansion into Austria and Czechoslovakia. Halifax was Britain's foreign secretary when Nazi troops bloodlessly crossed the border into those countries, and he held the job of ambassador to the United States as the trial of the Nazi leaders approached.

Göring told Kelley that he had sent a letter to Halifax in 1936, a prewar peace overture. "He states that Halifax received this letter, which could have prevented the war," Kelley informed Donovan. In the same memo, Kelley detailed Schirach's admission of guilt as a Nazi Party member, his acceptance of responsibility for developing the Nazi youth movement, and his acknowledgment that he signed persecuting decrees against the Jews of Austria. Jodl, Kelley reported, pointed out that the Russians committed atrocities of their own on the Eastern Front and planned to defend himself by asserting his duty to follow military orders. He strenuously denied enriching himself with looted civilian property. Frank, on the other hand, appeared to welcome his prosecution and "has become immersed in the belief that the accused are to be subject to a divine punishment," Kelley wrote. "He has become extremely enthusiastic in feeling that the entire group has been weak in not shooting Hitler at least two years ago." The Nazi leaders, Frank declared, worked "in league with the devil" and now faced punishment from God "in a form more devastating than any punishment man has yet devised." From their conversations, Kelley knew that Frank criticized his fellow prisoners for trying to save their necks instead of accepting God's judgment. "He seems to be at about the point where he might be willing to place the blame on other 'weaker' members of the accused group," Kelley wrote to Donovan. "He has stated twice that if they plead not guilty he at least will plead guilty."

Kelley's communication with Donovan inspired another missive to the prosecution's special assistant, from someone only identified by the initials J. E. S.:

> When Major Kelley dictated his report to you today, he talked with me some about the defendants, and I thought the following bits would be of interest to you even though the major did not include them in his statement.
>
> It has become increasingly clear that the defendants are shaping up into a homogeneous group, all accepting Göring as their leader, with each of these good minds contributing to the general defense. This, says the major, will make the case much more difficult.

The writer went on to tell Donovan that Kelley believed the Nazis did not fear the prosecution's plans to convict them through the massive written documentation of their misdeeds. "A document, whereas it convicts one or two beyond a doubt, does equally well in exonerating the rest, in their opinion. . . . Dönitz made the remark: 'The Americans are preparing my defense for me—typical Yankee humor!'" the memo reported.

Kelley followed his first communication to Donovan on defense strategy with another a few days later. This time he wrote that Göring planned to cite a book he had published in 1933, *Aufbau Einer Nation* (*Building a Nation*), in his own defense. The book, Göring claimed, supported his defense that he formed the Gestapo only to fight communists and that the police organization held to that purpose while Göring controlled it. In the Reichsmarschall's estimation, the book also demonstrated that Hitler's rise was a revolution that "while slightly bloody was nowhere near as ruthless as similar Russian or French revolutions." A scribbled notation on the memo reads, "Can we get this?" (To translator Triest, Göring claimed to have written *Aufbau Einer Nation* in a single weekend.)

Acting more as a physician, on November 17 Kelley gave Donovan his medical opinion that the unforgiving and backless benches for the defendants in the Nuremberg courtroom "will prove a trying hardship if the trial is of much duration at all" for the older members of the Nazi leadership. He was especially concerned for Keitel, Dönitz, Funk, Göring, and former Nazi commissar in the Netherlands Seyss-Inquart, whose rheumatism would cause them suffering and who "after many days might well collapse." Kelley recommended better seating with backs and seat cushions, with which most of the other seats in the courtroom were already furnished. Photos of the courtroom in use show that the defendants did receive a backrest, although cushions aren't visible.

In the end, Donovan had little time left to make significant use of Kelley's information. He and Justice Jackson had begun clashing over the best approach to prosecuting the Nazis, with Donovan envisioning swaying the judges through skillful examination and cross-examination of courtroom witnesses, and Jackson wanting to rely on the piles of incriminating documentation that the Allies had discovered. Donovan was also skeptical about charging the defendants, especially the military officers, with membership in organizations that had committed crimes. After a series of prosecutorial quarrels, Donovan left the team and was on his way home by the end of November.

Back in Chattanooga, Dukie awaited her husband's return with her sister, Leora Brooke, and their parents. A newspaper photo showed her and Leora—whose husband served in the European theater as an army combat engineer—standing in their parents' living room. Dukie held an ornate silver teapot, an accessory for the home she hoped she and Kelley would soon share. Wearing a tailored jacked and knee-length pleated skirt, she looked far more stylish than her older and taller sister. She had not seen Kelley for three years and communicated with him only through letters and occasional reports from his colleagues in the army who had returned to the States.

Near the fifth anniversary of their wedding, Dukie was interviewed by a Chattanooga journalist about her husband's activities at Nuremberg. She was encouraged to comment on what it was like to be married to a psychiatrist. "Sometimes they know what you're thinking," she said, "when you don't want them to." With his marriage on hold, Kelley was applying that skill to the Nazi defendants.

7

THE PALACE
OF JUSTICE

The trial approached. All of the top Nazi prisoners had engaged lawyers and were preparing their defenses. The German attorneys "were legally and politically respected," Colonel Andrus acknowledged, but their
trips into and out of the jail greatly increased the prisoners' contacts with
the outside world, as well as opportunities for smuggling. The suicides of
Conti and Ley still weighed heavily on the commandant. He instituted a
new round of security measures designed to keep the prison secure and all
tools of self-destruction out of the hands of the inmates. Anytime a prisoner and his lawyer exchanged a document, a guard inspected it. Guards
removed from the prisoners' cells anything potentially dangerous—shoelaces, razor blades, and neckties—and even confiscated eyeglasses at night.
The Nazis underwent searches when they returned to their cells and when
they bathed, and guards turned their cells upside down while the prisoners
were out.

"And still we were finding contraband," Andrus lamented. A raid of General Jodl's cell yielded a nail concealed in a tobacco pouch, a six-inch-long
piece of wire, nine tablets made of unknown ingredients, and lengths of
rag. Keitel had hoarded a supply of aspirin, a chunk of sheet metal, a stash
of belladonna tablets (useful in treating digestive disorders), a screw, and

two nails, and he hid the shard of a metal heel-rim in his wallet. Questioned about the origin of the latter item, which had not come from his own shoe, Keitel with some pride would only say, "I have had it for a long time."

In Ribbentrop's messy cell, guards discovered nine unrecognizable pills (four hidden inside socks) and a sharp, two-inch-long piece of metal. Even the good-humored Dönitz had a forbidden collection: shoelaces, string, a screw, and a bobby pin. "We had no idea what he was planning to do with them," Andrus wrote. Schacht was surreptitiously holding onto ten paper clips. Sauckel hid a broken spoon. Elsewhere in the cell block guards found shards of broken glass, loose nails, and a fragment of a razor blade. Only the cells of Göring and Hess yielded no secrets.

Protective security intensified elsewhere on the Palace of Justice grounds. A German employee of the courtroom library, the young niece of Field Marshall Erwin Rommel, had warned of a possible attempt by "werewolf" Nazis to blow up the building—defendants, prosecutors, judges, evidence, and all—to prevent the trial. "There is so much that they do not want exposed and they are so bitter," Christine Rommel said. Allied authorities knew of similar threats and rumors. In response, five tanks equipped with 75 mm guns assembled outside the building in a show of force. Soldiers took positions along the perimeter of the structure and in the hallways, on the roof, and at entrances. Sentries demanded official entry passes from everyone coming or going, including the judges.

Room 600, the second-story courtroom for this first-of-its-kind international tribunal, had been transformed. It no longer lay in shambles. A set of new high-intensity ceiling lights shone brightly, allowing photographers to record the scene without using disruptive flashes. Old walls had vanished to create a bigger public space. The room was quite large, able to accommodate more than five hundred people, but all of the judicial action was concentrated in a small area at its south end.

The defendants' dock was next to the main entrance of the courtroom, with two long rows of seating for the Nazi leaders. Directly in front of the defendants were chairs for their defense attorneys. The judges' seats faced them all, filling a bench beneath four large windows with green curtains drawn to keep out sunlight. The flags of the four Allied powers stood behind them. Translators given the difficult job of instantly interpreting the proceedings into German, English, Russian, and French would occupy glass booths along the wall to the right of the judges. Wires connecting the translators with speakers' microphones and headphone outlets spread across the floor and would trip up participants for the duration of the trial. Nearest the judges were the court reporters. (Defendant Schacht soon observed these tribunal staff, many of them chewing gum, and fell into the "optical confusion" of imagining they were chewing on words.) Areas for the prosecution teams, segregated by nationality, clustered around four tables in front of a press section. Nearby was the podium from which prosecuting and defense attorneys would address the court. Press members covering the trial had the finest seating of all, upholstered and widely spaced chairs, and there was a booth in the back of the courtroom reserved for newsreel cameras. All spectators had to sit in the more spacious north end of the courtroom or in the balcony above. One chair, dwarfed by the judges' dais and the large seating areas for spectators and tribunal staff, stood by itself like an insignificant piece of furniture. It was for witnesses. But it was very important, as Göring would eventually remind everyone.

More than thirteen hundred people contributed to the International Tribunal through the delegations of the four Allied powers and the teams of the defense attorneys, and over two hundred journalists were accredited to report on the trial for radio stations and publications around the world. Cafeteria workers at the Palace of Justice served about fifteen hundred lunches to trial participants each day.

In their cells the prisoners typically wore a motley assortment of garments, but Andrus wanted these men when in court to represent the careful care and attention they had received as inmates of his jail. "We do not want them to be in a condition where they might inspire pity," he said. He made sure their uniforms and suits were cleaned and pressed daily during the trial. He ordered tailors to produce new suits for several prisoners. More discriminating than most of his colleagues, Schacht complained that the prison-supplied suits were sewn from "very inferior material."

Andrus directed a somber rehearsal on the day preceding the start of the trial. He led the inmates the several hundred yards from the prison, through the covered passageway that he had ordered built as protection from outside attack, up the elevator, and into the courtroom. He ordered the sentries to remove the prisoners' handcuffs and lined up the deposed Nazi officials like schoolboy performers in the order in which they would fill the double rows of the defendants' dock. The order matched the listing of the defendants in the tribunal's indictment: Göring first, followed by Hess, Ribbentrop, Keitel, Rosenberg, Frank, Frick, Streicher, and the rest.

On the morning that the tribunal opened, November 20, 1945, guards distributed suits, belts, ties, and the eyeglasses that the prisoners had surrendered the previous night. Amid tension that Andrus noticed caused "an unusual stir in the prison," the inmates dressed themselves. Naturally no mirrors that could be broken and turned into daggers graced any of the cells, so Göring devised a clever procedure for the all-important examination of his own appearance. He used the backdrop of his lawyer's dark suit behind the glass partition that separated the two men as a surface that reflected his image. Göring scrutinized himself in the glass, giving special attention to his hair.

Judged by later security standards, the courtroom was remarkably free of weapons. Andrus feared the prospect of a prisoner grabbing a gun from a guard and doing something disastrous. The commandant made certain he was one of only two people in the room who would have a firearm while the tribunal was in session. Beneath his jacket, he kept a pistol and shoulder holster. Another prison officer wore a handgun. The many guards who escorted prisoners and watched over the courtroom proceedings carried white billy clubs, weapons threatening enough "to dissuade any prisoner if he got out of hand, or to prevent any spectator from making an attack," Andrus hoped.

Göring entered first. He wore his pearl-gray, brass-buttoned Luftwaffe uniform, stripped of all insignia and symbols of rank, and he appeared energized to retake the world stage. His months of confinement, which had cured him of his drug addiction and obesity while giving him time to reflect on his past and plan his defense, had left him mentally sharper than he had been in the final months of the war. But spectators also detected a softness within his undeniable strength that seemed disturbing. His garb draped his leaner physique more than clothed him. His face—pale, lined, yet strangely youthful—had the impassive and frightening look of a mannequin's. At times he seemed to appraise the visitors in the gallery, looking for an early sign of the mark he would leave on history. *New Yorker* reporter Rebecca West, describing Göring's blend of calculation, mean humor, and femininity, noted that he resembled madams of brothels with "the professional mask of geniality still hard on their faces though they stand relaxed in leisure, their fat cats rubbing against their spread skirts. . . . He was the only one of all these defendants who, if he had the chance, would have walked out of the Palace of Justice and taken over Germany again, and turned it into the stage for the enactment of the private fantasy which had brought him to the dock." He took the most prominent seat, at the far left of the front row in the defendants' box.

Hess entered the courtroom with a desultory shamble, appearing almost indifferent to the court's proceedings. His strange manner fascinated observers. With a face that reporter John Dos Passos thought "has fallen away till it is nothing but a pinched nose and hollow eyes and chinless mouth," he looked up into the corners of the ceiling like a trapped animal and sometimes gave an odd, anxious laugh. To West, he appeared "plainly mad; so plainly that it seemed shameful that he should be tried. His skin was ashen, and he had that odd faculty, peculiar to lunatics, of falling into strained positions which no normal person could maintain for more than a few minutes. . . . He looked as if his mind had no surface, as if every part of it had been blasted away except the depth where the nightmares live." In this first public appearance since he had piloted his Messerschmidt from Germany years earlier, he bore scarcely any trace of the Nazi rally speaker, pulsing with fanatical assurance, whom people remembered. Hess did, however, occasionally shed his sickly reserve to share brief comments with his seated neighbors, Göring and Ribbentrop, who was wearing sunglasses.

Other defendants made lasting impressions upon entering the court-room. Dos Passos wrote that Streicher looked like "a horrible cartoon of a Foxy Grandpa," and Rebecca West judged the young Schirach as "like a woman in a way not common among men who looked like women. It was as if a neat and mousy governess sat there, not pretty, but with never a hair out of place." Frick, who in his checkered jacket was the only defendant not wearing a military uniform or banker-gray suit, stood out like a circus per-former. There was a slapstick air to some of the entrances, as Fritzsche had to shove past other defendants who mistakenly emerged in the courtroom ahead of him. Schacht looked like an angry walrus. While they waited for the proceedings to start, a few of the prisoners read newspapers. Taken together, the Nazis looked dull and deflated, as if sheer ordinariness had driven them to lead the world into war. Guards in white helmets stood behind them at attention. Only Kaltenbrunner, still convalescing from his cerebral hemorrhage, was missing. He would be absent for the first fifteen days of the trial, while his attorney represented his interests.

Once the judges called the court into session at 10:00 a.m., the tribu-nal's first business was to present the indictment against the defendants, a recitation that took prosecutors hours to complete. For most of this time, amid the heat of the packed room and the smell of fresh paint, the Nazis chatted with one another and watched with boredom—they had already read the indictment—although Göring beamed when the indictment ac-cused him of the theft of a memorable bit of French property: eighty-seven million bottles of champagne. He also made faces, shook his head, and commented to others throughout the first day. Hess passed much of this time engrossed in a novel titled *Der Loisl, the Story of a Girl* and broke his concentration only to smile when prosecutors first spoke Hitler's name. Later, during a court recess, he grimaced from one of his periodic attacks of abdominal cramps. He gripped his stomach, rocked in his seat, and brought his head down to the rail of the dock. Kelley approached him but gave him no medicine, advising Hess to keep rocking. He soon recovered and sat up straight, appearing "alternately politely interested and bored" with the proceedings.

Few of his colleagues took an interest in Hess's brief display of agony. Schacht, one of the few defendants paying close attention to the proceedings, laughed aloud when prosecutors mentioned the charge of conspiracy. Some of the Nazis entertained themselves by flipping from one translation to another on the headphones with which they were supplied. The defendants ate lunch together in the courtroom during a break while everyone else fled the closeness of the space. It was the first group meeting during their captivity. A magnanimous Göring distributed cigarettes to his codefendants. The men discussed the events of the morning as they ate, but they all snubbed Streicher, refusing to include him in the chatter. He tried to engage Gilbert in small talk, noting that of the twelve or thirteen previous times he had been put on trial for crimes, one had been in this very courtroom. Ribbentrop tried to explain the atomic bombs dropped on Japan to Hess, who said he knew nothing about them and complained of what he believed was the illegality of the tribunal. The former foreign minister later suffered an attack of vertigo and tinnitus in the courtroom, collapsed, was given a sedative, and returned to the defendants' dock. Sometime during the day Hess leaned over to Göring and whispered, "You'll see, this apparition will vanish, and you will be Führer of Germany within a month." Göring remarked to Gilbert that now he was sure Hess was crazy. By the end of the day most of them were fatigued, and many were snoring in their cells by 7:00 p.m.

The next day the defendants had to make their pleas in response to the charges in the indictments. Göring, the first to rise, began to read a lengthy statement justifying the Nazi government and defending the actions of the accused. Chief Justice Geoffrey Lawrence silenced him and demanded the Reichsmarschall enter a simple plea, which was "not guilty in the sense of the indictment," a phrase that soon passed the lips of all the Nazi leaders in the dock.

Chief prosecutor Robert Jackson delivered an opening address that was admired for its eloquence and declaration of the international legal significance of the trial. The Allies, he said, were not accusing the German people of high crimes, but hoped to establish international standards for conduct in war and peace that would bind rulers, generals, and armies in the future. "We must never forget that the record on which we judge these defendants today is the record on which history will judge us tomorrow," Jackson told the courtroom.

The trial continued, focusing on the German leaders' planning for war while making false overtures of peace, Nazi aggression against Russia, wartime propaganda, the atrocities in Poland, and the suppression of Jews and Christian opponents. The press reported minutiae of the defendants' activities. "If Göring swore under his breath at a witness (and he often did), the oath would be ringing around the world within minutes," Andrus noted. "If Hess changed the book he was reading in court, millions would know the next day the title of the replacement."

By the time the trial had begun, Göring craved the chance to give Nazi Germany one last display of brilliance before a world audience. Any glory gained would be mostly his, and he had nothing to lose. He made it his goal to rally his codefendants to defend themselves, be proud of their actions, and accept the punishment of the victors as a unified group—which he at first rosily predicted would be exile from Germany and later presented as a likely group execution that would grant them all an afterlife as national martyrs. He persisted in this vision of honorific monuments and the adulation of future Germans. All this could be theirs if they only cooperated at the trial. Months spent passively behind bars had made him thirsty to act aggressively and defiantly. Unlike many of the others, Göring did not try to blame Hitler or pin the responsibility for the actions of the Nazi regime on colleagues. He repeatedly admitted to his own decisions and portrayed himself as a moving force of the Reich. Several weeks into the trial, he summed up his attitude in a remark audible to spectators in the courtroom: "Damn it, I just wish we could all have the courage to confine our defense to three simple words: 'Lick my ass.'"

The Nazis continued to eat lunch together on trial days, and Göring took advantage of the gatherings to rein in opinions that he considered damaging to their common cause. "When the trial began he demonstrated his peculiar abilities of leadership immediately by assuming his place at the head of the dining table," Kelley observed. "No one questioned this. His right to command was apparently taken for granted by all of the prisoners. . . . He said to me: 'We are sort of like a team, all of us who have been accused, and it is up to us to stick together to accomplish the strongest defense. Naturally, I am the leader, so it is my problem to see that each of us contributes his share.'"

Göring did not want to hear in court any admissions of wrongdoing or public denunciations of the Nazi regime. When Keitel tentatively suggested during lunch that Hitler should bear most of the blame for their country's downfall, Göring cut him off. "You men knew the Führer," Göring said. "He would have been the first one to stand up and say, 'I have given the orders and I take full responsibility.' But I would rather die ten deaths than have the German sovereign subjected to this humiliation." Frank angrily took up Keitel's cause. "Other sovereigns have stood before courts of law. He got us into this," he declared, "and all that there is left is to tell the truth!" Then Frank and three others stood up and left the room. Some defendants, including Frank, expressed dismay over the charges in the indictment that Göring had stolen artworks and other valuables from conquered nations; in their minds, these were selfish, criminal acts that tarnished the Reichsmarschall's credibility.

Despite such setbacks, Göring retained influence over most of the defendants by tailoring his arguments to their concerns and insecurities. He told some that he would shoulder responsibility for their misdeeds. Others he plied with heart-to-hearts about the indignity of casting aspersions on their previous government. To a few, Göring declared absolute defiance against the Allies, saying the victors had no moral right to judge Germany's internal decisions. In his cell between court sessions, he repeated to Kelley the same arguments about Nazi Germany's war preparations during the 1930s, which were in violation of the Treaty of Versailles agreement that concluded World War I: "Of course we rearmed," Göring, seated once more next to the psychiatrist on his cot, said. "We rearmed Germany until we bristled. I am only sorry we did not rearm more. Of course, I considered treaties as so much toilet paper. Of course, I wanted to make Germany great. If it could be done peacefully, well and good. If not, that's just as good. My plans against Britain were bigger than they ascribe to me even now. When they told me I was playing with war by building up the Luftwaffe, I replied I certainly was not running a finishing school."

Kelley counseled some defendants on how to resist Göring's dominance. When Fritzsche questioned the physician about Göring's intentions and the degree of cynicism in his admonitions to the defendants, Kelley replied that Göring wanted to be long remembered as a hero of the German state, a goal that prevented him from acknowledging the defendants' collective moral guilt. "If he wants to play it that way, let him speak for himself," Fritzsche observed, "but he doesn't have to rope the rest of us into his heroics." But Göring actually felt impelled to do exactly that.

Kelley and Gilbert monitored the prisoners' conversations at lunch and in the courtroom. Sometimes Kelley felt compelled to correct the prisoners' perspectives. On one occasion he debated a group of defendants about a comparison of the racial problems of Germany and the United States. Assured that America had no laws that were as racially repressive as those of the Third Reich, Rosenberg replied, "Oh, but you will. You wait and see. If you don't have a Jewish problem, you will at least have a Negro problem." Streicher mentioned a Negro leader who wanted to spark an American revolt, and Kelley responded that he had never heard of him. Such crackpots, the psychiatrist said, "come and go, and decent people don't pay attention to them." Streicher's reply: "Oh, but you're bound to have a racial problem. It's in the Talmud." To which Rosenberg added, "It's a biological necessity." Having had the last word, the Nazis returned to the dock for the afternoon sessions of the tribunal.

On the afternoon of November 29 everyone in the courtroom was transfixed by one of the most dramatic moments of the trial. The prosecution showed filmed footage of concentration camps shot during their liberation by British and American troops less than a year earlier. As the room darkened and a projectionist began the whirred spinning of the reels of film, Kelley and Gilbert took positions at the ends of the defendants' dock. Spotlights illuminated the prisoners, allowing the psychiatrist and

Kelley's grandfather Charles F. McGlashan, chronicler of the ill-fated Donner Party and collector of butterflies.

The astounding McGlashan home and museum (perched atop the Rocking Stone) in Truckee, California.

Douglas Kelley around 1938, when he was a graduate student at Columbia University.

A note that Göring wrote to Kelley in prison in September 1945. It quotes the Book of Psalms: "He caused an east wind to blow in the heaven, and by his power he brought in the south wind."

Nürnberg Sept. 9. 1945

An Major Kelley.

Ich bin am 12. Januar 1893 geboren.

Ich habe drei Stiefbrüder, von denen einer gestorben ist. Eine verstorbene Stiefschwester. Zwei richtige Brüder (einer gestorben) und zwei Schwestern. Ich bin der zweit jüngste. Ich war zuletzt Reichsmarschall und Oberbefehlshaber der Luftwaffe.

Er liess wehen den Ostwind unter dem Himmel, und erregte durch seine Stärke den Südwind. Psalm 78 / 26.

Seelisch fühle ich mich natürlich durch die derzeitige Umgebung sehr bedrückt. Körperlich abgesehen von zeitweiligen Herzanfällen leidlich.

Hermann Göring.

Former Deputy Führer Rudolf Hess: "Henceforth my memory will again respond to the outside world."

Kelley decided that Nazi Party philosopher Alfred Rosenberg "had developed a system of thought differing greatly from known fact."

Kelley called Nazi publisher Julius Streicher's anti-Semitism "an almost true monomania."

Hermann and Emmy Göring with their daughter Edda during the early years of World War II. (Courtesy of Corbis Images)

After Robert Ley's suicide, security tightened in the Nuremberg prison wing housing the top Nazi suspects.

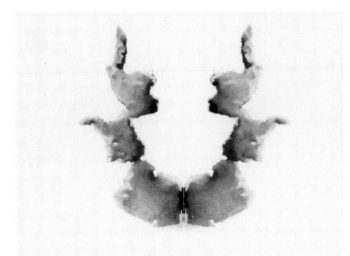

Julius Streicher perceived "the substance taken out of an operated knee" in Card VII of the Rorschach inkblot series.

Card IX of the Rorschach inkblot test, in which Göring saw "a spook with a fat stomach."

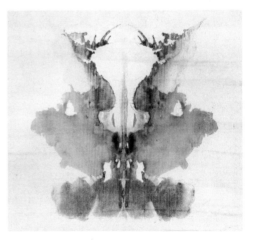

The portrait of Göring that the Reichsmar-schall inscribed, signed, and gave to Kelley.

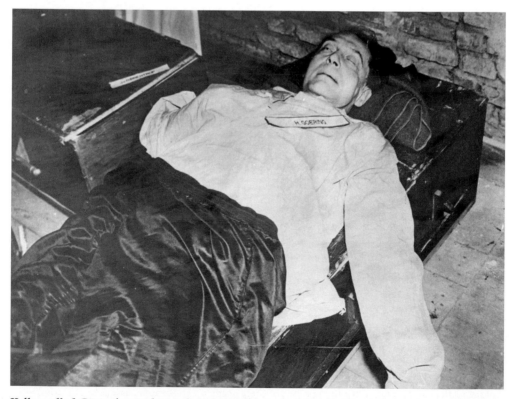

Kelley called Göring's suicide an admirably defiant act against the Nuremberg prison authorities.

The young psychiatrist, soon to be a criminologist.

Nancy Bayley (right), a Terman Study researcher, visits Dukie and Douglas M. Kelley, with their children Alicia and Doug, in the living room of their home on Highgate Road. (Photograph by Gene Lester © 1952 SEPS licensed by Curtis Licensing, Indianapolis, IN. All rights reserved.)

The principles of general semantics found their way into several of Kelley's criminology courses.

On the set of Kelley's successful educational television series *Criminal Man*.

psychologist to scrutinize their faces for traces of emotion and other telling reactions. The scenes of stick-limbed camp inmates, haunted faces, yawning crematoria doors showing incinerated skeletons, stacked corpses, and bulldozers tumbling mounds of bodies into mass graves—images all too familiar to people today—hit the uninitiated in the courtroom with terrific force. Sobs and soft cries from the spectators' gallery mixed with the hum of the projector. Coughing nervously, Göring leaned on the railing of the dock and covered his face with his right arm. Hess bewilderedly stared at the screen, but betrayed no feelings. Funk and Fritzsche were crying, and some who noticed their tears assumed they were grieving for themselves and their fate. Schacht, who had spent time in a Nazi concentration camp before his arrest by the Allies, turned away from the screen. Ribbentrop covered his eyes with his fingers but sometimes peeked through them. Moving restlessly in his seat, Rosenberg sneaked looks at his fellow Nazis. Dönitz kept averting his gaze and returning it to the screen, removing and restoring his sunglasses to his face. Alone among the Nazis, Streicher seemed keenly engrossed.

At the conclusion of the film, the defendants "remained seated, as if turned to stone," one person present recorded. "They were slow to rise when the judges filed out in disgusted silence." Stunned, Chief Justice Lawrence had neglected to officially adjourn the court. Slowly the prisoners regained their senses. Hess began to protest, "I don't believe it," and Göring shushed him. Guards finally led them all out of the courtroom, and Frank needed assistance dredging up the energy to move. When Kelley and Gilbert visited the prisoners in their cells that night, they saw weeping and heard protests that others were responsible—they knew nothing of such atrocities. Frank, however, put those declamations of innocence in perspective: "Don't let everyone tell you that they had no idea. Everyone sensed there was something horribly wrong . . . even if we did not know all the details. They didn't want to know." Streicher icily called the film "terrible," then asked for the guards to quiet down so he could go to sleep.

The screening of the camp films blew a hole in Göring's plan for the trial. "It was such a good afternoon, too, until they showed that film," he said. "They were reading my telephone conversations on the Austrian affair, and everybody was laughing with me. And then they showed that awful film, and it just spoiled everything."

At such times, Göring only reluctantly conceded the power of the evidence arrayed against him and his colleagues. "You're having a hard time keeping your group in fighting trim, aren't you?" Kelley remarked during the third weekend break of the trial. Göring admitted it was true. "Well, it seems to me the evidence is pretty damaging," Kelley pressed on. "You must admit that for yourself." Göring would not answer that directly. At last he responded: "Do you suppose I'd have believed it if somebody came to me and said they were making freezing experiments on human guinea-pigs— or that people were forced to dig their own graves and be mowed down by the thousands? I would just have said, 'Get out of here with that fantastic nonsense!' . . . It just didn't seem possible. I just shrugged it off as enemy propaganda." The evidence presented in court, however, established that Göring knew about the atrocities and details of the "final solution" planned for the Jews. The Holocaust had occurred with his assent and assistance.

On the day after the screening of the concentration camp films, the ninth day of the trial, the court took up the matter of Hess's amnesia as the former Deputy Führer sat alone in the dock. The judges wanted to know whether Hess had been mentally competent to enter his plea, and the prisoner's lawyer, Gunther von Rohrscheidt, presented a request to remove Hess temporarily from the trial proceedings until he could more actively take part in his own defense. (The court had already followed such a course in delaying the trial of the infirm industrial magnate and armaments manufacturer Gustav Krupp von Bohlen, whom the tribunal's prosecutors had indicted in 1945. Krupp died in 1950 without ever facing trial.) Rohrscheidt reluctantly conceded that Hess believed himself competent. The judges debated legal aspects of Hess's competence and fitness to stand trial. Chief prosecutor Jackson added that Hess should not be able to use amnesia as part of his defense or as a reason to delay his trial because he refused to undergo the narco-hypnosis treatment that Kelley had recommended to restore his memory. "He is in the volunteer class with his amnesia," declared Jackson, who was clearly persuaded that Hess had intentionally blocked his recollections.

During the two hours of debate, Hess scribbled notes and whispered and waved his arms at various times to draw the attention of his lawyer. He had grown visibly restless and agitated. Finally Lawrence looked at Hess and said, "The tribunal would like to hear Hess on the subject." Hess arose and strode to the center of the courtroom. Three guards leaped up to stop him, led him back to the dock, and handed him a microphone. Hess then asked to read aloud a statement he had just prepared on his mental state. He continued in a measured but high-pitched voice that suggested barely repressed excitement:

> Henceforth my memory will again respond to the outside world. The reasons why I simulated loss of memory were tactical. The fact is that only my ability to concentrate is somewhat reduced. However, my capacity to follow the trial to defend myself, to put questions to witnesses, or even to answer questions is not being affected thereby. I emphasize that I bear the full responsibility for everything that I have done or signed as signatory or co-signatory. My attitude in principle that the tribunal is not competent [to try and judge me] is not affected by the statement I have just made. So far in conversations with my official defense counsel, I have also simulated loss of memory. He has therefore represented me in good faith.

Astonished silence met Hess's revelation, and then, weirdly, Rohrscheidt laughed, and many others in the courtroom joined him. Justice Lawrence abruptly adjourned the court. Rohrscheidt exasperatedly told reporters he was completely surprised by his client's statement, but he added that this courtroom spectacle strengthened his belief that Hess was not sane. Hess went back to his cell, where Andrus told him, "I'm glad you're not going to fake anymore." Hess replied, seemingly in agreement, "*Ach,* I feel unburdened—I feel better."

Then Hess bragged to Rohrscheidt that he had made Kelley and Gilbert look ridiculous because they believed in his amnesia. Hess continued his elated recounting of the day's events. He could now recall events from his past that he had previously said were inaccessible. When Kelley asked why he had made this courtroom statement, Hess glowed with excitement "like an actor after a first night" and appeared not to realize that he had upset his own attorney more than any of the prosecutors.

"How did I do? Good, wasn't I?" Hess exclaimed. "I really surprised everybody, don't you think?" Kelley replied that not everyone was surprised. "Then I didn't fool you by pretending amnesia?" Hess asked. "I was afraid you had caught on. You spent so much time with me." Kelley then reminded Hess of the screening of the Nazi rally films in November, during which Hess had claimed to recognize nobody, not even himself, in the movies. "I thought then that you knew I was pretending," Hess recalled. "All the time you looked only at my hands. It made me very nervous to know you had learned my secret."

Kelley later wrote: "I had not, of course, learned his 'secret' in quite the way he thought. I knew only that he remembered more than he admitted." The psychiatrist was unwilling to give up the belief that Hess still suffered from some genuine amnesia, which began, as Kelley had earlier suspected, during Hess's interrogations while he was incarcerated in England, when it was easiest for him to feign lack of memory. Kelley continued to believe that over time "large sections of his life simply slipped below the threshold of memory. . . . In the end, he was a genuine victim of an induced, even rationalized, amnesia state." Yet, in defiance of Kelley's opinion, some of what Hess had claimed was lost he could actually recall.

Gilbert and Kelley informed some of the other prisoners about Hess's admission. Ribbentrop's confusion was immense. "Hess, the Hess we have here? He said that?" Ribbentrop exclaimed. Schirach declared the fakery amusing but beneath the decency of a sane German. Though undeniably amazed at Hess's pretense, Göring felt resentful that he had been fooled along with everyone else. When Göring and Hess met in the courtroom dock the next day, they initially bantered about the ruse like schoolboys who had fooled the headmaster. Hess now felt free to boast to the former Luftwaffe chief about the dangers of his clandestine flight to Britain. Göring quickly tired of the conversation "as he looked around the courtroom and saw that Hess was now the center of attention," Gilbert noted. "Hess was enjoying it immensely."

To some observers, Hess's statement may have made Kelley look foolish for having taken seriously mental disturbances that were faked. The psychiatrist, however, insisted to anyone who asked that Hess's words had come as no surprise to him. The courtroom declaration, Kelley told reporters, was expected given the prisoner's hysterical personality. Kelley repeated that he believed some of Hess's forgetfulness to be genuine and some intentional, "but it is obvious he has been using amnesia as a defense." Later Hess admitted to Gilbert and others that his declaration in court was false and that some of his amnesia was real. Hess continued to deteriorate mentally as the trial went on, failing to take the stand in his own defense because "he was too insane to testify," Kelley later said.

Privately, Kelley blamed Gilbert for Hess's unexpected statement. Right before that court session, Kelley wrote, Gilbert had told the prisoner that the tribunal might declare him insane and remove him from the trial. Hess wanted to remain a defendant "since he felt that to be denied a trial would indicate mental inferiority and he felt that he must stand trial with his companions," Kelley noted. "This sort of reaction again emphasizes his hysterical nature and his desire to thrust himself into the limelight, fatal as it might be, instead of attempting to escape by continued pretense."

Despite the drama of Hess's admission, the judges quickly determined that Hess was faking his forgetfulness, that he was fit to stand trial, and that they would order no further medical examinations. Kelley agreed with these decisions. When he completed his final assessments of the Nazis facing trial, including Hess in mid-December, he wrote of each defendant: "This man is competent and demonstrates no evidence of psychopathology. He is able to face trial."

Later, when the defendants grew too fractious and Göring too domineering, Andrus directed Gilbert to separate them into groups in different lunch rooms. The psychologist established eating groups designed to weaken Göring's dominance, based on the ability of various defendants to counter his arguments. Göring had to eat lunch in a chamber all by himself. "He was furious to be eating alone and let it be known that he thought I was 'a nobody'," Gilbert recalled, "while he and the others were 'historic personalities'." A few other factors played into Gilbert's seating assignments; historians Ann and John Tusa have noted that "Hess and Ribbentrop were put together because Gilbert thought they would hardly find anything to say to each other and this would neutralize them." The new seating arrangement had the immediate effect of empowering such defendants as Schacht and Speer to openly criticize Nazi policies and to blame Hitler, not the Allies, for Germany's defeat. As the trial lumbered toward its 218th day, several of the Nazis broke out of Göring's orbit and distanced themselves from him. Not even the Reichsmarschall could railroad his colleagues and hold the public's imagination that long. "*Gott im Himmel!*" he would sputter on his bad days, along with hissed oaths and exclamations of "*Schweinehund und verraeter!*" (Pig-dog and traitor!), which he would fling at damaging witnesses.

Even in the tribunal's early weeks—with nine months of argument and evidence still to come—the weight of damaging information arising in court dragged down the defendants. Keitel confessed to Kelley that the military atrocities he had heard about mortified him with shame, and he lamented the time he had spent away from the field, insulated in Hitler's headquarters. After one visit, when Kelley and Gilbert prepared to leave Keitel's cell, the former supreme commander of the Reich's armed forces stood at attention and begged, "Please let me talk to you once in a while, as long as I am not yet a sentenced criminal. Don't despise me altogether. Come around once in a while. It gives me a little moral support to stand this ordeal, just to be able to talk to someone." Gilbert found Keitel's plea so humiliating "that I did not translate it to Kelley until we had left the hall."

Sometime at the end of December, Kelley announced his intention to leave Nuremberg and return to the United States. The psychiatrist had heard enough confessions of frightened men in solitary cells and had taken in enough courtroom drama. Kelley had not seen Dukie since 1942, and he wanted to go home. The couple's letters during the waning months of 1945 kept anticipating Kelley's return to the States. In addition, Kelley yearned to restart his civilian career and get to work on a book written with Gilbert about the psychology of the Nazi leaders. He had not yet formed his conclusions, but he sensed he had gathered enough information for that future volume. The Rorschach scores, IQ tests, and interview notes filled file folders. Kelley's personal goals for his sojourn in Nuremberg had never been about the court inquiry. The psychological makeup of Göring and his Nazi colleagues concerned him more than their judicial fate. To the psychiatrist, the guilt of the German prisoners was never in doubt. Only their psychiatric workings and the causes of their abhorrent conduct as leaders—any thread that could possibly connect all twenty-two defendants—interested Kelley. He could predict the court's verdicts against most of them, but he had to remove himself from Nuremberg to dissect their minds.

Kelley had fulfilled his responsibilities to the tribunal, and his official duties wound down. He judged the prisoners to be in "good mental health" after a month of trial proceedings. "They are not the same lot of cocky, almost jaunty, individuals who entered the prisoner's box," he told a reporter. Before the trial, some had laughed about the odds of their swinging from the gallows, but now they were terrified that imminent execution awaited most of them.

During his last days in the prison Kelley made the rounds of the prisoners to hear their final thoughts and to offer his predictions for their future. Hess admitted to feeling distressed by his unending suspicions that his food was being poisoned. Sometimes, Hess said, he had tried to overcome his obsession by eating the suspect food, but he would get stomach cramps or attacks of giddiness as a result. "He wanted to know if an individual with a strong mind could possibly entertain such ideas or did they indicate a process of insanity," Kelley wrote. How the psychiatrist responded to Hess's concerns is unknown, but by this time Kelley could do nothing to help. Hess was the only defendant who did not thank Kelley for his attention during the previous months.

One expression of gratitude came from an unexpected source. On December 26 Rosenberg wrote a long letter that began with uncharacteristic warmth. Addressed to "the General Staff Doctor, Major Kelley," it started, "I regret your departure from Nuremberg, as do the comrades confined with me. I thank you for your humane behavior and also for your attempt to understand our reasons." Continuing with, "I hereby express my conviction that many conflicts would not have come to such a pass in the world if one had observed the laws of nature in politics," Rosenberg returned to form and was off and running on a five-paragraph discourse against Judaism, "respect" for the natural dominance of some races over others, and the inevitability of a Jewish and Negro catastrophe in the United States unless Americans mobilized to protect the "white race." Only in the letter's final line did he return to the personal tone in which he had begun: "I wish you luck in your later life." Then he signed off, "with best regards and repeated thanks, Alfred Rosenberg."

In one of their last meetings, Kelley and Göring pushed aside talk of politics or the trial. Göring described a conversation he had recently had with Hess, who commented on the sound of electric generators beneath their cells. Hess believed the noise was intended to keep the prisoners awake at night and ruin their nerves for the trial. Although Göring laughed off the incident, he wanted Kelley to know about it.

When Göring learned that Kelley was leaving the prison, he broke down and wept.

To Kelley, the trial and its run-up had served as fascinating laboratories for the study of the group dynamics of aggression, criminal motivation, defense mechanisms of the guilty, depression, and the response of deviant personalities to the judicial process. Kelley was with the prisoners as they faced their impending judgment and for the disturbing surfacing of their emotions. He saw the victors release their anger, and perhaps cleanse their own guilt for wartime brutalities they, too, had committed, through the accumulation of nose-rubbing evidence against the Nazis and the prosecution of the German leaders in court. The imprisoned individuals were set up to bear the responsibility for the war and its accessory horrors, perhaps so others could begin to feel less responsible. The deadly mess and blistering hatred of battle morphed into a logical and calculated game of strategy in the courtroom, complete with the prospect of a satisfying verdict in the end. Kelley found himself in the service of a nation that, in battling an ideology intent upon ruling the world and taking charge of the tribunal's administration, now emerged to lord over much of the planet.

Leon Goldensohn, a thirty-four-year-old physician from Newark, arrived on January 8, 1946, to replace Kelley as Nuremberg jail psychiatrist. The new man impressed the prisoners and jail staff with his congenial manner, unaggressive style, and willingness to listen to the defendants for long stretches without challenging them or saying much at all in response.

❧ • ❧

Douglas Kelley reunited with Dukie in Chattanooga in late January 1946, and he came home with boxes full of his records, memos, notes, and files from his time with the Nazis. When Gilbert became aware of the range of materials Kelley had taken—which included the handwritten autobiographies that the psychiatrist had asked the prisoners to compose and copies of Gilbert's notes from his interviews with the Nazis—the psychologist was furious. His rage grew when he learned that Kelley had left no forwarding address. A couple of months later, Gilbert received a letter from Kelley saying that he now intended to write a book about Nuremberg without Gilbert's participation. Gilbert could not fathom this change in their plans, but Kelley had likely concluded that as the officer superior in rank who had supervised the other man, he had moral ownership of all their research. With Gilbert still working with the prisoners in Nuremberg, Kelley could grab a head start in writing psychological profiles of the Nazis and an assessment of whatever personality traits they might share. He had leaped months ahead of his colleague.

He promised Dukie a second honeymoon after five years of marriage in which they had barely seen each other. By this time he had earned a promotion from major to lieutenant colonel. When reporters interviewed him, Kelley quickly discovered that the press was most interested in hearing him recount the peccadillos of the Nuremberg Nazis. And Kelley delivered: he noted that he had "practically lived with Hess" during the previous months and expressed his continuing resentment that Hess had refused to undergo narco-hypnosis. Moving on to Göring, he detailed the Reichsmarschall's drug habit—repeating, as he would for many years, that Göring snacked on paracodeine tablets "like peanuts, throwing them in his mouth as he read or talked"—and reporting the Nazi's cooperation in ending his dependence under the psychiatrist's care. "These people without Hitler are not abnormal, not pervert[s], not geniuses," Kelley said. "They were like any aggressive, smart, ambitious, ruthless businessman, and their business happened in the setting up of a world government."

The trial ground on without Kelley. Though deprived of much of his influence over his codefendants, Göring stuck to his plan to vigorously defend the Third Reich as the trial progressed and to preserve its honor in the minds of his fellow Germans. He took the witness stand in his own defense in March 1946 and jousted famously with Jackson. At first Göring did not defend himself effectively against Jackson's evidence that he knew about the concentration camps, prompting prisoner Schacht to tell Gilbert, "The fat one is sure taking a beating so far." But the atmosphere in the courtroom soon changed. Göring's manner shifted from defensive to assertive, and he succeeded in using the witness chair as a pulpit for long justifications of his role in the Nazi regime. "The only motive which guided me was my ardent love for my people, their fortunes, their freedoms, their life, and for this I call on the Almighty and the German people as my witness," he proclaimed. "He might have been addressing the Nuremberg Rally, not the Nuremberg Tribunal," wrote Airey Neave, an observer in court.

In one torrent of words that lasted twelve hours over two days, Göring portrayed Nazi Germany and his part in its government in the most radiant terms. His passion and expertise astounded many in the courtroom. Thanks in part to Kelley's physical care and patient ear, the old Göring— the Göring who in years past had designed a lightning-fast air force, earned the trust of a suspicious Führer, and maintained discipline within the Nazi Party—was back. Without Hitler watching over his shoulder, he was perhaps more assured than ever. Animated, smiling, and clearly enjoying himself, he exhibited his former magnetism. "Somehow he makes me think of a captured lion," wrote US prosecutor Thomas J. Dodd. Hesitant admiration for Göring's political acumen began appearing in press accounts of the trial. "His fellow prisoners followed him with rapt attention," Neave wrote. "Some of them, notably Rudolf Hess, now his inseparable companion in the dock, were carried away. I half expected them to rise, salute and cry, '*Sieg Heil*'! I realized then why he had commanded such influence in the early years of the National Socialist regime." Göring's spellbinding testimony lifted the legitimacy of the Nazi regime to its highest point in the trial.

Robert Jackson now had the unenviable job of cross-examining this master manipulator who was suddenly in the ascendant. Göring was ready for him. He anticipated Jackson's questions, offered to assist when he lost his place in his documents, and smugly corrected the prosecutor's errors of fact. He answered Jackson's questions with dismissive and off-topic lectures that Chief Justice Lawrence did not interrupt. According to some courtroom witnesses, Göring's obvious contempt and the court's refusal to head off his harangues nearly reduced Jackson to tears. "When the former Reichsmarschall strode from the witness stand to the prisoners' box after his last session with Mr. Jackson, he was congratulated and smiled upon by his fellow-Nazis there, like a gladiator who had just won his fight," Janet Flanner of the *New Yorker* reported.

It took weeks of work for the prosecution to repair the damage and to tarnish Göring's character. A turning point occurred during the presentation of evidence that Göring allowed the execution of fifty captured British officers in 1944, a scandalous war crime. Göring denied any participation in the atrocity, but he lost his temper on the witness stand. In contradiction to much of the assembled evidence, he claimed to have had no knowledge of the "final solution" against the Jews and astounded everyone by absolving Hitler of any knowledge as well. Nobody could believe that, and Göring's credibility dropped sharply.

From then on the Nazi defendants were on the run. Yet Göring remained devilishly defiant, a reaction Gilbert called "oral and incipient
overt aggression." In mid-June, for example, when tribunal judge Francis
Biddle rose from the bench to use the restroom during a court session,
Göring spun around in the dock to whisper a snide comment to one of
the other defendants. A guard grasped his shoulder to prevent Göring's
movement, and the Nazi leader ostentatiously brushed and flicked at his
coat in a mock demonstration of cleaning the soiled fabric. The collapse of
the defendants' group solidarity seemed to sour Göring on everybody and
everything. "It was interesting to compare notes with some of the other
officers who were seeing him at this time," Gilbert wrote, "to see how he
was maligning the psychologist to the psychiatrist, the Catholic chaplain to
the Protestant chaplain and vice versa, both chaplains to the psychologist
and psychiatrist, and vice versa, while fawning on each in turn."

Göring turned against most of his companions in the dock. Frustrated
and stressed, "he could not ask for drugs now, but we felt that he would
have given his right arm for a good shot of cocaine or a big dose of paracodeine," Gilbert observed. In the end Göring was beaten down by mountains of evidence and arguments that even the force of his personality and
courtroom theatrics could not overcome. Equally bad from his perspective, the press and public had grown weary of the tribunal's proceedings.
Göring "was no longer news; all that could be said for him was that he
stuck it out to the last bitter day," wrote his biographers, Roger Manvell
and Heinrich Fraenkel, "sitting with his head in his hands or with his chin
resting on his chest, deep in thought or lost in depression."

Jackson had meanwhile recovered his eloquence in the courtroom. He
ended the prosecution's case with a speech that many observers found mas-
terful. He noted the defendants' assertions of their innocence, and added:

> It is against such a background that these defendants now ask this
> Tribunal to say that they are not guilty of planning, executing, or
> conspiring to commit this long list of crimes and wrongs. They
> stand before the record of this trial, as bloodstained Gloucester
> stood by the body of his slain king.

He begged of the widow, as they beg of you: "Say I slew them not." And the Queen replied, "Then say they were not slain. But dead they are."

If you were to say of these men that they are not guilty, it would be as though to say there has been no war, there are no slain, there has been no crime.

On June 21, 1946, the judges of the tribunal began their private deliberations on the guilt of the defendants. Two more months passed, and then the prisoners had a chance to make their final pleas to the court. Göring made several unbelievable claims in his statement. "I should like to state clearly once more before the Tribunal," he said, "that I have never decreed the murder of a single individual at any time, and neither did I decree any other atrocities or tolerate them while I had the power and the knowledge to prevent them." Hess's statement was notable for its incoherence. He accused the prosecution of fabricating documents and producing dishonest witnesses. An "abnormal state of mind," he claimed, prompted the Nazis to lead Germany as they had. As he rambled on, Göring tried to get him to stop talking. "I do not regret anything. . . . No matter what human beings may do, I shall some day stand before the judgment seat of the Eternal. I shall answer to Him and I know He will judge me innocent," Hess said before Justice Lawrence told him his time was up.

One thing gave Göring comfort: news that his wife and daughter were free. In March 1946 Emmy and Edda walked out of the Straubling detention camp and settled in as tenants at a hunting lodge about forty-five miles northeast of Nuremberg. Their new residence, where they would live for the next two years, was so far from a school that Emmy taught the little girl, now six years old, at home. Emmy soon petitioned the International Tribunal:

I am submitting herewith a great request. Would it be possible for me to see my husband for a few minutes? I haven't seen my husband for a year and a quarter and I am longing so terribly for him that I don't see any way out; I need strength to carry on without my husband. A few minutes when I could see him and could hold his hand would help me no end. From the depth of my heart I implore you not to refuse my request.

The tribunal's administrators had no objection to Emmy's visit, but with the trial still in progress and the heavy security at the prison, Andrus refused to allow it. "It was contrary to prison regulations," he noted. It was also contrary to Göring's wishes. He consistently refused to let Emmy or other relatives come to Nuremberg to meet with him or testify on his behalf.

Once the trial ended, Andrus permitted family members of the prisoners to visit the defendants before they were sentenced. Hess refused to allow visits from his family, but Göring retracted his former refusal. "Whatever I thought about Göring, it was hard at that time to push the pathos of separation from my mind," Andrus admitted. Emmy and Edda arrived in Nuremberg on September 14, intending to stay with Göring's lawyer for two weeks, and photographers eagerly captured them walking the city's streets. Emmy visited her husband every day except Sundays, and she brought along Edda after the first several visits. "You mustn't cry, whatever you do," mother cautioned daughter. A wire screen separated Göring from his family. Emmy's requests to kiss her husband or at least hold his hand were denied. Physical contact "meant one more chance to pass a suicide weapon," Andrus noted. Upon seeing Edda, Göring, with security officers flanking him, lost control and cried. "You've grown," he got out. Edda recited to him poetry that her mother had taught her.

The families of the defendants had to leave Nuremberg on September 29, 1946, and a few days later, after a courtroom announcement signaling the end of the tribunal's historic 218 days in session, the judges returned to deliver their verdicts. Sharpshooters manned the roof of the Palace of Justice as the judges pronounced eighteen of the defendants guilty, while acquitting Fritzsche, Papen, and Schacht. Seven of the convicted Nazis—Hess, Funk, Dönitz, Raeder, Schirach, Speer, and Neurath—were given prison sentences ranging from ten years to life, and the rest—including

Martin Bormann, tried in absentia—were condemned to death. Those to be hanged were Göring, Rosenberg, Streicher, Ribbentrop, Jodl, Keitel, Kaltenbrunner, Frank, Frick, Seyss-Inquart, and Sauckel. Emmy could not avoid telling Edda about her father's death sentence, but she added, "The sentence probably won't be carried out. Papi will probably be exiled to an island somewhere," like Napoleon. Allied authorities scheduled the executions for October 16.

By imposing a life sentence on Hess, the judges gave a nod to the prisoner's long-standing mental aberrations. Despite his assertions of its falsity, Hess lapsed back into amnesia when faced with all the evidence of the barbarity of Hitler's leadership and the criminal acts and policies of his colleagues in the dock. Kelley approved of the judges' relative leniency toward Hess. The Nazi was hysterically deviant, paranoid, emotionally stunted, and deluded in his view of the Third Reich as a heroic regime. "Death sentences for insane persons are not a part of civilized, democratic law," he wrote, "so the Tribunal compromised by a sentence which will place him behind walls for life." Kelley made a prediction: "Later, as he realizes that he will not hang, he may relax and appear to recover. Such response will, however, be only superficial; and Hess will continue to live always in the borderlands of insanity."

In public Kelley expressed his overall satisfaction with the sentences, complaining only that Papen's acts also justified a guilty verdict. "A nice long prison term would have done him a world of good," Kelley said. He predicted trouble for the three acquitted defendants. "They are dead ducks. The German people will see they pay—not for their sins, but for having lost the war. They were the three smoothest talkers. They talked themselves right out of jail. But they'll not be able to talk themselves out of trouble." His forecast for the freed men was partially born out: a German court later convicted Hans Fritzsche of Nazi crimes, and he died of cancer soon afterward; Papen also received a guilty verdict from a denazification court before winning his freedom on appeal. But Hjalmar Schacht never again faced a judge and remained active in German banking until his death in 1970.

Sentenced to the indignity of hanging, Göring asked Allied authorities to allow him instead to face a firing squad. Gilbert gave him the news that his request had been denied. The Allies wanted to hand him an ignominious death. Göring acknowledged to Gilbert that his sixteen-month-long effort to keep alight the glory of the Nazi years and to retain the admiration of the German people had failed during the course of the trial. "You don't have to worry about the Hitler legend any more," he said. "When the German people learn what has been revealed at the trial it won't be necessary to condemn him. He has condemned himself." Gilbert warned Allied officials of the possibility of Göring killing himself. Hanging was for common criminals, so Göring revived an old contingency plan.

Uncharacteristically, he asked Chaplain Gerecke to give him Holy Communion the night before the scheduled executions. Gerecke, hearing from Göring that he believed in God but not in the divinity of Jesus or the holiness of the Bible, refused. A few hours later Göring sat at the table in his cell and wrote out a note. He then folded the paper and moved to the toilet in the concealed corner of his cell. After a few minutes there, he heaved himself onto his bunk and lay still, taking care to keep his hands visible to the guard observing him as prison regulations required.

Göring no longer needed his hands. A glass ampule, which he had just removed from his body or from the toilet, was already in his mouth. He shifted his eyes toward the watching guard for a moment, then ground his jaws together. Potassium cyanide trickled from the broken capsule and into his throat. Göring gasped, rattled, and convulsed. The alarmed guard called for help and flung open the cell door, but by this time the Reichsmarschall may already have been dead. Andrus was among the first to rush to the cell, and he observed that Göring's eyes were closed, his mouth hung open, and his skin was tinged green.

The Reichsmarschall had addressed to Andrus the note he scribbled in the minutes before his death. It managed to smartly dig at the colonel while freeing his subordinates of responsibility for failing to detect the poison:

To the Commandant:

I have always had the capsule of poison with me from the time that I became a prisoner. When taken to Mondorf I had three capsules. The first I left in my clothes so that it would be found when a search was made. The second I placed under the clothes-rack on undressing and took it to me again on dressing. I hid this in Mondorf and here in the cell so well that despite their frequent and thorough searches it could not be found. During the court sessions I hid it on my person and in my high riding boots. The third capsule is still in my small suitcase in the round box of skin cream, hidden in the cream. I could have taken this to me twice in Mondorf if I had needed it. None of those charged with searching is to be blamed, for it was practically impossible to find the capsule. It would have been pure accident.

Dr. Gilbert informed me that the control board has refused the petition to change the method of execution to shooting.

No other clues suggesting how Göring was able to hide the poison emerged until decades later, when Telford Taylor, who assisted and eventually succeeded Robert Jackson as chief counsel for the prosecution in later Nazi trials at Nuremberg, disclosed his belief that a US soldier and Nuremberg jail guard, First Lieutenant Jack "Tex" Wheeler, had helped Göring secrete capsules hidden in his stored luggage. A book by Ben E. Swearingen, *The Mystery of Hermann Goering's Suicide*, amassed considerable evidence that Wheeler had befriended Göring and may have performed this final favor in exchange for the Nazi's valuables. As recently as 2005, however, a new confession muddied the waters: Herbert Lee Stivers, formerly one of the white-helmeted guards in the Nuremberg courtroom, said he had secretly given Göring a pen containing the fatal capsule at the urging of his German girlfriend. Stivers claimed to have believed the capsule held medicine, not poison.

The Reichsmarschall's suicide surprised Kelley. In San Francisco to give a lecture, he had told the press on the previous day that owing to Göring's high IQ and stubborn character, he expected the Nazi to make a good showing at the end. "He'll never weaken at the gallows. He has an historic perspective," Kelley noted. "He'll swing through the trap shouting, 'Heil Hitler'—not because he's brave, simply because he can already see himself in the history books."

Kelley must have felt a chill when he learned that Göring had taken his own life. This compelling leader—a patient, subject, and close intimate with whom Kelley had discovered a communion of interests and personality—was gone. The magician had been taken in by one final sleight of hand. He had misjudged Göring, who had eluded his professional judgment. The psychiatrist may have detected a disturbing change in his own sense of permanence. Perhaps Kelley also felt a thrill that this great manipulator whose presence had dominated his life for five months had carried out an act that Kelley did not anticipate. But in retrospect, it wasn't really surprising that the Reichsmarschall insisted on making his death a statement of defiance. It matched Göring's ideals and image. Kelley did not see his suicide as cowardly. On the contrary, it "demonstrates how ingeniously clever he was," the psychiatrist told reporters, "and a last gesture to leave the whole American Army flat. In the German mind, his act is a fairly heroic one, placing him historically with the Big Four—Hitler, Himmler, Göbbels and himself." If all of the other highest-ranking Nazis avoided the shame of hanging, why not Göring? Kelley wrote:

> Göring, however, went a step further than his former associates. He stoically endured his long imprisonment that he might force down the Allied Tribunal and browbeat the prosecuting lawyers on their own terms. By these methods he established himself with the German people. His suicide, shrouded in mystery and emphasizing the impotency of the American guards, was a skillful, even brilliant, finishing touch, completing the edifice for Germans to admire in time to come.

This was a striking, surprisingly laudatory interpretation of the Nazi's final act, almost as if Kelley were describing a glorious twist to the curtain-closing of a play rather than the end of a life. A suicide, accomplished with skill, could wound enemies and build a grand legacy in one dramatic gesture. The image of Göring orchestrating his own farewell, on his own terms, burned in Kelley's memory for years.

❦ • ❦

The remaining condemned Nazis were led to the gallows in an operation that Andrus, insulted by Göring's escape, supervised. Ribbentrop's response to his approaching execution particularly impressed Kelley, who had previously speculated that guards would have to drag him to the gallows. Kelley wrote that the former foreign minister "showed some courage at the very end. Probably the news of Göring's suicide and the realization that he was now the leader of the death procession, holding the center of this final stage, stiffened Ribbentrop and made him a more competent person in his last seconds than at any other time in his entire life." Ribbentrop met the rope proclaiming his hope that Germany would remain united.

Rosenberg had refused to participate in or even hear prayers, and he approached the hangman shaky and weak, perhaps, as Kelley predicted, still internally debating some fine point of Nazi philosophy. Streicher, Kelley said, would "hang happy," and indeed he went down with Hitler's name on his lips. Frank, the psychiatrist supposed, would die "convinced that one drop of his body will wipe out all the 5 million black marks registered against his soul." As Kelley had predicted, none of the rest of the condemned men had to be dragged to the gallows. "Just as in a good deed well performed, so in a bad one well done, do men hold to the type of mentality with which they are endowed," he wrote, in what might have been a general epitaph for the convicted Nazis at Nuremberg.

The office of US Surgeon-General Thomas Parran Jr. asked for samples of the brains of the hanged Nazis. Andrus called this "a macabre request which was, of course, never granted." Instead, in an act of retribution, all of the bodies were trundled to the ovens of the Dachau concentration camp, incinerated there, and the ashes dumped into a river. There would be no vigils held by unrepentant Nazis at marble mausoleums. There would be no heroic funerary architecture.

Hess and his guilty compatriots who survived the tribunal's justice with their lives went to Spandau Prison in Berlin to serve their terms. In a final act of extinction, Andrus made sure that every remaining piece of jewelry that had been in Göring's possession was disassembled, melted down, and rendered unusable and beyond recognition. American authorities presented the hunks of precious metal and jewels to the treasury of the new Germany, then struggling back to its feet.

8

THE NAZI MIND

As the International Military Tribunal ran its course, questions arose about the men who had committed the atrocities and advanced the criminal regime that took shape in the evidence and testimony presented in court. Why did the Nazis and their followers do it? Were they insane? Could anyone find in them a specific mental disorder responsible for their criminal conduct? In the US House of Representatives, Congresswoman Emily Taft Douglas of Illinois raised those questions in 1945 during a committee hearing on the punishment of war criminals. Douglas doubted that Americans, or anyone else for that matter, understood much about the motivations for the enormities of which the Nazi defendants were accused. "We don't know about war crimes," she said. "We don't know at all. We know specifically of atrocities, but we do not understand the psychology of war crimes.... There has been a psychological sickness that has bred these crimes, which we must understand or we cannot cope with it in the future."

At the same time, many who worked in the tribunal or observed it realized that merely punishing the guilty would not make the proceedings a success. Something more had to emerge from the months of courtroom sessions: definitive signs that Nazi Germany and its ideologies had been crushed and that the world could learn from the horrors of the previous dozen years to prevent similar catastrophes from happening. "We have high hopes that this public portrayal of the guilt of these evildoers," declared President Harry Truman, "will bring wholesale and permanent revulsion on the part of the masses of our former enemies against war, militarism, aggression, and nations of racial superiority."

Back in Dukie's hometown of Chattanooga, Kelley had plenty to think about, much of it unconnected with the workings of Nazi minds. He "was anxious to forget the war years and get on with new plans and projects," Dukie later wrote, perhaps too breezily. Kelley certainly needed a job, and wanted one that would further his ambition of achieving a top academic position. He had a long-neglected wife to consider, as well as the possibility of their starting a family.

Still, Kelley's thoughts about the Nazi leaders did not fade. In his spare hours he had written down his musings about Nazis, the basis of their evil, and the lessons of the recent war for Americans. Upon his return to the United States, "a number of people urged him to write about his studies of the Nazis," Dukie wrote to an acquaintance. "He was reluctant to do so because after nearly four years at war with no respite, he was tired and wanted nothing more than for us to drive around the United States and see again the countryside we both love—which we did." But as they traveled, the book manuscript he had begun envisioning since his initial weeks in the Nazis' company slowly took shape. Kelley could not leave his Nuremberg experience behind. Indeed, it had followed him home.

To stimulate his thinking, Kelley had papers—mountains of them. The boxes he had shipped home from Nuremberg bulged with documents, many unique. He had also shipped to Tennessee a collection of books that their Nazi authors had signed; copies of letters he had conveyed between Hermann and Emmy Göring; a sampling of the Reichsmarschall's paracodeine pills; X-rays of Hitler's skull; and the wax-sealed specimens of crackers, cookies, and candies that Rudolf Hess had claimed were poisoned by his English keepers. A hoard of papers and artifacts, much of it medically intriguing or macabre, was close at hand. These materials taunted him. He wanted to make personal and professional sense of the past year of his life: experiences that countless other psychiatrists, psychologists, and academics would have done anything to have shared. Reluctantly Kelley began to sort out his own opinions on the Nazis. Now he could view them from a distance. What could he hypothesize from the evidence of cruelty and criminality?

Looking over his Rorschach data and interpretations, Kelley could see that none of the top Nazi prisoners, except the brain-damaged Ley, showed signs of any mental illness or personality traits that would label him insane. Here he came up against wartime popular myth. All of the men, even the disordered and forgetful Hess, were responsible for their actions and capable of distinguishing right from wrong. Göring, the charmer with whom Kelley had so much in common, presented special challenges. Kelley was astonished that such a clearly intelligent and cultured man so blatantly lacked a moral compass and empathy for others. Perhaps, Göring's example suggested, anybody with brains and weighty responsibilities—Kelley included—could lose his bearings and harm others. His intense interest in Göring was plain in the bulk of material on the Reichsmarschall he had brought back, which outweighed by far the material on any other defendant.

If Kelley had hoped to discover a Nazi "germ," a deviant personality common to the defendants, there was little evidence of one. Instead, he found in their personalities traits that he called neuroses, not uncommon psychiatric flaws that could certainly trouble the Nazis and increase their ruthlessness, but did not put them outside the boundaries of the normal. Kelley believed that countless men like Göring, unburdened by conscience and driven by narcissism, spent their days "behind big desks deciding big affairs as businessmen, politicians, and racketeers. . . . Shrewd, smooth, conscienceless speakers and writers like Goebbels, slick, big-time salesmen like Ribbentrop, and all the financial and legalistic hangers-on can be counted among the men whose faces we know by sight."

His long proximity to the prisoners had convinced him that they exhibited several qualities: unbridled ambition, weak ethics, and excessive patriotism that could justify nearly any action of questionable rightness. Moreover, the Nazis, even the most elite and powerful among them, were not monsters, evildoing machines, or automata without soul and feelings. Göring's concern for his family, Schirach's love of poetry, and

Kaltenbrunner's fear under stress had moved Kelley and persuaded him that his former prisoners had emotions and responses like other people. Anyone who dismissed them "because we look with disgust and hatred upon their activities and upon their actions, to sell the Third Reich short," was making a big mistake. Their relative normalcy left a portentous hanging question. How could their inexplicable conduct be understood? Without comprehending the Nazis or identifying their psychoses, Kelley could only reluctantly conclude that enormous numbers of people had the potential to act as the war criminals had.

Lacking psychiatric evidence, Kelley fell back onto sociology, history, and Korzybskian semantics to explain the Germans. "Insanity is no explanation for the Nazis," he wrote. "They were simply creatures of their environment, as all humans are; and they were also—to a greater degree than most humans are—the makers of their environment." Like many who wondered about the rise of the Third Reich, Kelley saw connections between the growth of Nazi ideology and the presence of long-standing barbaric tendencies and prejudices in German culture. From the late nineteenth century through World War I, German leaders had preached the necessity of slaughtering enemies, setting Germans above people of neighboring countries, and recognizing their destiny to conquer others. The Nazis did not have to invent notions of the Führer principle, the folk hero who would rescue the nation, and the existence of an elite who could lead everyone else. They simply tapped into what was already present in the national atmosphere. "It is an established scientific fact that a person who is thinking with the emotional (thalamic) brain centers cannot think intellectually (cortically)," Kelley observed, hearkening to general semantics. "Hitler had an entire people thinking with its thalamus. In such state they fell easy prey to Goebbels, Streicher, Ley, and the other propagandists." It did not require remarkable qualities to harness those ideas already embedded in the culture—merely leadership abilities.

If insanity was not the common factor among the Nazis, what was? Kelley could find only two areas in which the Nuremberg defendants shared traits. The first was an enormous energy they devoted to their work;

Göring and his colleagues were grade A workaholics. "They all worked for incredibly long hours, slept very little, and devoted their whole lives to the problem of Nazifying the world," he observed. "They worked slavishly and fanatically. It's too bad," Kelley added almost ruefully, "we don't have that much energy to spare in making democracy work." In addition, Kelley discovered, the Nazis focused on the ends of their labors and did not much care about the means that made them happen. Those ends varied from Nazi to Nazi and ranged from furthering the spread of Nazism to achieving personal power and glory.

As for Hitler, whose presence dominated the Nuremberg jail discussions yet who remained out of Kelley's reach, the psychiatrist made valiant efforts to understand his motivations and nature. At Mondorf and Nuremberg, Kelley had interviewed Hitler's associates, physicians, secretaries, and anyone else with intimate knowledge of the Nazi leader's life. He determined that "Hitler had a profound conviction of his own ability, amounting to megalomania. He firmly believed that he was the only individual who could lead the Third Reich to success, and at times he seemed to feel that he had been chosen by Heaven for this task." Anyone who crossed Hitler faced the leader's fearsome rage. To Kelley, it was not inconsistent with such megalomania that Hitler in private was often kind and soft-spoken with his staff; polite to women, children, and the elderly; and a lover of good food and other simple pleasures of life.

Kelley's analysis of the testimony he had gathered from Hitler's colleagues also convinced him that the German leader was less sexually driven than many other men, and like Göring may have channeled his sexual drive into work. "Hitler was just as normal in every way as any normal man," Göring had told Kelley. It was a rather chilling thought.

Douglas Kelley was far from the first psychiatrist or psychologist to attempt an analysis of Hitler's mind. In 1942 Cambridge professor Joseph MacCurdy had dissected the Führer's anti-Semitism, finding that it reflected Hitler's increasingly delusional and frustrated mental state as his fighters began losing on the battlefield. The psychoanalyst Walter C. Langer and the psychologist Henry Murray also produced profiles of Hitler that guided the planning of the US Office of Strategic Services during the war.

However, Kelley ultimately honed in on Hitler's well-known gastrointestinal disorders—a twenty-year history of gas and stomach pains—as a key to comprehending his behavior. Hitler's doctors never found an organic cause, and Kelley diagnosed the problem as "no more than a nervous bellyache." Kelley believed those symptoms pointed to "an anxiety neurosis and fixations centered on his stomach . . . nothing one could be committed to an institution for. He feared death. Many important decisions were made hurriedly and put into effect equally as hurriedly." Kelley had learned, for example, that Hitler told Göring in 1941 that a planned attack on the Soviet Union had to take place immediately because his stomach was getting worse; the Führer feared he had stomach cancer and that he might soon die. As a result, the Nazi leader turned his attention from successful assaults on Great Britain to a campaign in the east that resulted in defeat. "The horrors of this decision are well known," Kelley wrote, "and it is appalling to realize that an entire war was precipitated because of the severe hysterical stomach cramps and obsessive-compulsive fears of a psychoneurotic who happened to be in a position of command." In the same attempt to rush ahead before cancer struck him down, Hitler had demanded long hours of work from his underlings. There is no evidence that Hitler actually had stomach cancer, and the Führer refused to allow X-rays of his stomach because he did not want to confirm his fears. One of Hitler's doctors, Karl Brandt, had told Kelley that Hitler spent his final years continuously receiving shots of vitamins and glucose to stave off the imaginary illness.

Hitler's fear of death, evident in his employment of up to five physicians simultaneously, gave Kelley insight into the leader's attitude toward suicide. At first Hitler would not allow anyone to discuss the subject in his presence. For years, even as the momentum of the war shifted against him, Hitler often said, "No one but a weakling or a fool ever would commit suicide." But his opinion changed as the Nazi defeats piled up and his own health deteriorated. After 1944, now burdened with a tremor and weakness of his left hand and leg that doctors had diagnosed as hysterical in origin, "he was heard to say that he could easily understand how someone who was no longer healthy could kill himself. . . . [H]e expressed a terrible fear that this affliction might spread to his right hand," Kelley reported. "One day he said flatly that if this happened, he would put an end to himself."

Another factor in the attraction of suicide for Hitler was the fate of fellow fascist dictator Benito Mussolini, whose body his enemies strung up in public after his execution. After seeing photos of this desecration, Göring told Kelley, "Hitler went into a frenzy. He seized the pictures and went up and down the hall shouting, 'This will never happen to me!' And he waved the pictures in his hand. Afterward, Hitler several times brought up the subject spontaneously." Göring recalled, "He swore that he would never be taken alive and that no angry Germans would ever have the opportunity to befoul his corpse." For that reason, Göring maintained, Hitler declined to lead his army in a final stand against the Russians, fearing that the enemy would take possession of his body. Ultimately, in the days before he committed suicide in his Berlin bunker with Eva Braun, Hitler wrote in his last testament, "My wife and I choose to die in order to escape shame and overthrow or capitulation." Kelley found other peculiarities in Hitler's psyche—including his reluctance to touch animals without wearing gloves, his interest in and fear of horses, his obsessive repetition of daily routines, and his finicky attention to personal hygiene—but nothing that branded the Nazi psychotic or mad.

⬤ • ⬤

Kelley knew that the Nazis had committed atrocities and crimes of war on an unprecedented scale. Even the German leaders were surprised to realize what they had done and where they had ended up. But men whose personalities fell within normal parameters had set in motion the Nazi outrages, making Kelley worry that they could happen again. "With the exception of Dr. Ley, there wasn't an insane Joe in the crowd," he told a reporter for the *New Yorker*. The leaders "were not special types," he wrote. "Their personality patterns indicate that, while they are not socially desirable individuals, their like could very easily be found in America" or elsewhere. Consequently, he feared that holocausts and crimes against humanity could be repeated by psychologically similar perpetrators. His concerns differed from those of Hannah Arendt, who famously commented upon "the banality of evil" in her writings on the trial of Adolf Eichmann in Israel in 1961. Arendt asserted that Nazis followed orders from above, viewed those orders as routine, and accepted their own actions as unremarkable. On the contrary, most of the Nazis that Kelley had studied continued to see their regime and their own part in it as special, favored by the course of human evolution. That kind of thinking allowed Göring to liquidate former colleagues and issue murderous decrees—to revel in his power—even as he enjoyed a loving family life.

The psychiatrist could have easily accepted conclusions from his Nuremberg studies that cast the Nazis as psychopaths or as people in Arendt's mold. He could have rested easy believing that Germans were so culturally distinctive that such men could only have risen to power under unique circumstances. Instead, he reached a different conclusion, one that shocked and troubled him: the qualities that led the top Nazis to commit and tolerate acts of horror existed in many people, living in many places. True, the Nazis rose to power in Germany partly because of their nation's cultural training. But they "are not unique people," Kelley told American lecture audiences during the fall of 1946, following the execution of the condemned men:

> They are people who exist in every country of the world. Their personality patterns are not obscure. But they are people who have peculiar drives, people who want to be in power, and you say that they don't exist here, and I would say that I am quite certain that there are people even in America who would willingly climb over the corpses of half of the American public if they could gain control of the other half, and these are the people who today are just talking—who are utilizing the rights of democracy in anti-democratic fashion.

His observations of the Nazis in Nuremberg suggested to him that Germany's problems could, in theory, become America's. His countrymen commonly reassured themselves that in the United States the few could not control the many, civilization could not sink to such barbarity, and the nation's democratic traditions would not tolerate totalitarianism. Kelley found such optimism naive. He grew convinced that "there is little in America today which could prevent the establishment of a Nazi-like state." Even worse, fascistic bigotry already riddled American culture. "I found the same anti-minority feeling shot through the American population," he told one lecture audience.

American politicians, like white supremacists Senator Theodore Bilbo and Congressman John E. Rankin of Mississippi and Governor Eugene Talmadge of Georgia, Kelley maintained, exploited racial myths "in the same fashion as did Hitler and his cohorts. They use racism as a method of obtaining personal power, political aggrandizement, or individual wealth. We are allowing racism to be used here for those ends. I am convinced that the continued use of these myths in this country will lead us to join the Nazi criminals in the sewer of civilization." Although he declared the threat to America was not immediate, Kelley pointed to the political machinations of and harnessing of police control by such figures as Huey Long as evidence that Nazi power techniques were well advanced among demagogues in regional pockets of the United States, just as Hitler had launched his fascist movement from his ideological headquarters in Munich.

Americans, Kelley concluded, needed to look closely at their own culture and politics if they were to avoid the extremism and brutality of the Nazis. In a way, Streicher and Rosenberg had been right to warn of impending upheaval in the United States. Instead of the racial chaos involving African Americans and Jews that the two condemned Nazis had predicted, however, the biggest danger to America came from ideological demagogues. Kelley believed that Americans should scrutinize "our thoughts and our education, our policies and our political methods, if we are to avoid the sad fate of the Germans."

Consequently Kelley argued that Americans needed to prevent people with these kinds of personalities from gaining political control in the United States. With anticommunist hysteria and resistance to civil rights on the rise, he pointed out, America had ultranationalists and racial bigots aplenty. The Germans had long taught themselves ideas of Nordic superiority, tales of heroes who would arise from the masses to lead triumphantly, and the acceptability of an elite ruling class bulldozing the rest of society. "Americans are only [now] getting it ground in," Kelley declared. To combat this threat, Kelley advocated removing all restrictions on the voting rights of US citizens, convincing as many Americans as possible to vote in elections, and rebuilding the educational system to cultivate students who could, in Korzybskian fashion, think critically and resist using "strong emotional reactions" to make decisions. Finally, he urged his countrymen to refuse to vote for any candidate who made "political capital" of any group's race and religious beliefs or referred indirectly or directly to the blood, heritage, or morals of opponents. "The United States [would] never reach its full stature" until it had undergone this transformation.

While professing faith in America's traditions and potential, Kelley revealed his distrust of its politicians and the common Americans in their sway. Holders of public office were often manipulative and hungry for power, and their constituents were ignorant and gullible, he believed. Without the vigilance of intellectually evolved people, fascism could arise at any time. Authority was always nefarious. Without his realizing it, Kelley's suspicion of government institutions and officials mirrored that of many of his bigoted opponents.

● • ●

Starting in 1946, Kelley undertook a busy schedule of lecturing to spread his views on the Nazis and build demand for his yet-to-be-completed book. (He also wrote several articles, including an unfortunately titled essay for *Collier's*, "Squeal, Nazi, Squeal.") He focused on speaking engagements in California, where he had many contacts who could help him obtain bookings. Lecturing around the state, he covered a variety of topics, including psychological factors of the Nuremberg trials, the strategy of war psychiatry, and the physiological background of recent German history.

With his book manuscript mostly complete by the end of 1946, Kelley approached many New York publishers and, to his astonishment, was rejected. He ended up signing a contract with the Greenberg publishing firm for a meager advance of $300. Founded twenty-two years earlier by Jacob and David Greenberg, the company had a wide-ranging list, turning out Westerns, cookbooks, and gay erotica, as well as books on history, sociology, criminology, and architecture. It surely occupied a lower rung on the publishing ladder than Kelley had hoped to reach with his manuscript, but Greenberg's offer was the best he received, and he probably believed that any publication of his book would gain attention and advance his academic career. It took months, however, for Greenberg to edit and release the book, which was titled *22 Cells in Nuremberg*. Since his book was not going to make him rich, Kelley needed a job right away.

During 1946 he tried to land a teaching job at his alma mater, the University of California at Berkeley. Eventually he "was offered an instructorship at the University, and was told that if he was a good boy he could become an assistant professor in about 20 years," one of his friends and colleagues in the US Medical Corps, the neurologist Howard D. Fabing, later recalled. Kelley thought too highly of himself and his talents to accept such an offer, and he resumed his search for a position better befitting the former psychiatrist to the Nuremberg defendants.

Kelley soon found a new job 365 miles away from his home in Chattanooga, as associate professor of psychiatry at the Bowman-Gray School of Medicine, a part of Wake Forest University in Winston-Salem, North Carolina. There Lloyd Thompson, his old supervisor in the US Army, had founded a department of neuropsychiatry just weeks earlier. Initially the job focused on teaching responsibilities, but within a year Kelley was back to working with patients as the director of Graylyn, the medical school's thirty-five-bed psychiatric rehabilitation and convalescent center that opened during the summer of 1947. It occupied the Norman Revival mansion of Bowman Gray, the former president and chairman of R. J. Reynolds

Tobacco Company, and his wife Nathalie. After Bowman's death, Nathalie and her sons had given the estate to Wake Forest University. Visitors entered the fifty-acre estate on drives that curved among tidily trimmed lawns and gardens. Graylyn was huge and sprawling, "an English-style manor house of the type only an American with a long-accumulated bank account possibly could build," a newsman once reported. The house was filled with ironwork, fine tiles, and expensive furnishings.

This job gave the Kelleys their first real chance to settle down since their wedding. They moved to Winston-Salem in December and found a brick house with a library large enough to accommodate Kelley's six thousand pounds of books, which he described as one of the nation's largest private collections of volumes on psychiatry.

As a highly regarded thirty-six-year-old psychiatrist fresh from intriguing military experiences, Kelley was Graylyn's headliner, brought in to supervise all of the patient care. (Like the rest of the Graylyn staff, Kelley received a straight salary and did not maintain a private practice.) The university had filled the house with all sorts of testing apparatus and equipment. Graylyn could give patients a wide variety of treatments, including insulin shock therapy, occupational therapy, and electroconvulsive therapy. Doctors could even experiment with lobotomy, the technique of psychiatric surgery that Kelley believed brought improvements ranging from "considerable" to "spectacular" to half the patients operated upon. (The use of lobotomy eventually declined worldwide because of the procedure's significant side effects, its low actual effectiveness, and the greater benefits of psychoactive drugs.)

Kelley brought to Graylyn the group psychotherapy approach he had pioneered with traumatized service members during the war. When working with groups of patients, he displayed a mix of earnestness; all-too-apparent intelligence; and an adroitness in sketching graphs, pictures, and processes on the chalkboard. He planned to expand the treatment's reach by erecting at Graylyn a small stage with audience seating where scenes of a new form of treatment called psychodrama could be performed. There patients acted out their anxieties for discussion by fellow patients in the audience.

The point of these group interactions was to relieve patients' feelings of isolation. "A neurotic person invariably thinks his problem is a unique one," Kelley told a reporter soon after his arrival in Winston-Salem, "that no one else ever had such a problem. We point out—and other patients point out—that many persons have had the same trouble and try to show them how they can overcome their own worries."

Under Kelley's supervision, Graylyn accepted no "mental defectives" or psychopaths, whom he regarded as beyond the therapeutic reach of psychiatry. Most of the institution's patients were neurotic or mildly psychotic, and Kelley felt these people could benefit most from Graylyn's help. A small number of alcoholics would be admitted—those without psychopathic tendencies.

Although Kelley himself frequently enjoyed a drink, he did not professionally ignore the problem of alcoholism. For many years he advocated treating problem drinkers with a new compound called Antabuse, available experimentally in tiny white tablets. "No man," Kelley declared, "will fight through the effects of Antabuse to drink enough whiskey to make them [*sic*] drunk. Few can get beyond a first drink, once the drug has sensitized them to alcohol." The drug reacted with alcohol in the body to form acetaldehyde and caused headaches, shortness of breath, and extreme nausea. Kelley believed that the resulting intense sickness would condition drinkers to keep their glasses empty. Antabuse, which Kelley tested at Graylyn, "guarantees that any alcoholic who sincerely is interested in a cure will find great help," something that threats of damnation or laws restricting the sale of liquor could not accomplish, he told a reporter in 1948. Researchers could discover many other viable treatments for alcoholism if only there were enough money, and Kelley frequently proposed new taxes on liquor sales to fund such research.

General semantics, the use of words and their meanings to shape behavior, which Kelley had studied with Alfred Korzybski before the war, became part of the psychiatric toolbox at Graylyn as well. Just before Graylyn opened, Kelley had accepted the vice presidency of the Institute of General Semantics, which Korzybski himself had founded to advance the discipline. Kelley continued to believe that general semantics was valuable in psychiatry as an approach to communicating the use of reason against emotion in the treatment of illnesses. "We actually will retrain [patients] in thinking, so that they can intelligently and scientifically face the problems of life," Kelley explained.

In addition to patients suffering from neuroses and mild psychoses, Graylyn admitted many discharged military veterans in need of Kelley's expertise in treating battle-shocked fighters. In the fall of 1948 Chester S. Davis, a writer for the *Winston-Salem Journal and Sentinel*, witnessed the treatment of one such patient named Jonathan Worth (probably a pseudonym that Kelley asked Davis to use), who had survived an explosion in combat on Attu in the Aleutian Islands chain of Alaska, the scene of fierce fighting in 1943 after Japanese forces occupied the island the previous year. (The Battle of Attu was the only land engagement of World War II fought on US territory.) The fighting left Worth physically unharmed but psychologically scarred, and he complained of weakness and chronic headaches while having no memory of the blast that had disabled him. He was diagnosed with psychoneurosis, indicating symptoms without organic cause, and went through a treatment regimen typical for Kelley's Graylyn patients just out of the military. Worth received injections of insulin for three weeks, a treatment intended to produce episodes in and out of coma and a thorough rest of the patient's mind and body. Kelley believed that insulin overdose would also sharpen Worth's appetite, help him gain weight, and rebuild his central nervous system.

The insulin therapy left Worth feeling and looking better, but his headaches persisted. Now Kelley began the next phase of the treatment, which involved using one of his favorite antipsychotic aids. Moving the patient to his office, he gave him either sodium amytal or sodium pentothal to spiral him into the drowsiness of narco-hypnosis and played an unusual recording on a phonograph. As Worth slumped in half-sleep, the sounds of battle filled the room at high volume. Landing craft hit a rocky shoreline, airplanes dove and shrieked, bombs whistled and pulverized their targets, and machine guns spit bullets. The noises of Attu, or something much like them, surrounded the somnolent Worth.

Suddenly he rose up on the sofa and "in a moment, Jonathan Worth began to relive the Attu landing, a matter which, until then, was a blank in his memory," Davis wrote. Under Kelley's prompting, Worth said he believed himself transported back to his position as a machine gunner at the front of an invading US landing craft. He was firing at Japanese positions on the shore, and he saw many soldiers fall under his attack. After he landed, however, he discovered that the "enemies" he had killed were really US soldiers. He approached them and saw that one looked like his father. Overcome by shock, he collapsed on a heap of rocks and was later taken to a hospital.

"When Jonathan was free from his drug sleep, Dr. Kelley talked to him," Davis wrote, "made him see that what he had done was accidental and that his feelings of guilt were normal enough but unnecessary." Sent back to his room to recuperate, Worth found that headaches still troubled him. Kelley turned his attention to Worth's relationship with his father. He considered it unlikely that the dead soldier really looked like the elder Worth, and Kelley wanted to understand why the machine gunner had superimposed his father's face on the slain man's. In psychotherapy sessions, Kelley learned that Worth's father was a drunk who treated his wife and son violently "and, on occasion, backhanded baby Jonathan halfway across the room," Davis wrote. Worth grew up professing love for the man while harboring murderous feelings toward him.

"Doctor Kelley reconstructs the story in this fashion," Davis recounted. "When Jonathan hit the actual beach and ran toward the huddle of bodies, he had two shocks—first, that he had killed Americans, and second, to protect himself from that blow, he told himself that he had killed the one man he had always wanted to kill, his father. The treatment, with these facts in hand, was easy enough." Kelley suggested to Worth that his father deserved his hatred, and that Worth had indeed hated him. Worth's angry feelings toward his parent were completely normal and justified, Kelley said. "Once this lesson was accepted consciously, Jonathan's muscle tensions relaxed, the powerful cords of the neck released their grip on the base of the skull and Jonathan Worth felt the merciful relief of life without a driving headache." (John Hersey recounted an astonishingly similar tale of recovery from wartime trauma using narco-hypnosis in "A Short Talk with Erlanger," a *LIFE* magazine article published in October 1945.)

Davis's account of the diagnosis, treatment, and resolution of Worth's problem proceeded dramatically and logically, and Kelley actually did emphasize the rational and scientific basis of his general semantics-based work. He took pride in his skills in leading patients to replace deluded perceptions with rational ones. General semantics continued to figure prominently in his treatments, as in his use of battlefield recordings and the beneficial power he foresaw in moving Worth to use and own the word "hate" in describing his feelings for his father. Combined with all of the other treatments Graylyn offered, the application of general semantics could bring patients back to health much faster than other variety of psychotherapy alone. If people thought more rationally, they "wouldn't act so nutty," Kelley was fond of saying.

Throughout his sojourn at Bowman-Gray, Kelley continued lecturing, mainly in nearby mid-Atlantic states. He traveled through the Carolinas, Georgia, Pennsylvania, and Virginia, with occasional detours to the Midwest and West Coast, talking on such topics as lessons from Nuremberg and horizons in psychiatry. Between 1947 and 1949 he gave forty-six lectures, including a neurological talk at a convention of magicians.

Kelley often spoke of the emotional immaturity of the American public. "The average emotional age level of the American people is . . . appallingly low," he told an audience in San Francisco. "I hate to say it—I'm almost afraid to admit it—that everything we know seems to indicate that the emotional age of the great number of Americans lies somewhere between 5 and 7 years. If we elevate that to the level of 15 years, then we are safe—as a people and as a nation."

He focused entire lectures on what he seemed to believe was the sickly mental health of the American public and recommended changes in child-rearing techniques to lower the incidence of Americans who "are not very bright or are emotionally immature. You can see them every day—the adult who has temper tantrums like a child, another who resorts to tears to get what she wants, a third who merely sits like a hunk of proto-plasm, indifferent to all around him, and a fourth who just won't play," he told an audience. It was neither a sympathetic nor an optimistic portrait of his compatriots. Kelley also acknowledged that many of his psychiat-ric colleagues were "odd," a circumstance he called "unfortunate but rea-sonable. . . . The unstable will frequently go into psychiatry. The field has attracted more of the odd than perhaps any of the various branches" of medicine, he noted in Wilkes-Barre. But in defense of his colleagues, he deplored the "myth that psychiatrists are always trying to interpret at a dinner party their associates' behavior. We only interpret behavior during office hours."

Members of his audiences sometimes asked him how Göring acquired the cyanide capsule that he used to commit suicide. He replied that he did not know for certain but guessed that the Reichsmarschall's attorney might have passed it to his client along with some legal papers. Kelley felt certain that Göring had no poisonous capsules with him during the months he was the Nuremberg jail psychiatrist, because his own thorough physical examinations of the prisoners had turned up no foreign objects.

In other lectures, Kelley proposed blocking visitors to the United States who might try to spread a totalitarian ideology. If it were up to him, all politicians and statesmen would undergo psychological scrutiny before beginning their work. "The main thing to do," Kelley said in a 1947 ad-dress to the Anti-Defamation League of the B'nai B'rith in New York, "is to admit and recognize the danger. We shouldn't be like patients who suspect they may be sick and put off going to see a doctor because they fear he'll tell them that they are. The roots are here—you see them in anti-minority action of any kind, against Negroes in the South, against Jews in this area, against Orientals on the West Coast." But what went unsaid was the highly

authoritarian impulse that lay behind his demand for screening and scrutiny. Who would be the one to scrutinize if not the good doctor himself?

Although Kelley dramatized his findings on the Nazi personality when
addressing live audiences, he never expressed such certainty about identifying potential Nazis in his book. Greenberg at last published *22 Cells in
Nuremberg* in early 1947, and a second printing soon followed. Kelley had
fashioned the book as a survey of his professional opinions of the Nazi defendants plus Hitler, not as a chronicle of the Rorschach scores and interpretations he had developed at Nuremberg. He wasn't yet ready to explain
the test results.

Many of the book's buyers wanted to read Kelley's demolition of the
commonly held myths that the Nazis were madmen, that Göring and Schirach were clownish homosexuals, and that Hess's amnesia was completely
feigned. The author's assertions that the top Nazis who took control of
Germany were highly intelligent and psychiatrically normal men drew attention at the time, but seem to have faded from the public's imagination
in the decades since then.

Kelley hoped the book's publication would combat rumors that he had
somehow become attracted to the Nazis' ideologies or personalities during
his months at Nuremberg. He "was in no way sympathetic with the Nazis
or their philosophy or actions—far from it!" Dukie wrote loyally. "However, being a true scientist, he knew how to control his aversion in order to
elicit the information he needed for an unbiased study, which those who
think him sympathetic probably couldn't have done."

Meanwhile, Gustave Gilbert had not lightly accepted Kelley's departure
from Nuremberg with the psychologist's papers, test results, and observations. After the trials ended and he left army service, Gilbert rushed to
edit his notes and prepare his own volume for general readers about the
personalities of the Nazis and events behind the scenes at the jail and the
trial, which appeared as *Nuremberg Diary* a few weeks after the publication
of *22 Cells*. Like Kelley's volume, Gilbert's book steered clear of directly
referencing the Rorschach tests he and the psychiatrist had administered,
perhaps because of the author's inexperience in interpreting such results.

Nevertheless, Gilbert delved deeply into the Nazi personalities and produced a chronicle of his months with the prisoners in Nuremberg that influenced many later psychologists and historians. His interpretations of the German leaders often differed from Kelley's. Gilbert wrote that he did not see several of the Nuremberg defendants as normal or commonplace in their characteristics, but as psychopaths, possessors of a dangerous and distinctive type of personality. Göring, Gilbert insisted, was impulsive, egocentric, and deficient in moral courage, prone to lash out against opponents when he wasn't presenting his façade of geniality. He cared little for anyone outside his family. To Göring, war was merely a vehicle for asserting supremacy over others, not some lofty conflict over national interests. His yearning for power brought out his cynicism, sadism, and greed. Gilbert explained Göring's loyalty to Hitler as merely a superficial formality, a way for the Reichsmarschall to satisfy his craving for vast personal power. Göring's suicide, Gilbert maintained, was simply theatrical cowardice. Whereas Gilbert displayed Göring's unsavory traits as signs of a psychopathic personality, Kelley had held them up as qualities common to many people successful in business and politics. And unlike Kelley, who was suspicious of the aims of all political authorities, Gilbert regarded Nazism as a uniquely pernicious form of political domination that needed special conditions to thrive.

Gilbert's book received an unusual endorsement from a Nazi source, Albert Speer, now serving his twenty-year sentence in Spandau Prison. "I must admit that [Gilbert] reproduces the atmosphere with amazing objectivity," Speer said. "His judgments are on the whole correct and fair; I would hardly have put it very differently." Speer had always voiced approval of Gilbert's work at Nuremberg, confessing that the psychologist had left the Nazi feeling "something akin to gratitude." (Gilbert followed up with a second book, *The Psychology of Dictatorship*, a more systematic appraisal of the Nazi regime and its leaders, in 1950.) Perhaps the most important distinction between Kelley's and Gilbert's books was that Gilbert's offered an explanation that self-righteous and victorious Americans wanted to hear. It caught the mood.

Greenberg licensed 22 Cells to a British publisher and hoped for decent sales throughout Europe. "However, we discovered brother Gilbert had been there before us," one of Greenberg's representatives wrote to Kelley. "You probably noticed in the Times that Gilbert's book will be out the end of March. It's some comfort and a real advantage to have beaten him to the gun." When Leon Goldensohn, the psychiatrist who succeeded Kelley at Nuremberg, complained about the claim on the jacket of 22 Cells that Kelley was the only psychiatrist in the prison who had had intimate contact with the defendants, Greenberg removed it from the cover. "I don't think we need worry about him," the Greenberg staffer added. (Goldensohn kept his own detailed notes of his extensive encounters with the Nazis, but did not publish them. They came out in 2005 as the book The Nuremberg Interviews: An American Psychiatrist's Conversations with the Defendants and Witnesses, edited by the World War II scholar Robert Gellately, forty-five years after Goldensohn's death.)

Ever willing to speak to the public, Kelley tirelessly promoted 22 Cells. He believed he had an urgent message to deliver. In March 1947 he spent four days touring with the book in New York City; appearing on four live radio programs, recording another show for later broadcast, and headlining a press conference. He emphasized that his book was not for psychiatrists, other physicians, or academic specialists—he intended it to influence the thinking and behavior of the American public. Kelley hoped readers would understand the qualities that allowed a group of men to cruelly dominate a country and let them believe they had the right to do so. He wanted people to see that anyone could become those men, that America could become Germany. The United States was at a crucial moment of change, and the understanding he had brought home from Nuremberg could shine a light on the right path to follow. The Nazis, he warned, were you and me— given the slightest twist of fate. In broadly optimistic postwar America, he sounded slightly paranoid.

So strongly did Kelley believe in these principles that several years later, he required his young son to read 22 Cells in Nuremberg. "That was important to him," Doug Kelley Jr. recalls. "He set me down and had me read the last part of the book, so I could understand that anybody in any place and in any culture could create a regime like this."

● • ●

Lewis Terman, in his review of *22 Cells* for a psychology journal, looked forward to the future publication of Kelley's Nazi Rorschach transcripts and records, which the psychiatrist had promised were forthcoming. Kelley and Gilbert soon scuffled over the terms of a jointly published report and could not come to an agreement that met the demands of each that he receive primary authorship.

Kelley's faith in the value of the Rorschach test never weakened, and he continued using it as a tool for diagnosis for the rest of his career. He served a term as president of the Rorschach Institute during the late 1940s. He felt a professional responsibility to do more with the Nazi Rorschachs than presentation for laypeople in *22 Cells* had required. So starting in 1947, he shared the Rorschach information on seven of the Nazis with a group of international experts whose opinions he respected, including Marguerite Loosli-Usteri, the first president of the International Rorschach Society; S. J. Beck, a Chicago psychiatrist who often wrote about the Rorschach technique; and Bruno Klopfer, Kelley's old Rorschach collaborator. "I am not concerned with differences in scoring or interpretive methods or using these records for validation of the Rorschach method," Kelley told them. "I am only interested in gaining from as many experts as possible the completest patterns of personality which can be elicited from the records." He also said that he hoped to publish a paper that gathered and synthesized their findings.

Many of these correspondents returned their comments—sometimes written at great length and with obvious care. But Kelley never published the paper he had planned. This failure to make use of the contributors' work did not sit well with Loosli-Usteri, who complained to Kelley six years later and lamented that the window for such research had closed. "Nobody will anymore be interested in the psychology of those seven men," she wrote.

A separate effort to assess the Nazi psychiatric records had already begun among attendees of the First International Congress of the World Federation of Mental Health, held in London in 1947. The clinical psychologist and Rorschach expert Molly Harrower had invited ten fellow authorities to examine seventeen records gathered by Kelley and Gilbert for their assessment, along with eight unrelated control test results. (Gilbert was the source of these records.) Nothing came of the committee's examination of the Rorschachs. Harrower was among those who did not provide the interpretation they had promised. In 1976 she explained this dropping of the ball by recalling that the tests "did not show what we expected to see, and what the pressure of public opinion demanded that we see—that these men were demented creatures, different from normal people as a scorpion is different from a puppy. What we saw was a wide range of personalities, from severely disturbed neurotics to the superbly well adjusted." The members of the assessment team, she realized in retrospect, saw good and evil in black and white terms, with no room in their beliefs for more uncertain delineations of the personalities that could commit atrocious acts. So in the end Kelley remained the only investigator willing publicly to declare that people like the worst of the Nazis live among us.

Slowly, Kelley's focus on clinical psychiatric work began to weaken. Outwardly he appeared devoted to his teaching at Bowman-Gray and his direction of the treatment of patients at Graylyn. But his months at Nuremberg and inability to discover psychiatric triggers in the Nazis, or even a common personality type, left him yearning to better understand the minds of criminals. If, after months studying the prisoners responsible for the worst horrors of modern history, he found that evil was contained within people who in other ways seemed normal, then what could the tools of psychiatry usefully uncover? Kelley turned to criminology to illuminate these men.

In embracing criminology, Kelley ran a risk. Searching for the seeds of badness in others would force him to confront his own sinister aspects. As it offered answers for aberrant behavior, criminology could stir up the dark, untrustworthy world, so stingy in its appreciation for a great man's accomplishments, that Kelley's mother June had revealed to him years ago. When he turned to this new discipline, Kelley risked exposing his deepest fears.

● • ●

Starting in 1947, for the first time in his career Kelley accepted consulting work with a city police force, teaching psychiatric techniques to members of the Winston-Salem Police Department and helping the police investigate criminal cases. In the spring of 1947 he testified in court on behalf of an accused rapist, Ralph Vernon Litteral, and described his diagnosis of organic brain damage, probably indicated by Rorschach testing. Litteral was eventually convicted. In a development that captured headlines in North Carolina newspapers, Kelley publicly sparred with Governor R. Gregg Cherry over the politician's denial of clemency for Litteral. After personally interviewing Litteral, Cherry rejected Kelley's assertion that the convicted man was legally insane, and Kelley countered by suggesting that the governor should get a medical license if he wanted to practice psychiatry. "This business of being governor is not an exact science, and I think psychiatry is equally nebulous," Cherry replied. To which Kelley responded: "If he is competent to determine whether this man knew right from wrong, then we've solved the shortage of psychiatrists." Litteral was executed in November 1947.

Kelley refined his use of narco-hypnotic drugs for application in criminal investigations, especially in cases of amnesia or hysterically repressed memory, by replacing sodium pentothal and sodium amytal with Somnoform, a commonly used dental anesthetic. He counted the drug's subtle smell among its many advantages—it did not require hypodermic needles for administration, and in gaseous form it had a faint odor that often went unnoticed until it had intoxicated the patient. By that time the recipient was unlikely to worry about what it smelled like. Somnoform could take effect in ninety seconds and intoxicate the subject for ten minutes. "Take a whiff," Kelley once invited a reporter. "Well, come on and smell it. It won't hurt you. Sometimes it makes you feel like you had one drink too many." Kelley was speaking from actual experience. He had experimented with all of the "truth serum" drugs on himself. "After a few whiffs," he said of Somnoform, "your body begins to feel numb except for a little tingling sensation. Then you get sleepy and imagine you are floating away. A bit later about everything in the world seems wonderful and you relax. There is a constant feeling that something or someone is dissolving before your eyes." He hoped to discover a narco-hypnotic drug that could be delivered even more easily than Somnoform, either in small bottles or some other container, perhaps for on-location use at crime scenes.

Whether using traditional drugs or new ones, narco-hypnosis was experiencing a brief popularity in law enforcement. Evidence that police obtained using "truth serums" resulted in the release of murder suspects in California, Oklahoma, and elsewhere during the late 1940s and early 1950s. The drugs, Kelley and other proponents maintained, could elicit confessions, help rule out falsely accused suspects, and draw from witnesses details of crimes that their memories had suppressed. Even as Kelley acknowledged that people could lie while under the influence of the drugs, he emerged as perhaps the treatment's most loquacious advocate, and he frequently regaled journalists with his own dramatic stories of success. One such case involved a teenaged girl who in a fit of hysteria had lost her memory of her parents. They were strangers to her. Kelley's application of Somnoform wafted the girl into a suggestive state that allowed the psychiatrist to plant in her mind the imperative to remember all important events of her life, including experiences with her parents. Kelley asserted that the girl awoke from her narco-hypnosis, looked at her parents, and declared, "Hello, Mother and Daddy!" Kelley diagnosed her as suffering from "parental denial," a rejection of her mother and father. That disorder still required treatment, but the narco-hypnosis had freed the patient from her worst symptoms.

For years a specialist in the study of psychiatry and criminals, Herman Morris Adler, had worked on plans at the University of California at Berkeley to start a new and groundbreaking academic program in a relatively new discipline: criminology. After Adler died suddenly in 1936, the proposal became moribund. It regained momentum after the war, and university administrators cast about for candidates to lead the school, which would be the first academic program for the study of criminology on the West Coast and one of the first in the nation. With *22 Cells* published and attracting attention, Kelley's name came up. In a dramatic turnaround from its offer of an instructorship with weak prospects for advancement only a few years earlier, the university now offered Kelley a full professorship in criminology, to begin in the fall term of 1949. Kelley admitted that he was "seriously considering the offer" but would wait until he discussed it with Bowman-Gray's administration before making a final decision.

The Kelleys had their first child, Doug, at the end of 1947. (Two more, Alicia and Allen, followed in 1951 and 1953, respectively.) But because Dukie had recently inherited $400,000, the couple could now afford Kelley's changing the course of his career. A move to Berkeley would involve more money and prestige, but it also would alter Kelley's long-cultivated national image as a clinical psychiatrist. "It would be an exclusive teaching and research position," Kelley said while he was considering the offer. "If I accept, I will retire from psychiatric practice and devote full time to research work." He could not resist. He handed his Bowman-Gray supervisors his resignation, effective July 31, 1949, just two years after Graylyn had opened with him as its director. He had supervised the care of more than 560 inpatients during his time there, and an additional 1,600 veterans had come for outpatient care.

22 Cells in Nuremberg had gone out of print a few months earlier, and Greenberg sold the publication rights back to Kelley for $250. Tired of the war, its aftermath, and the trial, readers did not have much appetite for more information about Hitler and company. The book dropped from the limelight, although it continued to lend Kelley prestige. That prestige carried him a long way in Berkeley, until the day it changed to notoriety.

9
CYANIDE

Kelley never lost his love of being the center of attention. A natural ra-
conteur and entertainer, he adored teaching. His move to the School of
Criminology at UC–Berkeley in 1949 gave him the chance to immerse
himself in the field of study that had gripped him at Nuremberg. It placed
him before law students, future law enforcers, and soon-to-be judges, those
whose world he had increasingly inhabited as a consultant for the police
department and attorneys in Winston-Salem. From the cigarette-littered
police stations and coffee-scented law offices of North Carolina, he moved
to the bell towers and landscaped lawns of California's largest university
(and to a princely annual salary of about $9,000). He would quickly bur-
row his way into the grimy dens of justice that he so liked. His switch to
criminology intrigued many of his psychiatrist colleagues. "Do you accept
armchair detectives in your course?" wrote one physician. "If you get a
chance some time, I would very much like to hear about this venture of
yours, as what avid follower of Ellery Queen, Nero Wolfe, etc., would not?"

In his first semester at Berkeley, Kelley taught courses in criminologic
psychiatry and the detection of deception. Students could see that the
physician-professor did not match the common picture of a psychiatrist.
He joked in class, made dramatic pauses during lectures to let his authority
and good looks sink in, and filled chalkboards with bubble-filled diagrams
that resembled works of abstract art. He was developing a new collection
of criminal paraphernalia, which included sharpened spoons and other

felon-crafted weapons that he acquired from the warden at San Quentin Prison.

In the course "The Detection of Deception," Kelley taught the concept that different perspectives and points of view could rationally lead to different conclusions. And he was happy to resort to sleight of hand to teach those lessons. He often used what he called the "water trick" in the classroom. Kelley set up vessels of water that were hot, at room temperature, and cold and asked volunteers to plunge in their hands. Then, after they had acclimated to a temperature, he told them to withdraw their hands and immerse them in a bucket of cold water. The class was always amused to hear how the cold water felt frigid, medium cool, and warm to different students. Kelley's point was that the perception of what was legal or criminal—not to mention what we perceive as just—varies according to the perspective our senses afford us.

He still enjoyed playing the magician, letting on that "by learning the techniques of the magician in deception one can recognize the same maneuver in the deliberate lying of the criminal." As he had baffled the denizens of Berkeley two decades earlier by driving a car blindfolded and making his escape from locked boxes, he now produced simpler but no less effective tricks. He sometimes pulled out a deck of cards in class, surreptitiously drew the same card from the bottom of the deck time after time, and convinced his students that all of the cards were identical. He then let them examine the deck and discover that it held fifty-two different cards. The senses, he impressed upon them, can deceive us. "All the students come to class," he said, a point of pride for a teacher who hoped never to bore. He soon began planning to write a book on deception that would powerfully meld his experiences with Nazis, common crooks, and magic.

Now in his forties, Kelley had aged into a ruddy, solid, meat-slab sort of man, with a beer belly and fleshy thighs that supported his 165 pounds. Many mornings before going to campus, he stared at his face in the bathroom mirror and intoned the vowels a-e-i-o-u, exercising the voice that was such a commanding part of his presence. Before anyone (except Kelley) realized it, the newcomer was an international leader of his field, a previously low-profile discipline populated by attention-shy academics that one criminologist noted "contained nobody but us chickens." Kelley took pleasure in pulling the study of criminology down to earth, and he assigned students such street-level texts as Joseph Mitchell's *McSorley's Wonderful Saloon* and David Maurer's *The Big Con*. "He also picks up a tidy bit of scratch as a medico-legal expert, as a lecturer, etc.," wrote friend and fellow criminologist Howard Fabing admiringly to a colleague.

A lot of that income came from the Berkeley Police Department, which engaged Kelley as a psychiatric consultant in November 1949, almost as soon as he hit town. The local law enforcers had taken advantage of nearby academic expertise for many years, and a legendary police chief, August Vollmer, had taught criminal justice at the university. Another School of Criminology teaching star, Paul L. Kirk, frequently volunteered as a police consultant. A former chemist with the Manhattan Project who turned his scientific talents to the microscopic examination of physical evidence in criminal cases, Kirk later conducted blood analysis for the defense in the infamous Sam Sheppard murder case in Ohio, helping overturn the defendant's conviction.

Throughout the 1950s Kelley worked closely with police superintendent John Holstrom, who administered the police oath to Kelley, gave him the title Psychiatric Chief of Police, and issued him a chief of police badge from Alameda County, which Kelley could produce, as necessary, with the same dexterity with which he could deal a card from the bottom of the deck. Once while speeding along a highway in Northern California with his son, Kelley was stopped by a state trooper. "The Old Man popped out his wallet and showed him the badge," Doug remembers. "The officer said, 'Oh, I see. Excuse me.' I thought, 'What a hypocrite! How do *I* get a badge?'"

Kelley earned his badge for the most part for psychologically evaluating Berkeley police recruits. Among his first tasks for the force was to examine thirteen candidates for patrolman and patrolman-clerk jobs, and he found three of them "sufficiently unstable to be considered potential hazards in these positions." That high percentage of recruits that the psychiatrist rejected prompted Holstrom to let Kelley schedule regular psychiatric evaluations of all recruits, and as the doctor's proficiency in weeding out bad candidates increased, he gained fame around the country as an exponent of the rigorous screening of prospective police officers.

Strangely, Kelley also took it upon himself to evaluate the psychiatric health of certain citizens of Berkeley who reported crimes. In 1950 alone, he examined seven residents who had made frequent reports, plus the families of two of those people. He concluded that several of these people were mentally disturbed and should be "either committed or referred for psychiatric treatment." As a result, he predicted, "bizarre calls for aid" would dramatically fall. "I don't really think Berkeley is any crazier than any other city," he said in a press interview, "but Berkeley has a high percentage of psychotics and lunatics wandering the streets. We find about two new ones a week." Kelley launched a similar campaign against chronically bad drivers in 1953 and asserted that frequent traffic offenders could be classified as mentally unfit.

He capitalized on his police department expertise by frequently writing and speaking on law enforcement themes. One of his topics was "dumb cops." "About one-third to one-half of the policemen in this country are totally unfit to protect you or to solve crimes," he declared sweepingly in one article. "They are emotionally unstable, low in mentality and psychologically unsound." Even worse, he claimed that many cops on the beat were paranoiac, sadistic, and actually insane. "They're just as dangerous as the thug who steps out from behind the shrubbery in your garageway and sticks a gun in your back." His solution to this perilous situation was for more police departments to subject officer candidates to screening tests like those he championed in Berkeley, including IQ and Rorschach examinations. In speaking engagements, he sometimes told the story of a police recruit he examined who looked at a Rorschach inkblot and said he saw "a bisected, stomped-on rabbit." That candidate, Kelley noted, advanced no further in pursuing police work. He often berated police chiefs whose departments lacked scientifically based barriers to entry. "That's awful," he scolded. Over time, as he immersed himself more in the world of crime and detection, Kelley seemed to develop a progressively bleaker view of the criminality of society in general and a dimmer view of the competence of detectives.

Sometimes his targets shot back. In the summer of 1954 members of the New Jersey State Association of Chiefs of Police placed on their meeting agenda a discussion of one of Kelley's recent "dumb cops" articles and complained about it to the FBI. An agent found Kelley's views "highly unfavorable to law enforcement generally" and irrelevantly added that Kelley's book *22 Cells in Nuremberg* had received a good review in a publication of the Washington Cooperative Book Shop Association, an organization identified as politically subversive. When Kelley attended a conference of the International Association of Chiefs of Police a few weeks later, FBI agents monitored his talk on traffic offenders, found that he said nothing about unqualified police officers, and filed a memo on the incident.

Lecture audiences could not count on Kelley to keep to a narrow range of topics. In Los Angeles he told a crowd that the Russians were as dangerous as the Nazis and that the United States should use firmness, not appeasement, in handling Soviet involvement in Korea. In 1951 he informed an audience in San Francisco that many of his colleagues in psychiatry were in over their heads, and that they used big words "to conceal the fact that they don't know what they're talking about." He often discussed psychopaths, declaring that the personality type, like an elephant, was difficult to define but "you can sure tell one when you see one." A listing of his lectures in a promotional brochure issued by his lecture representative included "Fact and Fable in Psychiatry," "Fear: Its Facts and Fictions," "Fads, Frauds, and Fools," "How to Keep Young in Mind," and "Nothing But the Truth." He spoke animatedly about juvenile delinquency, and he blamed rising crime rates among the young on modern parenting, which too often ignored teaching children to limit their impulses to do wrong and to feel remorse when they strayed from right. Kelley found a lot wrong with the human condition.

● • ●

Kelley applied his psychiatric expertise to many prominent criminal cases. Working sometimes for the prosecution and sometimes for the defense, he consulted and testified in the cases of such notorious Bay Area defendants as Ray Cullen, tried for killing his wife and father-in-law in 1949; Mary Edna Glenn, charged in 1952 with murdering her two children; Hildegard Pelton, who murdered her husband after he repeatedly abused her; Rodney Sheran, convicted in the 1955 murder of his wife; and Saul Sidney Klass, a jeweler convicted in 1957 of shooting a physician to avenge his wife, who had died under the doctor's care. With the aid of prosecutors, Kelley examined Stephen A. Nash, who had committed a series of "thrill murders" in Los Angeles, without disclosing that he was a psychiatrist. Kelley then testified that Nash was legally sane. In many cases such as these, he put his Rorschach expertise to good use, and he made the psychological test a centerpiece of his consulting arsenal for the remainder of his career. The book he had written in 1942 with Bruno Klopfer, *The Rorschach Technique*, stood prominently on a shelf in his home office. Kelley insisted publicly that the test was a valuable tool, despite the mystery that continued to surround it—though on occasion he let slip a doubt about exactly why the Rorschach test worked. "The Rorschach method has come fast in the 29 years of its existence," he wrote in 1951. "Whether it has come far is harder to say. We still have little notion as to why it seems to work—theories, yes, by the pound, but [few] facts measured in the microbalance."

Similarly, Kelley held fast to his conviction that various forms of truth serums and truth detection were effective. He continued to champion Somnoform as a treatment to elicit criminal confessions and to overcome amnesia. Pathological liars, he admitted, would continue to dissemble under Somnoform's influence, but those people were uncommon. He still hoped for a truth drug that was even better. "I'm hunting a drug which can be contained in a container as small as, say, a pencil," he told a reporter. "When I get it, then I'll be really happy."

The murder of a fourteen-year-old girl named Stephanie Bryan in 1955 drew Kelley into the most notorious case of his career. Walking home from her junior high school only a few blocks from the UC–Berkeley campus, Bryan, the daughter of a local doctor, had vanished while taking a shortcut through a wooded area. The girl's body eventually turned up in a hurriedly dug grave in Trinity County, in far northern California. A twenty-seven-year-old former Berkeley student named Burton Abbott was the chief suspect. Abbott was something of a cipher, a skinny, smart, dapper, and bespectacled man with a thin mustache and well-manicured fingers whom one reporter likened to "a pencil standing on end." The police brought in Kelley and polygraph expert Albert Riedel to grill Abbott, and their work slowly broke through the suspect's glib and nonchalant façade. After Riedel's insistent lie-detector interrogations, Kelley took over and put his questioning and listening techniques to use. In the middle of many other questions, he asked Abbott if he had attended a coin collectors' convention at the Claremont Hotel, a building near Bryan's fatal shortcut. "Do you collect coins?" Kelley prodded. "No," said the suspect, who then mentioned that his wife did. "What kind?" Kelley asked. "The spending kind!" Abbott joked. Kelley did not laugh, but he took note of Abbott's inappropriate hilarity. In another interview, Kelley subjected Abbott to a detailed description of the scene of Bryan's grave and the state of her decomposed and animal-mangled body when her remains were found. Abbott took it all in with no sign of emotion: "Damn you, O'Meara," Abbott said to another person in the room, "where is that ham sandwich you promised me?" Kelley later observed that "Hermann Göring and Burton Abbott were the most self-centered" of all the people he had professionally interviewed during his career.

Abbott grew to dislike and fear the psychiatrist, calling him a brainwasher and complaining that Kelley "put me through hell." He responded disdainfully to Kelley's suggestions that he lacked a conscience and was emotionally immature. "He's all wet," Abbott said. "My conscience is quite well developed. If anything, I am rapidly developing a persecution complex. Dr. Kelley seems to be impressed with his own importance." Such remarks must have convinced Kelley that his questioning was getting close to the truth. Denying his guilt to the end—even after the murdered girl's clothing and purse turned up in his basement—Abbott was convicted and sentenced to death in 1956, and he perished in San Quentin's gas chamber the following year.

Such cases propelled Kelley into prominence as a consultant, and he won jobs advising authorities on personnel selection and criminal matters at Travis Air Force Base, San Quentin Prison, Letterman Army General Hospital, the California Attorney General's Office, the Atomic Energy Commission, and the Oakland Police Department. In the few spare hours he left himself, he took on freelance consulting gigs in Central and South America, Pakistan, Thailand, and other parts of the world. He stretched his time thinner by shouldering the responsibilities of the presidency of the East Bay Psychiatric Association. During the mid-1950s Kelley was considering adding further to his workload by starting a new business as a psychiatric consultant in corporate management.

With his return to California, maybe the call of Hollywood was inevitable. In 1954, before the production of the film *Rebel Without a Cause*, director Nicholas Ray contacted Kelley to consult on the criminological soundness of Stewart Stern's screenplay (which Ray and Irving Shulman had adapted from Robert Lindner's novel). Ray wanted Kelley to focus on the script's portrayal of youth gangs and juvenile delinquency. Kelley pointed out to Ray only a few inaccuracies in the script, including police dialogue and interviewing techniques that struck him as wrong, an unrealistic encounter between the James Dean and Sal Mineo characters, and insufficient attention to juvenile psychiatry, although he acknowledged that giving psychiatry its due "might slow down the action."

Also in 1954, Kelley consulted on a TV program about stage magic for NBC. He splurged with his earnings from that work and bought a color television—an expensive and rarely seen home electronic appliance at the time. For a long time the storytelling techniques and potentially large audience of television had drawn his interest, and over the years he had sketched several proposals for TV shows about crime and psychiatry. One nascent show he discussed with friends, *Fakes, Frauds and Fools*, would each week feature an infamous con, quack, or carnival cheat, along with the frauds they perpetrated. Kelley's inspiration for the series was a letter his father had received of the "Spanish prisoner" type—an ancestor of the Nigerian 419 scams that later invaded e-mail inboxes. Turning the tables, Kelley convinced the Mexican swindlers who had targeted his father to wire him $50 to travel south to complete a transaction. "He figures he has enough script ideas," one of Kelley's friends said of the con show concept, "to go five or ten years without straining himself to think or read. . . . Kelley would wind it up, title and all, as Professor of Criminology, scientist, doctor, psychiatrist, magician, etc., who knows all the answers to everything dealing with human cupidity, including the basic psychology which motivates both the mark and the con." That itself sounded a bit like a con, but the University of California seems to have been an enthusiastic supporter. The School of Criminology would gain credibility and publicity for its programs and faculty, as well as credit for advancing the notion "that crime does not pay, for the thought that the shepherds of Berkeley are watching over the little sheep of America," Kelley's friend reported to a colleague.

However, the series never got off the ground. Kelley appeared in some other programs, including ten episodes of a series titled *Science in Action* and another, sponsored by the California Medical Association, called *Why, Doctor?* He received nearly $50,000 in funding for another program, titled *Criminal Man*, from the Educational Television and Radio Center of Ann Arbor, Michigan. His teammate in the production was a local writer and producer named Gordon Waldear, a former test pilot who had become a journalist after he was injured in a crash. The two had previously collaborated, with Waldear as ghostwriter, on a book manuscript gathering much of Kelley's experience and wisdom on the intersection of psychiatry and criminology. Kelley came to view Waldear as "a psychopath," as Dukie later recounted. While working on the book, "Doug had had a rough time with him," she said. "It would be hard for you to imagine the degree of frustration and pressure he suffered because of Waldear's lack of ability to work with any degree of speed, his inability and at times complete failure to get to work at all, his not showing up for appointments, his constant lies, and his complete irresponsibility both in his contractual arrangements and in his finances." Kelley's judgment was excessive: Waldear may not have been as rigorously productive as Kelley had hoped, but he was far from psychopathic. In later decades, Waldear became a beloved and respected figure among Bay Area documentarians and TV producers.

Waldear's undeniable talents as a television producer ensured that *Criminal Man* proceeded smoothly and achieved a stunning success. In twenty episodes the series covered the history of crime, its causes, various categories of criminal acts, crime-fighting strategies, and solutions to criminality. The series strove to "bring about a better understanding by the public of the person who commits a crime so that attention in the future may be shifted from what Dr. Kelley calls 'simple vengeance' to true rehabilitation of the offender," explained the original proposal for the program.

Kelley believed that TV programming, even shows on academic topics, could interest a mass audience. "Why shouldn't all educational programs be as dramatically interesting as a play?" he wondered. On camera, he worked hard not to look or sound like a tweedy professor. He put his considerable powers of persuasion to use, modulating his voice, turning up his speaking volume at times, grimacing and smiling, and raising his bushy eyebrows. "No!" he exclaimed to the audience in an episode that investigated whether criminals have physical features in common. "There is no such thing as a criminal type. It is simply folklore. It is like saying the world is flat. You can't tell by looking. Criminals are not born." In another episode about the causes of violence, Kelley's son Doug appeared as a child whose incessant beating on a drum drives his father into a frenzy. Kelley played the exasperated father.

Shot at the studios of KQED in San Francisco, *Criminal Man* did not reach completion until the end of 1957 and was scheduled to air nationwide on educational television stations, the forerunners of today's PBS network, during the summer and fall of 1958. Kelley never saw his programs broadcast to the screen of his beloved color TV set or to any other. The show was the final professional project of his career.

●　•　●

The Kelley kids knew that when the Old Man was upstairs working on a sensitive police or legal project, he was immersed in darkness, lost in an inaccessible state of mind. He wanted no interruptions and often played loud tribal or classical music when holed up in his office at those times. "To us, the music was synonymous with Daddy's most important cases," Doug remembers. Often police officers, criminal suspects, and prosecution or defense lawyers would visit the house to meet with Kelley. The psychiatrist had equipped his desk with a hidden drawer that contained a tape recorder and an ashtray with a concealed microphone, and he used them surreptitiously to record his interviews. One time a man came to the house for a psychiatric evaluation, a criminal "who had shot people from his overcoat with a shotgun," Doug recalls. The boy played with the visitor in the living room for a few minutes until Kelley came down from his study. The two men went upstairs, closed the study door, and the loud music came on.

Even as a child, Doug detected the dual allure that attracted his father to psychiatric criminology. The intellectual puzzle of these cases merged with Kelley's need to feel like "the big man on campus." The combination made police and criminal consulting irresistible. But police work also awakened fear in Kelley, almost paranoia. The crimes of others disturbed him, stirring the anger he felt from the buried emotions and view of the world that he could never acknowledge or confront. He expressed his anxieties in the fear that criminals would invade his home to harm him and his family. He had two handguns from the Berkeley police that he kept handy with ammunition, and he installed high-quality locks on the first-floor windows.

His fame as the Nuremberg psychiatrist persisted, and his interactions with Nazis sometimes reemerged unpleasantly. In 1952 he received an angry letter from Christa Schroeder, a former secretary to Hitler whom Kelley had interviewed during her incarceration in the Nuremberg jail.

Schroeder objected to Kelley's characterizations of her, which had appeared in newspapers four years earlier and in *22 Cells in Nuremberg*. In the book Kelley had called her "a motherly, maiden female in her late forties, of medium height, stocky, sloppy, non-Nordic in appearance." He had also reflected on her loyalty to Hitler: "[E]ven when the evidence of his brutality became undeniable, he remained a hero. Her comments, consequently, though frank, are those of a person who refused to see anything but greatness in Adolf Hitler."

Schroeder accused Kelley of breaking a promise not to use his interview with her in any published work, and she took him to task for inaccuracy and unkindness in his observations. Of all people, she wrote, he should have understood that the harsh conditions in the prison made it impossible for women to keep up their appearance. She noted that when they met she had already been behind bars for six months, had been traumatized by Germany's collapse, and had no personal articles such as "combs and hair pins, shoe laces, creams and manicure things not to be mentioned." At the time, she asserted, she was thirty-eight years old. "My appearance is absolutely not 'unnordisch.'" She stood 1.7 meters tall. She demanded from Kelley an apology and "a settlement and reparation of the insult" if he wished to avoid unfavorable press coverage in Europe. Kelley's reply, if he made one, is unknown, and he never faced a campaign against him in European newspapers. Schroeder went on to work for several German businesses and died in 1984.

Kelley's consulting income, plus his professor's salary, allowed for plenty of spending money. And Kelley spent it. He bought specimens and equipment for his home laboratory, folk art and crafts from his travels, books, and kitchen doodads. He made the money, he thought, and he should spend it. Saving for the future did not often enter his thinking, although Dukie thought differently.

Meanwhile, Kelley and Dukie settled into a striking house on Highgate Road in Kensington, a well-to-do community of university professors, doctors, and lawyers just north of Berkeley. It was a Spanish-style house with red tiles on the roof, stucco on the outside walls, and an expansive brick patio between the wings of the U-shaped layout. A green gate opened to the yard's eucalyptus and redwood trees, plus a grove in which grew almonds, cherries, peaches, and persimmons. The property cascaded in terraces down to a lawn, to a road, and finally to the neighboring cemetery. Stone walks snaked among the plants. A hired gardener tended the yard, although Dukie sometimes sought out the gardens for their sunshine and to work the earth.

Inside the house, living areas and bedrooms branched off from long and expansive hallways splashed with sunlight from tall windows. The rooms nevertheless gave an impression of darkness, perhaps because of the attention-seeking hodgepodge of Donner Party artifacts, fossils, plant and animal specimens, and other weird collectibles that filled the many nooks and crannies. Vials of wood splinters from the Donner cabins, labeled and certified authentic by Charles McGlashan, were holy relics in this household. The second-floor closet held a mysterious assortment of objects, including straitjackets, card decks subtly marked with tiny wheels and other symbols, and Oscar, the comical wooden duck mounted on a small pedestal whose head and bill Kelley could manipulate mechanically to pick cards from decks held in the hands of his audience members. Kelley no longer performed his magic tricks professionally, but he could not pass up opportunities to dazzle others as a showman and continued to display his talents in legerdemain to friends and neighbors, at class reunions, and in his lecture classrooms.

Upstairs Kelley set up an office commanding a magnificent view. Fog often flowed between the hills enclosing Golden Gate Bay and shrouded Alcatraz Island. Rosy sunsets set the office on fire with color. This was Kelley's private preserve, a room that the children—Doug, Alicia, and Allen—knew they should not enter without permission. Kelley's desk, spotless and tidy, stood in front of the windows. Across the room, behind a door, was the doctor's lab—a wondrous cabinet of curiosities that contained bones, plant specimens, cranial saws, stoppered jars of chemicals, minerals and rocks, and an assortment of scientific investigative equipment. Kelley's library had only enlarged since he had moved from North Carolina, and it now boasted a notable collection of books on such topics as Southwestern art, mythology, and witchcraft, in addition to texts on biology, zoology, chemistry, and astronomy. Kelley also kept handy the autographed volumes by Nazi leaders that he had collected at Nuremberg.

A black staircase led down, its descent interrupted by a large, white-railed landing six feet above the first floor that was visible from anywhere in the living room. Kelley relaxed in the living room when he managed to push professional concerns from his mind. Alcoves beneath the stairs housed a well-stocked record collection and a high-fidelity music center equipped with a phonograph, radio, and speakers, all enclosed in a custom-made wooden cabinet that had been hauled to Berkeley from North Carolina. Music could entrance Kelley, and he liked Hawaiian, African, and classical recordings. Across the room was a baby grand piano. A horned toad and a lizard stood as still as statues in a terrarium against one wall.

Wearing boxer shorts and a white T-shirt, Kelley liked to decompress in a green leather chair that faced the TV. He had the piece of furniture specially designed to allow him to sit with Doug and Alicia on the arms of the chair, with little Allen on his lap. At other times he occupied the chair for long periods while he watched boxing matches on television; a can of Pabst Blue Ribbon beer invariably sat on the table at his side. The more he drank, the more closed-off to the children he grew. He would often end the day in a condition "between squiffed and smashed," according to Doug.

The kids watched the beer cans pile up and wondered whether Kelley was investigating a new scientific question: How much Pabst Blue Ribbon could a man consume in a day and continue to think and function? Their father, however, labored under a different preoccupation. How could he escape from the turbulence he felt from the torments of criminology, the discipline that agonized and attracted him? Pabst provided the simple answer.

The living room, and the dining room down the hall, with its large cherry table and leather-armed chairs, were the scene of all sorts of board game sessions, chess matches, and spontaneous mental play. Kelley and Dukie were both quick to laugh, and their wordplay and slightly manic, competitive punning filled the house. It was up to the kids to keep up. "If you didn't know what a word meant, you had to look it up," Doug says.

Wearing socks, the children could take a running start and glide the entire length of the living room's polished brick floor. Outside, hay bales stacked against the outside wall of the kitchen pantry served as archery targets, at least until an errant arrow once sailed through the window.

The kitchen, down the hall from the living room, was Kelley's domain—the place in which he exercised unrestrained control. "Dad was like a Boy Scout, always prepared for anything," Doug remembers, and his father kept the kitchen and adjoining pantry stocked with fifty-pound sacks of beans and rice and a hoarded supply of water. Using a hand-cranked grinder, he pulverized prodigious quantities of meat. His larder filled two refrigerators and three freezers, and he maintained an extensive stock of spices. Kelley believed that cooking food required continual modification and frequent sampling, and he liked to proclaim, "Beware the lean and hungry cook." He adored making his signature recipe, Indian curry, but he also dished out pressed duck, bird's-nest soup, great big slabs of bacon, and even stuffed bear paws that he made with two stoves bristling with eight gas burners and equipped with a fast-food style griddle that seared at 450 degrees.

Kelley often cooked up ambitious meals when he and Dukie hosted dinner parties for neighbors and friends. Dukie had never really learned how to cook, and Kelley insisted on taking charge of the preparation. The psychiatrist could not resist making himself the center of attention at these gatherings. He often prepared a prized duck recipe at such meals, and the fanfare with which he displayed the duck press, dropped the bird inside, and started cranking the big handle to extract the juices was an important part of his staging and performance. He would pour gravy into a special tureen and proudly ladle a serving onto each plate. He found other ways to grab the spotlight, as well. At one gathering outdoors on the Kelley patio, the visitors noticed a large animal—a badger or a possum—creeping through the yard. Kelley, ever the master of ceremonies, astonished the guests by rising from the table and cornering the animal, which triggered its instinct to play dead. Not content to leave the creature alone, Kelley grasped it by the tail and raised it high for everyone to admire. Or perhaps it was so they could admire him. Kelley was a showman to the end, ever eager to place himself center stage, at the heart of the action—no matter how strange.

Here and elsewhere, the Kelleys never discussed politics, and the children never learned which political candidates they favored, except during the 1952 presidential election, when Kelley and Dukie wore Ike buttons. It was the McCarthy era of academic intimidation, and Dukie warned Kelley never to sign any petitions; they would come back to soil his reputation. Your name was your most valuable possession, they believed, and you had to guard it. It was a tense, watchful time.

● • ●

The native westerner and Bay Area boy came out in the frequent road trips Kelley took during summers and academic sabbaticals with his kids. Suddenly he would declare a four-month vacation and would pile the children and an assortment of camping gear into an old DeSoto that he had modified by removing the jump seat in the back, thus transforming it into something like a four-wheel-drive Jeep. Visiting Arizona and New Mexico, the family would tour Native American land; gather archaeological and craft collectibles; and dig into whatever the local cuisine, culture, and religion set in their path. These were serious pursuits of knowledge that Kelley designed for his children, intended to spark the sort of ravenous curiosity that afflicted him.

He tried to make the kids eat any exotic foodstuff they encountered, including, on one occasion, abalone. Alicia drew the line there, and none of her father's attempts to get her to swallow the sea creature succeeded. He tried to make each excursion into a learning opportunity for the children. They were never at rest. When the family returned home, they carried as many artifacts as they could fit into the DeSoto, objects that Kelley would add to his collections of souvenirs that opened windows into science, anthropology, and history. "He was like a spider gathering a lot of different things," son Doug recalls, and the psychiatrist's predatory collecting soon filled the house on Highview Road. Kelley told a friend that he coveted a whale fetus to add to his artifacts and that he would "swim across the Bay" to get his hands on one.

Kelley felt reenergized after these trips. He was like his grandfather, who decades earlier had often hiked to the sites of the moldering Donner cabins near Truckee in search of inner calm. Kelley similarly believed in the benefits of escaping from familiar surroundings, and he felt stronger after immersing himself in another place, new hunting grounds for artifacts, fresh physical and cultural worlds to ponder. And, like his attorney grandfather, Kelley tapped the power of attentive listening: the technique of making a show of concentrating on everything an interviewee, patient, or client says, of drilling his green-eyed gaze into the souls of the people around him, to kindle flattery and crumble secrets.

The family was often dragged to Truckee and Donner Lake. That was the place he identified as his origins. As throughout his life, he considered his mother's family, the McGashans, to be his worthy, heroic ancestors. He never sought out his father's roots. On one trip into the mountains, he cradled a beer can while driving and got drunk. His aggressive driving frightened the children. "He was a great driver, but he took risks," Doug says. Dukie often sat next to him, grimly quiet, with her knuckles bleaching white. The risks Kelley took as a driver, and the anger that seeped out when he spent time with his family, revealed a painful ember in his soul. Teaching, consulting for the police, writing a torrent of articles on psychiatry and criminology, marriage, and fatherhood all weighed upon him. Convivial but stubborn, he clashed with some of his university colleagues, and academic politics stressed him. He could be prickly and petty, turning minor disagreements into disputes. On one occasion he took umbrage at a $17.50 fee that a hospital billed to give Dukie an X-ray. He wrote to the hospital's chief administrator, no less, in sneering terms, that the charge seemed "a little high as I interpret the ethics of professional courtesy. However, I suppose you have your own private standards."

● • ●

Kelley's inner rage, however, involved far more than type-A stress. The household he had grown up in was loud and full of dissatisfied commotion. June Kelley, the brilliant and precocious lawyer who had devoted herself to her father's reputation and welfare, had grown hard and embittered in her final years. She reared Kelley never to feel satisfied with what he had, always to crave to know, obtain, climb, and deserve more. The roots of

June's mental tumult are unknown, but she lived in darkness, anger, and fear. Danger lurked everywhere, and June taught her son to think fast and find the threats. Kelley's filial role was to support June emotionally and keep her going.

From childhood, part of Kelley was fun-loving, quick witted, jovial, and a player of tricks and games—that joy came from his father, Doc, the dentist to whom he never felt very close. Doc was no man of accomplishment, and he practiced from the same office on Irving Street in San Francisco for nearly fifty years. His home, frozen in time with its linen-draped furniture and heavily curtained windows, was upstairs. The other part of Kelley was a furious achiever for whom praise was essential, a man who could not find contentment no matter how high he scrambled. June pulled those strings. "He didn't know how to let little Douglas Kelley Sr. come out and play with big Douglas Kelley Sr.," son Doug observes. Learning and acquiring information fueled him, but never to a conclusion that satisfied him. From criminology he really needed an explanation for his own emotional blow-ups and craving for recognition. But his research and teaching left him at a loss. He careened wildly in his work and vented frustration. "He was a cross between a sponge and a rampaging bull," Doug says. "He was a Renaissance man on speed."

The discovery that had dawned on him at Nuremberg—that the behavior of some of the worst criminals of modern times could be attributed to no psychiatric type or any specific mental illness—continued to rattle him and animate his ferocious output of research and work. And fueled by alcohol, he lashed out unpredictably against his family. The children feared him.

Dukie tried her best to love and support her volcanic husband. She was strong, and Kelley knew he had a good partner in her. They shared an actual family melody, a high-low-low musical phrase that Kelley would pucker and whistle when he was looking for her in or out of the house. When Dukie responded, it signified a connection that went beyond words. Dukie knew her husband loved her, but she quietly regretted his inability to provide attention that felt soft and gently affectionate, too. Most of the time she could handle his moods and keep him from collapsing beneath his burdens, although she resented Kelley's bond with his mother, who was still very much alive. Dukie complained that he was closer to his mother than to her. Many times, though, the Kelleys' arguments escalated without logic or apparent reason. They could argue about anything, the meaning of a clue on *What's My Line?* or the reason for the newspaper boy's misplacing their paper. Kelley's voice grew more stentorian during their altercations. Dukie's voice was shrill, by no means weak, but his vocal blasts overpowered anything she said.

Anything could happen between them. A dinnertime dispute resulted in a smashed glass, and Dukie, who didn't realize that she was hurt, served Doug a plate smeared with her blood. When the boy pointed it out, she carefully wiped off the blood with a towel and calmly handed the plate back to him. The children watched transfixed one day when Kelley and Dukie shouted at one another in the sun-drenched corridor on the second floor that ended at the psychiatrist's office. They faced each other outside the magic closet. The kids lived in a near-constant state of apprehension, but they did not expect to see Kelley level a gun at her. His finger tightened on the trigger and a shot reverberated around the house. He had lowered the gun at the last split-second before he fired, and the bullet left a neat hole in the wood-paneled floor at Dukie's feet. She later covered the spot with a rug. It was all just a tremendous piece of showmanship, wasn't it? But the children's minds raced: "If he had shot her, would he have shot us?" Doug remembers thinking. "That was the secret our family kept: Periodically, the Old Man went crazy." He often would go upstairs "to look at the bullet hole in the hallway floor."

Dukie believed she had her own cause for anger against her husband. In 1950, soon after the Kelleys' move to Berkeley, Dukie's father witnessed one of the psychiatrist's rages, an explosion in which the potential for violence was obvious. A quiet and placid man, Mr. Hill was outraged by the treatment he saw his daughter receiving. He remained upset for a long time, soon suffered a stroke, and died. Dukie blamed Kelley not only for her father's death, but for destroying her ideal of family life, a picture of love, warmth, and growing devotion derived in part from the sunny novels of Clarence Day. She wanted this sort of emotional environment for her own family with Kelley, but his outbursts and pent-up fury made that impossible. When her own anger boiled over and she sank too low, she would pack up some clothing, grab her purse and the youngest children, and spend a day or two with relatives in the Bay Area. "Once I told Dad I really missed them," Doug remembers. "He said, 'Me, too—let's go and get them.' We got them and drove back home."

Perhaps inevitably, Kelley—the collector, analyst, pursuer of insight into the dark corners of the human mind, and one-time magician—made it his goal to rear an exceptional eldest son. Young Doug would be a guinea pig for aggressive techniques to spur mental development from the moment of his discharge from the hospital maternity ward. The son replaced Göring, Hess, and Rosenberg as the father's experimental subject. At home the boy received a barrage of tutoring, information, and insistent exercises in brain-building. To this day, he still feels the pain and pressure of Kelley's observation exercise, which would be set up as a contest for his son. Sitting in the living room, he would ask Doug to inspect their surroundings, taking note of as many details as he could. After telling the boy to leave the room, Kelley would make a slight change in the room's arrangement—even as slight as nudging a pencil across the coffee table. "What's different?" Kelley demanded when his son came back in. The exercise inspired dread and panic in Doug, as well as excitement and satisfaction when he identified the difference. It was a strange combination of feelings.

"I practiced IQ tests all the time," Doug says. Kelley reported Doug's IQ scores—usually in the mid-150s—to school officials and to his old acquaintance Louis Terman, who still directed his influential study of gifted children at Stanford. In 1952, when Doug was four years old, the *Saturday Evening Post* featured the family in an article about high-IQ people and Terman's study. The accompanying photo showed Dukie leaning over Doug, who clutched a baby doll as he sat on a sofa and looked back expectantly. Sister Alicia sat at his side. Kelley hovered above them all, the only standing figure and the brainiest looking of the bunch. Wearing a silk tie that glistened in the light, Kelley's eyes bored into the top of Doug's head.

Kelley put his son through memory training, and Doug regularly visited the Stanford and UC–Berkeley campuses to take psychological and intelligence tests from the best in the business: Bruno Klopfer, Alfred Korzybski, and S. I. Hayakawa. If he suddenly decided Doug needed to learn about astronomy, Kelley would bring in an astronomer who ran the nearest planetarium to give the boy home lessons. He skipped Doug over three and a half years of school. Despite his own overbearing authority, which brooked no challenges, Kelley taught his son to question the authority of others. Every day young Doug was subjected to some aspect of his father's regimen: "When I woke up, Dad would hand me a protein shake, stand next to the heater, and hold out the paper with words for me to memorize for the day." Kelley performed his fatherly tasks with sternness, anger, and absolute inflexibility. He aimed to create a high-level thinking boy, the sharpest observer and intellectualizer one could possibly make from a child. As a guide and expert on rational thinking, Kelley exuded the confidence that he knew everything. His ultimate end was to teach Doug how to arrive at rational conclusions "and then distance yourself and see how others are viewing you," Doug recalls.

On one level, the reactions of others were important to Kelley, because only from outsiders could praise—and thus a smidgen of something approaching gratification—come. But he had bigger principles in mind when he inculcated in Doug the benefits of closely observing other people. Scrutinizing the behavior of others, paying close attention to what they say and how they move, leads to predicting their behavior, Kelley believed. The psychiatrist told his son that forecasting people's behaviors after carefully examining them can result in something called tele-empathy, the ability to feel what others are feeling and thinking. Kelley himself was a master of this skill, able to attract everyone's attention at a party, speak persuasively, project sheer competence, and read the crowd at a magic performance. If nothing else, Kelley's domineering mentorship passed on to his son that ability to interpret the feelings of others. He absorbed how to gauge the atmosphere of a place, the mood of its inhabitants, and ways to circumvent people who stood between him and his goals.

"I can get a good sense of how a room feels. . . . The value of that is staggering, but the weight and burden of it is terrible," Doug says. He used the talent Kelley brought out in him to sniff the air of his own home to forecast whether this would be the day of one of his father's explosions or not. But a child has enough to worry about in his own thoughts and feelings without trying to understand a world of adult complexes and impulses. As a result, as Doug neared adolescence, he began rejecting the basic premises of his father's teaching. "I didn't want to achieve, lead, or take control," he says. He refused to grow up to become the person Kelley imagined he would be, and he continued "to love a part of myself," he says. Doug, who resented his father's refusal to accept any opposing points of view, began drinking and smoking pot when he was eleven years old. Secretly he retrained himself *not* to focus on figuring out what was going on around him. Slowly Doug learned to value something his father never understood, the individuality of others. Kelley's doomed attempt to create a brilliant, perfect son—a true McGlashan heir—was the one continuous project to occupy him from soon after he returned from Germany to the end of his life. It was as if, having looked into the dark Nazi minds and found nothing there to fundamentally separate them from himself or anyone else, Kelley was determined to try to create in his son a better, stronger, more ideal creature, someone who was not vulnerable to whatever weaknesses in the human condition had permitted the staggering wartime atrocities. Perhaps, too, Kelley invested so much hope in his son's future because he had begun to realize his own failures. He was clearly a man in torment; perhaps Doug would be spared if his father could prepare him for and fortify him against a world of criminality, ignorance, pettiness, and—evidently—evil.

● • ●

"The Old Man always gave us presents for our birthdays. He would take us wherever we wanted, and he was often playful," Doug says. But Kelley's own frustrations left him with few tools for good fatherhood. "He never understood that we were different from him and not just his children." Doug, at the age of seven, found himself coolly planning ways to escape his father. "If I get on the refrigerator with a hatchet, will I be fortunate enough to cleave him in the head before he knows it is coming?" he remembers thinking. But he was not a violent child, and instead he "learned to shut up and hunger and survive, but I needed to be let go and be free."

Having Douglas Kelley as a father proved both a boon and a curse. The boy learned the joy of knowledge and the adventure of curiosity. He acquired the gift of reading people and spent pleasure-filled hours cultivating his own mind. At the same time, he faced the full force of a terribly conflicted guide, a top psychiatric diagnostician in distress who refused to go see a psychiatrist. As a father, Kelley was capable of love but had little idea how to open himself to his children. When he drew close to them, the unresolved rage he carried chilled them. He careened through their lives like a runaway train.

This upbringing weighed on Doug as he pondered his fate in his basement bedroom. "I had rages and would go nuts and destroy my room, and then I would put it back together. I slept lightly because I didn't know if the Old Man would get drunk and come down and beat me." Doug felt confident that his father's violence would not get out of control, but he feared it nonetheless: "I knew it was sort of dangerous." Kelley could lose his temper for any reason, or for no reason at all. But sometimes the psychiatrist came down simply to kiss the boy on the forehead. Doug never knew which version of his father was approaching each time he heard the heavy footsteps on the stairs.

Doug engaged in angry imaginary dialogues with his father. "In the end [I would mentally say to the Old Man], you can think you know everything, but you can't get my essence. You cannot break me or get here," he declares, pointing to his heart. "That nugget you can't get—you'll have to kill me." Sometimes Doug stepped out of an upper window and sat on the roof to consider the enigma of his father. "It was hard to understand how someone with all that facility, who could give help to others, couldn't help himself. It's still somewhat baffling," he admits. Kelley's acquaintances and colleagues had little idea of the degree to which he was psychologically disturbed.

A closet that opened to the hallway adjoined the Kelleys' bedroom, and when thunderbolts flew between their parents, the children would close themselves in it and listen to the sharp voices as they penetrated the wall. "I'd go in there and wrap myself in her fur coat and listen," Doug says. "I thought they were crazy. Dad was angry, a cold intellectual anger, but hers was softer anger. He was so dominant. I remember a massive fight about something Bennett Cerf had said on TV. I knew Mom was right." But it was his father who prevailed. "I had the fear that one of them would die. Mother's fear was that he would end up destroying the family or himself. Such a big man couldn't say, 'I've got something wrong with me.'"

Seeking help from a fellow psychiatrist, in Kelley's mind, would have tainted his authority. Who could he possibly see who wouldn't know that he was a world-renowned authority on the Rorschach, a police consultant who screened out unfit cops, an expert on violence and criminal behavior? For God's sake, he must have lamented at his lowest and most angry moments, who could understand a guy who treated Nazis, the most notorious criminals of the century, and couldn't fathom his own fits of mayhem? Who would keep it quiet? He had built a magnificent public persona based on his competence, authority, rationality, and control—although at home he shed that garb to drink in his shorts and T-shirt and constantly threatened eruption. Dukie later acknowledged to her son that his father was "too prestigious" to be caught visiting a psychiatrist.

So Kelley's frustration and anger remained bottled up. The emotions heaved in cycles of work and violence, amid continual demands from the responsibilities he had taken on to distract himself from his inner turmoil. He shuttled among classes, criminal consultations, TV appearances, lectures, police screening, his own writing, and husbandhood and fatherhood. He cooked dinner every night, met with and dissected psychopaths, tried to guide children not yet in adolescence into high intellectual achievement, and entertained audiences—all while leaving his own volatility and psyche unexamined. His weight crept up along with his stress. Over time he noticed the twinges of a duodenal ulcer—not the sort of thing that would curb his craving for spicy foods—and popped Tums much as Göring had snacked on paracodeine. His personal physician, Harry Borson, warned Kelley that the ulcer probably was the result of the strain of overwork. But never did Kelley waste thought on taking care of himself.

Others could see the dangers of Kelley's fast and brutal track. Lewis Terman warned him of the danger of spreading himself so thin. "I am amazed by the number of activities you are engaged in and can't help but wonder whether it is too many for your long-range professional good," Terman wrote to Kelley in 1955. Terman, an older man who had known Kelley since the psychiatrist's childhood, owned up to having the same workaholic tendencies himself, a habit he regretted. In reply, Kelley defensively described how he had increased his work efficiency by accelerating the pace of his activities to get everything done. "For example," Kelley wrote, "preparation for a speech or paper ordinarily takes [me] 20 to 30 minutes unless, of course, a major research project is involved." He admitted, though, that he could not continue to capably juggle the tasks of parenting, teaching, and researching, and he promised to heed Terman's cautions. But he never did—his inner demons proved too relentless. That same year, Kelley's mother June died, which—though he left no record of his feelings—must have devastated him.

George Dreher, a family friend, took notice of the load Kelley seemed to bear. Around the fall of 1957, he observed that Kelley "was feeling the weight of his exceptional workload," he wrote to Dukie several months later, "but only now am I sensing how much inner strain this signified. It is probable that not only I, but many others who should have understood and responded, were hindered by the impression of his obvious competence and vitality." By the time Dreher wrote his letter, however, it was too late.

● • ●

When he was forty-five, Douglas M. Kelley's professional pressures, internal grievances and disappointments, and marital unhappiness flared up in a violent ignition. Doug can project a flickering replay of the nightmare scene in his mind. It is New Year's Day 1958, late afternoon, twenty-four hours past his tenth birthday. The Christmas tree still stands in the corner of the living room, and Doug's younger siblings Alicia, then eight, and Allen, four, are playing together on the floor by the fireplace. A football game fills the screen of the color TV, and Doug and his grandfather, Doc, are watching it. Kelley and Dukie are preparing dinner in the kitchen.

There is a commotion in the kitchen. Something has happened. The voices grow louder. The words aren't understandable, but they rise in pitch. Doc looks up and listens. Kelley and Dukie are taking turns shouting at each other. They're fighting—there's no doubt. It goes on until the Old Man throws open the door and strides into the living room. He is talking gibberish, spouting sounds of anger. Won't take it anymore, he bellows. He spins round the corner and runs upstairs into his study and slams the door shut. A blue porcelain doorstop trembles, topples over, and rains pieces from the second floor into the living room. Dukie enters the room and looks at Doc. "This one's bad," she says.

Doc rises and begins to herd the children out of the room. Alicia and Allen go out, but Doug has taken a position behind the sofa, nestled in the crook of the piano. He feels compelled to witness what happens. Then, after seconds pass, it does happen. The Old Man marches out of his study and appears at the top of the stairs. He holds something in the palm of his hand. Gliding quietly, Dukie moves to the foot of the stairs. Kelley descends to the landing and faces his wife, father, and son like an orator. "I don't have to take this anymore!" he howls. "I'm going to take this potassium cyanide and I'll die in thirty seconds. I'm going to take this, and nobody will care!"

Dukie says, "Doug, don't." Doc cries out, "Don't do it!"

In an endless moment of quiet and slow motion, a monster—a roiling billow of the anger, stress, frustration, and fear within him—has forced itself out of Kelley, and it is as visible to the family as a storm cloud that rules the sky. This creature, which has never before dared show itself so brazenly, is now horribly present. It has taken over Kelley's soul. It understands the powerful drama of the situation and the thrall in which it holds its helpless audience. Under its control the Old Man opens his palm and places something in his mouth. He swallows.

"No, Doug, no," Dukie says.

Kelley drops like a slackened marionette and strikes the stairs below. The monster has risen up and away. Dukie runs up and reaches out to touch her husband. She pulls him down to the bottom of the stairs. He is still alive, gasping and staring in disbelief. She cradles his head; they talk, share a few words. Something in the performance has gone wrong. The illusion was not supposed to go this far. Together Dukie and Doc drag Kelley down the hallway to the bathroom by the entry. As Dukie runs off to call for help, Doc pours water into Kelley's mouth, trying to flush out the poison.

Still standing behind the sofa, Doug is stunned. Someone soon leads the children out of the house through the front door, and as he passes his father, who lies on the floor, his top half under the bathroom sink and his legs in the hallway, Doug glimpses Kelley's face. Racked by seizures, the eyes bulge red and the mouth trickles foam. The boy thinks, "I never want to die that way." Then he is yanked away from the man's shell, and the kids spend hours at a neighbor's house. "It never occurred to me that he would die until Mom came home and told me. . . . I thought he'd pull it out," Doug says. Doctors had pronounced Kelley dead upon arrival at 4:56 p.m. at Herrick Memorial Hospital in Berkeley.

Police superintendent Holstrom came to the house that night. He gazed at Doug, took him to his bedroom, and searched for words. "This is terrible," he told the boy. "Don't hang onto it. He can remain alive in your poor heart, but move on and take him with you." Move on—this won't define you. Doug has never forgotten the policeman's kindness.

Dukie later tried to appease Doug with a childish explanation of what had happened. "We were arguing, honey," she said. "Your father burned himself with the pan." Her words didn't come close to describing what Doug had witnessed. His father had not perished because of a kitchen spill, and he knew it. Dukie remained loyal to Kelley in her incomprehension. To her, the suicide remained forever inexplicable. Kelley left behind no note. "I never did know why. He wasn't unhappy," she insisted when a San Francisco reporter interviewed her more than forty years later. "I just put it out of my mind. I don't want to try to remember. . . . [I]t's not anything I want to think about. It is just a mystery."

Doug has never stopped pondering the suicide. He is his father's son —
he wanted to know more. He could have escaped the tragedy, Doug believes. Kelley could have stopped it up until the point he grabbed the
cyanide and created the possibility of an act with no return. A truly big
man could have contained his rage, could have put out the fire, but Kelley
was really no bigger than anyone else. Doug ultimately concluded that his
father had been grandstanding on the landing of that staircase, and that the
accumulated force of his emotions and inner pain had carried him away.
The son believes that the rational thinking that Kelley advocated through
general semantics had suddenly abandoned him.

Because Kelley's death had not been natural, county officials conducted
an autopsy, which revealed no diseases that might have sent the psychiatrist into despair. (Rumors had circulated that Kelley was distraught over
the advance of a serious stomach or intestinal disorder.) Kelley's cremated
remains found a final resting place two days after his suicide in Truckee, in
the McGlashan family cemetery plot. There Charles McGlashan's memorial dominates Kelley's marker and everyone else's. Few people attended
the memorial service, and Dukie, afraid of traumatizing the children,
would not allow them to go. The house on Highgate Road grew darker.

Kelley's suicide filled the pages of Bay Area newspapers for several days.
Nearly every article reported the shock with which his friends and colleagues learned of his death and their scramble for an explanation. They
raised the possibility that Kelley felt overcome by the burdens of work, a
fatal disease, or a sudden realization of the insidiousness of criminal behavior. Some suggested an inevitability to his death. A writer for the *Berkeley
Gazette* somberly recalled that "Dr. Kelley had once said that the professional life of a psychiatrist was about 15 years—after that he either went
crazy, or committed suicide. He had been practicing since 1940." Each article failed to mention the argument that had preceded Kelley's final act, and
many even reported that he had embraced Dukie and wished her a happy
new year just before swallowing the cyanide. The *San Francisco Examiner*
noted nonsensically that "as far as anyone knew, his life held not a single
dark secret."

Speculation quickly swirled about the source and significance of the cyanide. Had Kelley provided the Reichsmarschall with poison? Journalists covering the suicide variously reported that Kelley's fatal dose was a souvenir from Nuremberg or had been a gift from Göring. In some ways, perhaps it was, though certainly not literally. But Göring's example demonstrated that a man who fears he will need a poison pill will keep one handy.

Everybody tactfully, if somewhat negligently, spared Dukie any questioning. Although she gave a statement to the police, no official investigators or reporters ever followed up with her. Any direct connection between Kelley's and Göring's deaths "is ludicrously ridiculous and smacks of the sort of [irrational] association—certainly not informed cognition—of some ulterior motive which stems from the author's own problems," she declared. Noting that it would have been unethical and illegal for her husband to have assisted in Göring's suicide, she wondered "if that's the sort of thing these accusers would have done." And she dismissed the notion that Göring had given a cyanide capsule to Kelley as simply "nuts!"

Dukie even doubted that Kelley took his cyanide in capsule form. He held "what appeared to me from across the room to be a powder," she wrote in 1985. "I never saw the container, but from the way he held it palmed, I would say it was probably round and large enough for him to quickly grab some 'powder' in his other hand, put it in his mouth, and gulp it down." She also believed that Kelley perished almost instantly, while Doc was pouring water into his mouth, because "I heard a thud while I was talking [on the phone] and I think he must have dropped dead at that point—very quickly and painlessly." There was a lot of wishful thinking in her account. Kelley's death, as Doug could see, was not painless. Kelley's doctor had told reporters that nobody would plan ahead to swallow cyanide because the chemical "burns painfully" in the throat. Besides, the question that Dukie never addressed was the most obvious one: Why did the doctor use cyanide?

There were guns in his office—a self-administered gunshot would have been quicker, cleaner for the victim, at least, and more manly. If Kelley wanted melodrama that New Year's Day, why not display a gun or knife to generate a frisson in his anguished audience instead of holding some substance, unknown to the onlookers, concealed in his hand like a palmed coin? As a physician well acquainted with criminal practices, Kelley knew that ingesting cyanide led to one of the most painful and unpleasant deaths we can inflict upon the human body.

There was more behind Kelley's choice of that particular poison and that exceedingly rare form of suicide, a train of thought more complicated than grandstanding and letting the devilish drama of the moment carry him away. The cyanide was a deliberate evocation of Göring's defiant suicide and the Reichsmarschall's pose of a hero backed into a corner. When Kelley fetched the cyanide, he signaled the arrival of his final stand against a fate worse than death that lay ahead. Death provided the quickest and noblest escape for the overwhelmed psychiatrist from an ignominious future—a descent into incompetence in the face of his insecurities, responsibilities, and pressures. Just as Göring's high opinion of himself would not permit him to suffer the indignity of hanging, Kelley could not allow himself to appear as a bungler unworthy of praise or recognition. The pain of death would end the more intense pain of staying alive.

In his 1950 book *The Psychology of Dictatorship*, Gustave Gilbert had explained Göring's plunge into Nazism by observing, "It was the zest of high and fast living, of heroic playacting, that appealed to him." Kelley loved that same kind of high-emotion, fast-accelerating life journey before an awed audience—and their similarities probably account for the close bond that he and Göring formed. But in both cases, when their heroic rides approached their bitter, agonizing ends, they chose to bail out. It is no coincidence that cyanide, a poisonous agent with a uniquely dramatic effect on the body, was their selected means of escape.

Obituaries and public eulogies extolled Kelley's best qualities while unknowingly demonstrating how effectively the psychiatrist had hidden his private life from his acquaintances. "For almost 30 years we were extremely close friends," wrote Dariel Fitzkee, a fellow magician. "I had never known him to do an impulsive thing in all those years. . . . Doug had told me, as I presume he had told others, that no one really knows his own breaking point." Kelley ended his life, Fitzkee speculated, because he worked himself too hard and cracked under the strain. "Even for such a complex man, the answer is that simple."

Eventually the press stopped reporting on the suicide, the cards of condolence no longer poured in, and what remained of the Kelley family was left to itself.

10
POST MORTEM

After the police left, after her husband had been cremated and his ashes buried, when the remaining Kelleys returned to the home on Highgate Road, Dukie struggled to take control of her family. It was as if the stagecoach driver had been shot, and she had to grab the reins of the runaway horses. She found herself surrounded by Kelley's lab apparatus, books, artifacts, and gadgets, without the presence of the collector himself to give them meaning or life. Although she had always been a loving presence in her children's lives, she didn't know how to be an active parent. Her husband had done the disciplining, driving, earning, and idea making. The cooking had been Kelley's job as well. Dukie did not have the slightest idea how to make a meal.

She put many of Kelley's belongings up for sale within a year of his death, including crystals, mortars, beakers, pipettes, Bunsen burners, an autoclave, a microscope, slides of botanical specimens, an algae collection, a hoard of mounted poisonous plants, a bubble sextant, two human skulls, a relief map of California, a Polaroid camera with flash, the tape recorder from his desk drawer, an oil refinery model kit, and a model steam engine. But she kept much more, including the psychiatrist's large collection of medical records, papers, notes, Rorschach results, and souvenirs from his months in Nuremberg.

Dukie also tried to keep her husband's ideas and opinions in circulation. She authorized a reissue of *22 Cells in Nuremberg* in 1961. Accounts of the Holocaust, such as *The Diary of Anne Frank*, were starting to attract readers' interest, but Nazi war criminals still felt like tired news to many. Kelley's book sold poorly. Greater acclaim came to his *Criminal Man* TV series, which aired on educational television stations around the country during the year after his death and won KQED a Sylvania Award for excellence in television production. Dukie hoped to capitalize on that success by plugging the long-dormant criminology manuscript that Kelley had begun with Gordon Waldear. Waldear spent months completing and trying to interest publishers in this volume, but the book never materialized. Publishers noted that it had little chance of catching on without the dynamic Douglas M. Kelley around to promote it and feature it in his trademark spellbinding lectures.

After failing to generate interest among publishers for the Kelley-Waldear book, Dukie reached further. She did not want to see her husband's ideas and work disappear. She thought Kelley's career could form the basis of a dramatic TV series, so she contacted television writer Frank L. Moss—whose credits included episodes of *Route 66* and *U.S. Marshal*—and tried to reel in a TV producer. The premise of the series shrank to "a consulting psychiatrist and his adventures in the world of crime and criminology" before vanishing altogether.

● • ●

In the summer of 1961 the family left the house on Highgate Road and moved into another one higher up in the hills, with floor-to-ceiling windows that gave a view of the entire bay and admitted light, light, light.

Occasionally, as Kelley's suicide receded into the past, friends tried to set Dukie up with men. She took the kids with her on one notable date with a man who proposed a day trip on his boat. Things went wrong from the start—her son Allen toppled off the gangplank and fell into the water. "I'm fine on my own," she often grumbled to the kids. "Why are they setting me up?" As she forged ahead, she realized she did not need a man in her life to "bother" her. She believed she had already been married to the best she would find. A stoic, loyal southerner, she remembered all that had been exciting and satisfying about her marriage, and she buried the bad. She decided that she and Doug, as she always called her husband, had made the best of their fates.

Selective memory was not going to help all the family recover from Kelley's devastating death. Its members "blew apart, all affected in different ways by the suicide," Doug says. Allen, the youngest, remained Dukie's baby, and she watched over him closely. Alicia bonded closely with her mother and took care of her.

Doug, on the other hand, actively rejected what his father had taught him. "I was repelled by power and the idea of leading others," he says. His parents had greatly accelerated his progress in school, and he was nine years old when he started seventh grade. After a short stay in a military boarding school in Tennessee, he came back to El Cerrito High School to graduate. Doug cruised through hippiedom, college, jobs, and marriages for years, always avoiding standing out, excelling, or being the kind of achiever that his father had wanted. He finally stuck with a mail sorting job in the US Postal Service—a man with a reputation among his coworkers for knowing everything that was happening in the building. It was his tele-empathy still ticking away, still on alert. For a time, one of his postal colleagues was Georgia Abbott, the wife of Burton Abbott and the discoverer of the belongings of Stephanie Bryan in the Abbott basement. Doug's father had helped send her husband to the gas chamber.

George "Doc" Kelley continued practicing dentistry in San Francisco into his ninety-first year, and he outlived his son by nearly fourteen years. He joined Kelley in the cemetery at Truckee in 1971.

◆ • ◆

By then only three of the men who had occupied the twenty-two cells at Nuremberg remained alive. Half a world away, Rudolf Hess still lived behind bars in Spandau Prison in Berlin. In 1948 a Mayo Clinic psychiatrist working as a consultant for the US Army, Maurice N. Walsh, had evaluated Hess. Some years earlier Walsh had taken an interest in the minds of political tyrants when he encountered Dominican Republic dictator Rafael

Trujillo as a patient at Mayo. Trujillo was supposedly there for a general checkup, but actually needed treatment for syphilis. Talking with Trujillo, Walsh judged him "schizophrenic and . . . without any access to normal guilt feelings and normal emotions of love and tenderness." Walsh wondered how such a man could rule a country and attract loyal followers. He grew interested in the callousness with which he believed many despots regarded human life and human rights.

At Spandau, a crowd of Allied representatives occupied the visiting room with Walsh, making a normal psychiatric interview difficult. Hess, looking thin and still suffering from frequent stomach cramps, "was affable and pleasant during the interview, which lasted two hours and was largely carried out through the American interpreter," Walsh wrote. His amnesia appeared to have vanished, and Hess clearly recalled most events from his past. He only had difficulty remembering his episodes of forgetfulness in England, and he repeated his claim that his amnesia at Nuremberg had been faked. "Hess then asked permission to make a statement," Walsh recorded. "With considerable dignity and with great emphasis he stated in a very formal manner that he regarded his present imprisonment as dishonorable and unjust. He said that he and his comrades were at times insufficiently fed in the prison and were made to do hard labor which was contrary to the sentence at the Nuremberg tribunal. . . . He said that he wished to request that he be set at liberty." Walsh reported to the army soon after the interview that Hess did not suffer from hallucinations or delusions, that his mood was normal, and that he was not psychotic. He said that the depths of Hess's emotions were greater than he had expected to find. He called Hess "an individual of superior intelligence with schizoid personality traits" who had experienced hysterical amnesia in the past because of emotional stress.

Writing about the examination decades later, however, Walsh characterized Hess very differently. Hess, he recalled, "had a latent schizophrenia. There was no doubt about the basically psychotic nature of his psychiatric illness or that he had experienced recurrent psychotic episodes for several years past. This was indeed an astonishing situation," and Walsh objected to Hess's continued imprisonment. The psychiatrist disclosed that he had previously been "forbidden by the American Military authorities to release my diagnosis on Hess because, I was informed, this would irritate the Russians, and at the time of my visit during the Berlin Airlift, the Russians were very easily irritated."

The Soviets absolutely refused to allow any clemency for Hess, and his incarceration continued. Under normal circumstances in an American or British court, Hess might not have been put on trial at all, but the Russians insisted that his sentence was not alterable. In the 1970s—when the last of his fellow defendants remaining in prison, Baldur von Schirach and Albert Speer, had been released and Hess was Spandau's sole inmate—committees of concerned citizens in Britain formed to demand a review of the former Deputy Führer's case, and then Hess's wife and son joined efforts to put an end to his treatment as a criminal. Alone among the former Allied powers, however, the Soviet Union resisted making changes to the terms of Hess's punishment. The Russians never freed Hess from his sentence.

John Dolibois, Kelley's first translator at Nuremberg, caught a final glimpse of Hess in 1984. He and his wife were visiting the US Army's Berlin brigade and took a helicopter tour of the city. Flying low, the aircraft hovered over Spandau Prison. "From an oblique angle I spotted a single, lone figure walking slowly along a path in the prison garden," Dolibois recalled. Hess was sickly and shrinking within himself, refusing to speak with anyone or see his family. The stubbornly resistant man Dolibois remembered was gone. "Stooped, he shuffled along slowly." Three years later, at the age of ninety-three, Hess succeeded in committing an improbable suicide by strangling himself with an electrical extension cord. Spandau Prison was soon demolished to prevent neo-Nazis from making it a shrine.

◆ • ◆

As Hess deteriorated in prison, a controversy roiled over the best interpretation of the Rorschach tests that Kelley and Gustave Gilbert had given him, Göring, and the other Nuremberg defendants. Many psychologists pointed out problems with the records: the Nazi subjects—recently toppled from positions of power—were stressed from capture and time in prison, they probably were not representative of Nazis in general, and as prisoners they occupied subservient positions to their examiners. Even so, the tantalizing insights these records provide into the minds of leading Nazis have made them the most fiercely contested Rorschachs in history.

The debaters have fallen into two categories. In one camp are those who agree with Kelley that the Rorschach tests of the Nazi defendants reveal no distinctive "Nazi mind." Some in this camp also assert that many people regarded as mentally healthy are capable of behaving similarly to the Nazis under the right circumstances—the line of thinking that so overwhelmed Kelley when he reached the same dark conclusion. On the other side are investigators who point to data in the Rorschach tests that they believe indicate the Nazi leaders shared signs of mental disorder.

Gustave Gilbert was the early standard-bearer of the latter group. In 1961 Gilbert, by this time a middle-aged member of the psychology faculty at Long Island University, stoked the debate as an expert at the trial of Holocaust architect and Nazi fugitive Adolf Eichmann in Jerusalem. The court wanted to understand the mentality of the Nazi criminals. Testifying from the witness stand in Eichmann's presence, the bespectacled Gilbert carefully and formally asserted that his study of the Rorschach scores of the Nuremberg prisoners showed that they had fit a common and narrow personality profile that included antisocial qualities and a lack of interest in the suffering of others, contrary to Kelley's interpretation. (Gilbert tellingly titled two of his academic articles on Nazi psychology "The Mentality of S.S. Murderous Robots" and "Goering, Amiable Psychopath.")

Support for Kelley's view of the psychological characteristics of the Nazis as commonplace came from Stanley Milgram's famous 1963 experiment on the willingness of volunteers to follow orders to administer harmful and fatal levels of electricity to others. Personality, he demonstrated, was not important. The aftermath of World War II had inspired Milgram's research, according to his colleague Philip Zimbardo, who himself designed a renowned experiment on the brutal capabilities of subjects, the Stanford Prison Experiment. Milgram "worried about, you know, could the Holocaust happen in America?" Zimbardo says. "If Hitler said electro-cute somebody, would you do it? . . . And everybody said, no, Stanley, we're not that kind of person. What he said [even] as a high-school kid was, how do you know unless you're in that kind of situation?"

A decade passed after Milgram's initial work, and the Nazi Rorschach records only accumulated dust. Most of Kelley's records, in fact, which Dukie kept in boxes at her home, had vanished from the sight of research-ers. Molly Harrower, the same Rorschach researcher who had tried to gather a consensus of opinion on the Nuremberg tests during the late 1940s, made another, more successful effort some thirty years later. Now a professor at the University of Florida, with a direct gaze and regrets that she had suspended her earlier investigation, she gave a group of fifteen ex-perts in Rorschach interpretation the records that Gilbert had collected on Göring, Hess, Ribbentrop, and five other Nazis—unidentified to avoid bias—along with eight Rorschach records from hospital patients and members of the clergy to serve as controls. Even as late as the 1970s, there was no standardized method of interpreting Rorschach scores, and Har-rower did not tell her experts how to evaluate the records. Although the experts could correctly pick out mental disturbances among some of the Rorschach test-takers, they could not find any similarities in their inter-pretations of the Nazis' results. "The fact that they didn't makes the no-tion that the war crimes were due to mental disorder untenable," Harrower concluded. In fact, they judged all the Nazis except Ribbentrop as either normally adjusted or exceptionally well-adjusted. Using the Rorschach records, there was no way to differentiate the Nazis from ordinary people. In any event, Harrower believed, personality traits had little to do with the brutality of the Nazi regime and the atrocities it perpetrated. More decisive in the rise of German fascism was the susceptibility of normal people to myths, propagandistic manipulation, deception, and fear. And that susceptibility was a part of our species' makeup. "It can happen here," she declared, echoing Kelley.

At about the same time, the research team of Michael Selzer and Flor-ence Miale, a student of Bruno Klopfer who had worked with Rorschach testing for decades and had been one of the experts Harrower tapped just after the war, began their own investigations of the Nazi Rorschach records. Selzer, who taught in the department of political science at Brooklyn College of the City University of New York, wrote to Dukie in 1975 seeking access to Kelley's results. Dukie put him off with excuses: Kelley's papers were too voluminous for her to go through, his shorthand was impossible to read, and he kept much of the information in his head. Her actual reason for keeping the records away from Selzer, as she later disclosed to a friend, was that Kelley would not have approved of the sort of elaborate psychoanalysis of the top Nazi figures that she believed Selzer envisioned. Deep down, Dukie may have feared letting the records out of her control. She similarly declined a request for the records from the Rorschach Institute in Switzerland.

Selzer and Miale gained access to Gilbert's records and wrote their book anyway, and the conclusions of *The Nuremberg Mind: The Psychology of the Nazi Leaders*, published in 1975, placed them in Gilbert's camp—so much so, in fact, that Gilbert wrote the book's preface. Gilbert took this opportunity to take some digs at Kelley. The psychiatrist, Gilbert wrote, had "spoiled" any efforts to obtain clean Rorschach records from the Nazis by administering "some of the tests through an interpreter, before he knew that a German-speaking psychologist was coming. This rendered both the completeness and the accuracy of those tests somewhat doubtful, and also interfered with the imagery." (Gilbert's preface was one of his last published works before he died in 1977.)

The authors then took over, first proclaiming that people like Arendt, Milgram, and Kelley "have not persuaded us that the major Nazi war criminals were normal, ordinary people fundamentally similar to you and us." On the contrary, they believed, the Nuremberg defendants shared a common personality profile of mental disturbance. Based on their interpretations of the Rorschachs, they labeled many of the Nazis psychopaths with a limited capacity to feel guilt or attach themselves to other people or even to political or philosophical standards of behavior. The Nazis' virulent self-interest was paramount in determining their behavior, set them apart from most people, and rendered them abnormal and psychologically unhealthy.

Although this conclusion seems to oppose Kelley's in every way—and Kelley would have furiously condemned Selzer and Miale had he lived to see their book—the divide is not as great as it may appear. The Israeli political scientist and historian José Brunner has pointed out that Selzer and Miale left open a door to the possibility that certain large and prominent groups of people—politicians, business leaders, artists, and others—might share the Nazis' traits. Kelley would have agreed.

Harrower declared the conclusions of Selzer and Miale fatally biased by their foreknowledge of the tested Nazis' careers and crimes, and she faulted them for not reviewing the records blindly or comparing them with a control group. She believed that "their interpretations of the Rorschach results reflected their own expectations about Nazi mentality." In other words, Selzer and Miale had assembled their book with a set agenda.

In 1978 a researcher new to the debate, psychologist Barry Ritzler of Long Island University, applied a quantitative and statistically based criterion to the Nazi Rorschachs to avoid arbitrary interpretations and standardized the responses for comparison with a database of thousands of other test results that had been similarly appraised in previous years. Ritzler fell somewhere between Harrower and Selzer-Miale in his interpretations: he determined that the Nazi responses indicated a difference from the norm, but not enough to brand them psychiatrically disordered. The Nuremberg defendants, he said, resembled "*successful* psychopaths" who selfishly took advantage of chances to advance themselves and their status without caring about the effects on the people around them, but they did not show the severe symptoms of psychopaths who actively harm others.

Ritzler's Rorschach appraisal method had been devised by Samuel J. Beck, a Chicago psychologist to whom Kelley sent some of his Nazi Rorschach records in 1947. Years after Beck died, in 1992, researcher Reneau Kennedy discovered those records among Beck's archived papers at the Institute for Psychoanalysis in Chicago. As a result, despite Dukie's best efforts to keep them under her control, several of Kelley's Nazi records emerged into the spotlight for the first time.

The appearance of Kelley's records set the stage for the most extensive review of the Nazi Rorschach results, by a collaboration of Ritzler,

Harrower, psychological assessment expert Robert P. Archer, and Drexel University psychologist Eric Zillmer, another longtime contributor to the controversy. In 1995 this team published *The Quest for the Nazi Personality: A Psychological Investigation of Nazi War Criminals*, which drew from Kelley's results, as well as Gilbert's. They concluded that it was impossible to use the Rorschach records to lump the Nazis into a distinctive psychiatric category. Göring, Hess, and their compatriots may have shared some personality traits—such as a tendency to vacillate in trying to solve problems, as do about 20 percent of the American public—but those traits did not make them abnormal or psychopathic and probably belonged to many political leaders and others. "In fact," the research team wrote, "the differences among the members of this group by far outweighed any similarities." They concluded that "many individuals . . . participated in atrocities without having diagnosable impairments that would account for their actions." Psychotic sadism may have offered one path to the top of the Nazi elite, but men of many other personality types sat in the dock at Nuremberg. Tides of thought famously cycle in psychiatry and psychology, and Gilbert's view of the Nazi records may again rise some day. But Ritzler, Harrower, Archer, and Zillmer decisively came down on Kelley's side in the debate. Until someone else refutes it, the latest study suggests that the Nazi personality that eluded Kelley, seduced Gilbert, and tempted so many other researchers is a myth.

It took Doug Kelley twenty-eight years after his father's death to feel that he could reconcile with Dukie. For so long he had blamed her for her role in his upbringing, for her inability to protect him from Kelley's emotional storms. Then, in the mid-1980s, he realized that his demand for justice from Dukie would come only at great cost to her. She did not want to remember the painful episodes of her life with her husband. Doug decided to stop hoping that she would acknowledge his father's faults and errors. In 1987 he visited her in Santa Barbara, California, where she lived in a house with beautiful views of the ocean. Ostensibly Doug arrived to help

Dukie figure out how to use a new computer. Their relationship began to mend. "It was a way of saying, 'I love you. We're a family,'" Doug remembers. "From then on I was Doug to her, not Douglas, not just her son, but an equal she could be more upfront with."

By then her memories of Kelley had frozen into images of his brilliance and boundless curiosity. Doug thought of him as a father with his own way of loving, as a man who led him down a path he couldn't stand, as one tormented by lifelong demons that escaped his control. When Dukie died in 2007, Doug inherited the ragged boxes of papers, medical records, and notes that his father had brought home from Europe sixty years earlier.

Doug's sister Alicia died in a car accident in 2006, and his brother Allen is seriously ill and disabled. So Doug remains the sole guardian of this hidden archive—yet another McGlashan collection with a stormy story to tell. Doug still has many of his father's collectibles: a meteorite, old leaves encased in glass, wood carvings from Africa, and polished crystals. Upon request he will bring out one of the splinters from a Donner Party cabin. Floating in oil in a tiny glass vial, a suspended sliver of hardship from the past, it is not much more substantial than an eyelash, and you have to blink to make sure you've seen it.

Now in his mid-sixties, wiry and strong, with a wrinkled face and thinning hair on his head, Doug has organized his father's jumbled papers and filed them in folders labeled with the names of the Nuremberg defendants. The collection exhales the scents of tobacco smoke, dry paper, and fading photos. Included are three small boxes, the size of necklace cases. They contain peculiar jewels. One holds a set of glass slides showing views of Robert Ley's brain. In another are six paper packets, still sealed with smears of red wax, maintaining a grip on the sugar, chocolate, and other foods that Rudolf Hess thought were poisoned. The final little box encloses a bed of cotton wool upon which lies a glass vial holding about a hundred white paracodeine tablets, a taste of Hermann Göring's personal pharmacy.

The whole collection belongs in a museum or archive, but Doug has not surrendered it. He keeps it close at hand. He is curious, and he still wants to know more.

ACKNOWLEDGMENTS

Without the help of Doug Kelley—the oldest son of my subject, Douglas M. Kelley—I would not have attempted to write this book. I tracked down Doug in 2008 with hopes that he would have recollections of his father's career, however faint they might be. I was overwhelmed to find that he possessed Dr. Kelley's extensive collection of papers and photos chronicling his time at Nuremberg, as well as the years before and after. Doug invited me into his life and welcomed my questions. Insightful and funny, he generously plumbed his memories of being Douglas M. Kelley's son, a journey at times painful and confounding. I am grateful to Doug and his partner, Christine Straub, for their enthusiasm and hospitality as I tried to make sense of Dr. Kelley's story.

How fortunate I was to interview the men who may be the last living people who worked at Mondorf and Nuremberg with Douglas M. Kelley. My thanks to John Dolibois and Howard Triest for their time, ideas, and patience. I am also grateful for my interview time with Steven Miles of the University of Minnesota and with Michael Gelles.

Several institutions and archives aided my research. I thank Luisa Haddad and her helpful colleagues at the Department of Special Collections and Archives at the University of California, Santa Cruz; Hilary Lane of the History of Medicine Library at the Mayo Clinic; the staff of the US National Archives in Silver Spring, Maryland; and the archivists of the William Donovan Nuremberg Trials Collection at the Law Library of Cornell University.

Many others contributed to my writing in a variety of ways. I thank them all: Fred Appell, Dr. Arnold E. Aronson, Maisy and Bert Aronson, Ann Bauer, Laurie Brickley, Katherine Eban, Karla Ekdahl, Cornelia Elsaesser, Nancy Gardner, Elizabeth Giorgi, Anne Hodgson, Eugene Hoffman, Peter Hutchinson, Jon Klaverkamp, Bill Magdalene, Mary Meehan, Brad Schultz and Marx Swanholm, and Laura Weber.

I first wrote about Douglas M. Kelley and Hermann Göring in an article published in 2011 in *Scientific American Mind* magazine. My thanks to my editor there, Karen Schrock, for her skilled guidance and for keeping an open mind toward an unusual topic.

The team at Mythology Entertainment—Brad Fischer, Laeta Kalogridis, and Jamie Vanderbilt—have my appreciation for their interest in my work and for their support.

As always, I have benefited from the confidence, experience, and suggestions of my literary agent, Laura Langlie, whose common sense and calm always prevail. I also thank my performance rights agent, Bill Contardi, for his wonderful work. Kenneth Weinrib's legal expertise has been essential.

Clive Priddle at PublicAffairs has supported this project from its earliest stages, and I feel lucky to write within the fold of this terrific publishing company.

Sometimes you need someone who will give you a place to write without asking questions. For that I have relied upon my local Caribou, Dunn Brothers, Quixotic, and Sebastian Joe's coffee shops. By now they've learned I'm a tea drinker.

Finally, I thank my wife, Ann Aronson, for entertaining my crazy ideas, studying my manuscript, and giving me so much to look forward to outside of my writing den. She and my daughters, Natalie and Sasha, put up with a lot while my obsessions overtake me. They have all of my love.

NOTES

CHAPTER 2: MONDORF-LES-BAINS

3 *He had evacuated* Manvell and Fraenkel, *Goering*, 310.

3 *Less than forty-eight hours* Ibid., 325; Stack, "Capture of Goering."

4 *Emmy was in tears* Emmy Göring, *My Life with Goering*, 131.

4 *considered himself the most charismatic* Manvell and Fraenkel, *Goering*, 324.

4 *American soldiers escorted Göring* Ibid., 325.

4 *"Don't worry if I'm away for a day"* Göring, *My Life with Goering*, 132.

4 *Göring spent the night* Andrus, *I Was the Nuremberg Jailer*.

4 *Yet Stack and his staff extended* Manvell and Fraenkel, *Goering*, 326.

4 *Someone found a slightly larger plane* Volz, "Montana Pilot, 99, Recalls Flying Goering."

5 *Emmy and Edda Göring* Lebert and Lebert, *My Father's Keeper*, 202.

6 *perhaps to make him more cooperative* Andrus, *I Was the Nuremberg Jailer*, 30.

6 *enjoyed attention from the international press* Manvell and Fraenkel, Goering, 327.

6 *"You will soon be free"* Gunkel, "How a Top Nazi's Brother Saved Lives."

6 *Göring chose his longtime servant* Manvell and Fraenkel, *Goering*, 327.

6 *US soldiers preparing for transports* Andrus, *I Was the Nuremberg Jailer*, 22–23; Dolibois, *Pattern of Circles*, 84.

7 *urgently requested female company* Tusa and Tusa, *Nuremberg Trial*, 45.

7 *spent his final days of freedom* Sprecher, *Inside the Nuremberg Trial*.

7 *Andrus took charge of fifty-two* Tusa and Tusa, *Nuremberg Trial*, 42.

7 *"either by fanatical Nazis trying to rescue"* Andrus, *I Was the Nuremberg Jailer*, 23.

7 *A group of 176 Luxembourgers* Dolibois, *Pattern of Circles*, 98.

7 *"plump little figure"* Andrus, *I Was the Nuremberg Jailer*, 14.

7   *the colonel was a lean water-polo enthusiast* Ibid., 15–17.

8   *disrespect he encountered from the gum-chewing American guards* Manvell and Fraenkel, *Goering*, 328.

8   *such items as jewel-encrusted military medals* Dolibois, *Pattern of Circles*, 88; Teich, "Inventory: Hermann Goering."

8   *He bragged that one of the rings* Kelley, 22 *Cells in Nuremberg*, 68.

9   *now empty except for a flimsy table* Andrus, *I Was the Nuremberg Jailer*, 29–30.

9   *"Had he sat on the table"* Ibid., 40.

9   *Concerns about suicide also prompted* Dolibois, *Pattern of Circles*, 94.

9   *"in very poor physical condition"* Andrus, *I Was the Nuremberg Jailer*, 31.

9   *he often imbued his rising* Dolibois, *Pattern of Circles*, 85.

9   *Just before Kropp's departure from Mondorf* Manvell and Fraenkel, *Goering*, 329.

10 *Göring asked Eisenhower to fly him out* Andrus, *I Was the Nuremberg Jailer*, 46–47.

10 *"Whereas I do not desire to stand in the way"* Dolibois, *Pattern of Circles*, 95.

10 *"This food isn't as good"* Andrus, *I Was the Nuremberg Jailer*, 40.

11 *"the fat man in endless screenplays"* Neave, *On Trial at Nuremberg*, 71.

11 *once shot down and was credited with destroying* Tusa and Tusa, *Nuremberg Trial*, 496.

11 *"You've got to have bayonets"* Gilbert, *Psychology of Dictatorship*, 92.

11 *"that meant I could soon be a big man"* Kelley, 22 *Cells in Nuremberg*, 56.

11 *"Hermann will either be a great man"* Gilbert, *Psychology of Dictatorship*, 88.

12 *"For Hitler, Göring was a warrior"* Davidson, *Trial of the Germans*, 67.

12 *Göring exploded with laughter* Neave, *On Trial at Nuremberg*, 66.

13 *he gathered tame lions* Davidson, *Trial of the Germans*, 63.

13 *Only Gestapo chief Ernst Kaltenbrunner's reluctance* Kelley, 22 *Cells in Nuremberg*, 66–67.

13 *"I felt you should see this, sir"* Andrus, *I Was the Nuremberg Jailer*, 30.

14 Göring had hoarded a much bigger stash Davidson, *Trial of the Germans*, 66.

14 *"a relatively rare narcotic"* Andrus, *I Was the Nuremberg Jailer*, 31.

14 *Hoover asked to be kept apprised* Hoover, "Hermann Goering."

14 *"Imagine my being featured"* Dolibois, *Pattern of Circles*, 102.

14 *"Paracodeine fills a gap"* "Therapeutic Progress."

16 *"from a Machiavellian villain"* Kelley, 22 *Cells in Nuremberg*, 51.

16 *As a boy he had visited the Grand Hotel"* Curnutte, "Interrogator Recalls Talks."

16 *"We didn't have to use artificial devices"* Dolibois, *Pattern of Circles,* 104.

17 *"12 lbs at birth"* Kelley, Bound Notebook of Interview Notes.

17 *The prisoner's collection of toiletries* Kelley, *22 Cells in Nuremberg,* 58–59.

17 *"truly massive baubles"* Ibid., 68.

20 *"When he was captured"* Kelley, "Clinical Summary."

20 *"not an unusually large dose"* Kelley, *22 Cells in Nuremberg,* 57.

20 *"It was the need to do something"* Ibid., 57–58.

21 *"he had whined and complained"* Andrus, *I Was the Nuremberg Jailer,* 34–36.

22 *"He fancied looking like the hero"* Dolibois, *Pattern of Circles,* 88.

22 *"This concession was granted"* Kelley, *22 Cells in Nuremberg,* 59.

22 *A doctor called it just a palpitation* Andrus, *I Was the Nuremberg Jailer,* 34.

CHAPTER 3: THE PSYCHIATRIST

23 *"You are to contact Captain Miller"* Executive Command, "Carrier Sheet."

23 *"Some went as far as to propose"* Pick, *Pursuit of the Nazi Mind,* 126.

25 *"Our house sang out from the hill"* McGlashan, *Give Me a Mountain Meadow,* 4–6, 95.

26 *"Give me a mountain meadow"* Ibid., 70.

26 *McGlashan tracked down Keseberg* Ibid., 105–107.

26 *In the decades that followed* Ibid., 96.

27 *This all-consuming project took a toll* Ibid., 109–113, 141.

27 *He collected splinters of wood* Ibid., 159.

27 *McGlashan's polymath interests* Ibid., 141–145, 152.

28 *They practiced together* Ibid., 183.

28 *When publicly challenged* Ibid., 217.

28 *Before arguing a case* Ibid., 182.

28 *"The ring of steel"* Ibid., 182.

29 *"Super-vitality, courage"* Kelley, "Personal File, to 1937."

29 *Douglas's measured IQ* Sears to Mandel.

29 *Terman kept close tabs* Friedman and Martin, *Longevity Project,* 53.

29 *the 1,444 children* Shurkin, *Terman's Kids,* 36.

29 *he had amassed collections* Kelley "Personal File, to 1937."

30 *These feats included driving a car* "Faculty Will Not Examine Float Entries."

30 *Kelley emulated Harry Houdini* "They Can't Tie Him."

30 *president of the San Francisco Society of Magicians* "Former Local Boy Given Major Scholarship in East."

30 *working as a magician strengthens* "Magic Helps Treat Insane."

31 *Guardians of the property* McGlashan, *Give Me a Mountain Meadow,* 247.

32   *he collaborated with colleagues* Kaempffert, "New Test for Drunks."

32   *the effect of the full moon* Kelley, "Mania and the Moon."

32   *"The average individual gives"* Whitman, "Blots on Your Character."

32   *"The method must always be considered"* Kelley, "Rorschach Technique."

33   *"And as any pie eater knows"* Whitman, "Blots on Your Character."

33   *two pet monkeys sitting on his lap* Kodish, *Korzybski,* 349.

33   *"This communication must be free"* "Experts on Semantics Deliver SF Lecture."

34   *he had become an officer* Alice Kelley to Starr.

34   *"Long before the name psychology"* Kelley, "Conjuring as an Asset to Occupational Therapy."

35   *"No other type of entertainment"* Ibid.

36   *"Magic gives the patient"* "Psychiatrists Using Shell Game to Treat Insane."

36   *safe even for suicidal patients* "Magic Helps Treat Insane."

36   *"After mastering three tricks"* "Magic and Mickey Mouse."

36   *He was quoted on topics* University of California, "U.S. Neglects Mental Disease Research."

36   *In such a state* "UC Doctors Use Drug to Aid Psychiatric Test."

37   *she had emerged from the Girls' Preparatory School* "Miss Alice Hill Weds."

37   *"Life isn't half so serious"* Kelley, "Personal File to 1937."

37   *in a lynx-trimmed, Venetian blue wool ensemble* "Miss Alice Hill Weds."

37   *Dukie gave him an ornately calligraphed* Kelley, "Faux Invitation."

38   *more than 1.6 million soldiers* Hale, *Rise and Crisis of Psychoanalysis,* 15.

38   *1.1 million disabling, psychiatric traumas* Ibid., 192.

38   *Fear and stress were most often responsible* Hastings and Hastings, *Psychiatric Experiences of the Eighth Air Force,* 206.

39   *He trained other doctors* "Kelley Teaches Battle Psychiatry."

39   *He put Oscar to work* Walker, "Lessons of War Will Help Now."

39   *After resting them with a hot shower* Case, "Army Doctors' New System."

39   *There Kelley and his colleagues* Kelley, "Use of General Semantics," 189–195, 217.

40   *Throughout the North African campaign* Barnes and Kelley, "Combat Neurosis."

40   *more than 95 percent of the soldiers* Davis, "How Graylyn Is Reviving Some of Our Sick Minds."

41   *"there was so much pure larceny"* Fabing to Byron.

41   *Aboard a flight originating at Ridgewell* Gaillard, Certificate.

41   *"I suspect in the not too far future"* Everts to Kelley.

42   *"senior Germans will be given"* Andrus, *I Was the Nuremberg Jailer,* 49.

42 *Reporters arrived and wrote about* Tusa and Tusa, *Nuremberg Trial,* 44–45.

42 *"Get up, that man!"* Ibid., 46.

43 *felt dread when guards moved him* Ibid., 48.

43 *frequently visited Mondorf* Dolibois, *Pattern of Circles,* 104.

44 *"Internee is sane and responsible"* Kelley, "Clinical Summary."

44 *deprived of belts, ties, and shoelaces* Overy, *Interrogations,* 65.

44 *the pilots watched with astonishment* Dolibois, *Pattern of Circles,* 135.

44 *Two guards, one carrying a .45-caliber pistol* Andrus, *I Was the Nuremberg Jailer,* 61–64.

CHAPTER 4: AMONG THE RUINS

47 *A single British air attack* Sprecher, *Inside the Nuremberg Trial,* 63.

47 *More than half of Nuremberg's homes* Gregor, *Haunted City,* 25.

47 *Many of those who remained* "Here and There with *Newsweek* Correspondents"

47 *Staircases led to empty air* Sprecher, *Inside the Nuremberg Trial,* 64.

47 *Lacking money* West, *Train of Powder,* 10.

47 *The water was undrinkable* Neave, *On Trial at Nuremberg,* 42.

48 *Previously the neighborhood* Urban, *Nuremberg Trials,* 48.

48 *Women lived in another hotel* "Here and There with *Newsweek* Correspondents."

48 *"To arrive at my room"* Sprecher, *Inside the Nuremberg Trial,* 65.

48 *The bar was well stocked* "Here and There with *Newsweek* Correspondents"

48 *"cheap and potent"* Neave, *On Trial at Nuremberg,* 43.

48 *The Russian occupiers sometimes broke out* West, *Train of Powder,* 13.

48 *an air raid had damaged the roof* Urban, *Nuremberg Trials,* 15.

48 *Allied soldiers had left the Palace of Justice's main courtroom* Neave, *On Trial at Nuremberg,* 46.

49 *Here in wartime a special court* Urban, *Nuremberg Trials,* 14–15.

49 *the courtroom noisily collapsed* Andrus, *I Was the Nuremberg Jailer,* 68.

49 *Meanwhile, tanks, armed soldiers* Neave, *On Trial at Nuremberg,* 45.

49 *Kelley thought the shape of the prison* Kelley, "Nuremberg Trial."

49 *the area that Andrus directed* Tusa and Tusa, *Nuremberg Trial,* 126.

49 *"There was nothing to stop them"* Andrus, *I Was the Nuremberg Jailer,* 66–67.

50 *The colonel soon went to work fortifying* Ibid., 75, 144.

50 *"I took it upon myself"* Kelley, *22 Cells in Nuremberg,* 12.

50 *"Of course we were not interested"* Schurr, "Gods Come Down."

51 *The top Nazi prisoners* Dolibois, *Pattern of Circles,* 147.

51   *"Cells lay on both sides"* Kelley, 22 Cells in Nuremberg, 8.

51   *"unsteady wooden erections"* Schacht, Confessions, 403.

51   *"A guy could go nuts"* Tusa and Tusa, Nuremberg Trial, 126.

51   *"The very air feels imprisoned"* Andrus, I Was the Nuremberg Jailer, 84.

52   *"the bitter gall of their own boastful words"* Kelley, 22 Cells in Nuremberg, 8.

52   *Prisoners were not allowed to turn away* Tusa and Tusa, Nuremberg Trial, 127.

52   *"these shakedowns were so thorough"* Kelley, 22 Cells in Nuremberg, 10.

52   *"If time permits they will call 'HALT'"* Andrus, "Prison Regulations."

52   *He said to their faces* Schacht, Confessions, 402.

53   *"the fire brigade colonel"* Neave, On Trial at Nuremberg, 69.

53   *Andrus's breath smelled of booze* Schacht, Confessions, 403.

53   *Joachim von Ribbentrop was notorious* Tusa and Tusa, Nuremberg Trial, 127.

53   *former propaganda minister Hans Fritzsche arrived* Ibid., 125.

53   *Andrus rescinded his ban on shoelaces* Overy, Interrogations, 71.

53   *sometimes repeating his favorite jokes* Dolibois, Pattern of Circles, 169.

53   *"a group of men who could probably be counted"* Andrus, I Was the Nuremberg Jailer, 17.

53   *Breakfast, often cereal, biscuits, and coffee* Tusa and Tusa, Nuremberg Trial, 131.

53   *former field marshal Wilhelm Keitel's flat feet* Ibid., 129.

54   *"were quite glad to talk to anybody"* Kelley, "Nuremberg Trial."

54   *some of the easiest Kelley had ever experienced* Kelley, 22 Cells in Nuremberg, 12.

54   *"If you wanted to know about A"* Schurr, "Gods Come Down."

55   *giving all of them the first mental examinations* Kelley, 22 Cells in Nuremberg, viii.

55   *Göring, for example, understood English well* Overy, Interrogations, 82.

55   *In one of the abandoned offices* Sprecher, Inside the Nuremberg Trial, 66.

56   *"The sudden change of environment"* Kelley, 22 Cells in Nuremberg, 70.

56   *"Psychologically, I feel because of the environment"* Göring to Kelley.

56   *"like that of a veteran star"* Neave, On Trial at Nuremberg, 69.

56   *"an air of pregnancy"* West, Train of Powder, 5.

56   *"Each day when I came to his cell"* Kelley, 22 Cells in Nuremberg, 51–52.

57   *"the rosy dawn of an always better future"* Ibid., 60

57   *"not by the tale, but by the teller"* Ibid., 71.

57   *"If you have one German"* Ibid., 72.

57   *He also enjoyed quoting from a notebook* Dolibois, Pattern of Circles, 103.

57   *On the table in his cell* Kelley, 22 Cells in Nuremberg, 59.

58 *"When her final illness came"* Ibid., 60.

58 *"Thus did Göring try to appease"* Ibid., 60.

58 *"I am quite convinced"* Ibid., 61.

59 *another soldier malevolently or mistakenly* Göring, *My Life with Goering,* 135–136.

59 *Edda resembled her father* Dolibois, *Pattern of Circles,* 169.

59 *"Germany has more diphtheria"* Kelley, "Nuremberg Trial."

60 *"For . . . his friends, for his family"* Kelley, *22 Cells in Nuremberg,* 62.

60 *"ability to carry out policy"* Ibid., 52.

60 *"complete lack of moral value"* "Goering Was Child in Adult World."

60 *which the Reichsmarschall valued* Ibid.

60 *"not the action of a man suddenly realizing he's a pauper"* Ibid.

60 *"Well, here is something just as good"* Alice Kelley to Mandel, September 1, 1985.

61 *"a dreary calling indeed"* Schacht, *Confessions,* 409.

61 *a tipsy fall while drinking* Tusa and Tusa, *Nuremberg Trial,* 36.

61 *"immensely paranoid version of history"* Brickner, *Is Germany Curable?* 221.

62 *a Nazi version of the Nobel Prize* Kelley, *22 Cells in Nuremberg,* 42.

62 *a hat, an overcoat, a handkerchief* Teich, "Inventory: Alfred Rosenberg."

62 *"a tall, slender, flaccid, womanish creature"* Kelley, *22 Cells in Nuremberg,* 38.

62 *"I was more than casually interested"* Ibid., 46.

62 *Rosenberg often could not complete his sentences* Dolibois, *Pattern of Circles,* 171.

63 *"lounging on his cot"* Ibid., 141.

63 *Newspapers described his pornography* "Streicher's Lewd Sex Library."

63 *"He was a dirty old man of the sort"* West, *Train of Powder,* 5.

64 *Streicher was no stranger to the Nuremberg jail* Davidson, *Trial of the Germans,* 44–45.

64 *"Twenty-four hours a day"* Kelley, *22 Cells in Nuremberg,* 142–143.

64 *Ley tried to commit suicide three times* Ibid., 168.

64 *"Fell 2900 meters, pilot killed"* Kelley, Bound Notebook of Interview Notes.

65 *He always claimed that a couple of jolts* Dolibois, *Pattern of Circles,* 118.

65 *"An inner voice drove me forward"* Kelley, *22 Cells in Nuremberg,* 152–153.

65 *"He gave the impression of being intellectually gifted"* Dolibois, *Pattern of Circles,* 118.

65 *"Often when I talked with him in his cell"* Kelley, *22 Cells in Nuremberg,* 154, 156.

65 *"who always saw the world through rose-colored glasses"* Ibid., 155–156.

66   *He told Allied interrogators* Tusa and Tusa, *Nuremberg Trial*, 47.

66   *Another nickname, "the movie actor"* Kelley, *22 Cells in Nuremberg*, 93–94, 98.

66   *"Doctor, what shall I do?"* Kelley and Whitman, "Squeal, Nazi, Squeal!"

66   *"He walks up and down his cell"* Schurr, "Gods Come Down."

66   *"He is like a little boy"* Schurr, "Gods Come Down."

66   *"a typical bully, tough and arrogant"* Kelley, *22 Cells in Nuremberg*, 133–134.

67   *the arrival in Nuremberg of more than a hundred American legal staff* Overy, *Interrogations*, 16.

67   *They reminded him of the directors of a business* Kelley, "Nuremberg Trial."

68   *These early investigators had thought* Halleck, *Psychiatric Aspects of Criminology*, 8.

68   *in attempting to measure the psychological states* Abrahamsen, *Crime and the Human Mind*, 8.

69   *By the 1930s, an enormous study* Bromberg, *Crime and the Mind*, 82–84.

69   *Brickner tried to view the crimes* Brickner, *Is Germany Curable?* 29, 151, 271.

70   *the German nation, including the Nazi regime* Ibid., 32, 42.

70   *Brickner took pains to keep from tarring* Ibid., 264–265.

CHAPTER 5: INKBLOTS

74   *"I had too much personal history"* Triest, Telephone interview.

75   *Göring possessed the most undiluted self-centeredness* Ross, "Dr. Douglas Kelley."

75   *"He reached his goal too late"* Kelley, *22 Cells in Nuremberg*, 71.

75   *"That may well be"* Ibid., 72.

75   *"In fact, when Göring chose"* Dolibois, E-mail interview.

76   *During one talk* Kelley, *22 Cells in Nuremberg*, 65.

76   *When the Reichsmarschall once declared* Gilbert, "Goering."

76   *informing Kelley that he felt relatively well* Göring to Kelley.

77   *"He's very anxious to be considered"* Schurr, "Gods Come Down."

78   *Prisoner Fritz Sauckel, who spent three years* Sauckel to Kelley.

78   *"For three months I have been writing"* Göring to Emmy Göring, October 10, 1945.

79   *"an honest and very humane man"* Göring, *My Life with Goering*, 136.

79   *"Finally, finally a letter from you"* Emmy Göring, to Hermann Göring, October 19, 1945.

79   *"You can well imagine how inexpressibly happy"* Göring to Emmy Göring, 10/28/1945

80 *"To see [Edda's] beloved handwriting"* Göring to Emmy Goring, October 28, 1945.

80 *"It is my opinion that Frau Göring"* Kelley, *22 Cells in Nuremberg*, 62.

80 *gave him a distinctive military deportment* Kelley, *22 Cells in Nuremberg*, 27.

80 *in accordance with a suggestion from his astrologer* Dolibois, *Pattern of Circles*, 175.

80 *"I had never flown that type of plane"* Kelley, *22 Cells in Nuremberg*, 24.

81 *even calling Hess insane* Gilbert, *Psychology of Dictatorship*, 123.

81 *Churchill's viewing of a Marx Brothers movie* Andrus, *I Was the Nuremberg Jailer*, 72.

82 *"I denied any knowledge of military events"* Kelley, *22 Cells in Nuremberg*, 25.

82 *he disapproved of Hess's drab taste* Davidson, *Trial of the Germans*, 111.

83 *it was rumored that Hitler had even selected Hess's wife* Neave, *On Trial at Nuremberg*, 77.

83 *Hess refused to submit to similar treatments in the future* Gilbert, *Psychology of Dictatorship*, 126.

83 *"such fallacious claims are typical"* Kelley, *22 Cells in Nuremberg*, 26.

83 *Hess flipped again* Andrus, *I Was the Nuremberg Jailer*, 121.

83 *Jews were hypnotically controlling people* Gilbert, *Psychology of Dictatorship*, 126.

83 *Hess tried to kill himself* "Rudolf Hess: Report of British Observations and Findings."

84 *The dull weapon* Neave, *On Trial at Nuremberg*, 79; Gilbert, Psychology of Dictatorship, 126–127.

84 *The Russians, however, insisted* Davidson, *Trial of the Germans*, 119.

84 *"Hess immediately recognized Göring"* Andrus, *I Was the Nuremberg Jailer*, 72.

84 *his personal articles included a pocket watch* Teich, "Inventory: Rudolf Hess."

84 *"He was—as I expressed"* Andrus, *I Was the Nuremberg Jailer*, 73.

84 *"where the only requirement"* Ross, "Dr. Douglas Kelley."

85 *during one of their earliest encounters* Kelley, *22 Cells in Nuremberg*, 27.

85 *"While his demeanor was strictly formal"* Dolibois, *Pattern of Circles*, 172, 174.

85 *"Hess smiled, agreed to sign"* Kelley, "Rudolf Hess."

85 *"a profound neurotic of the hysterical type"* Kelley, "Statement on Hess."

85 *"All through my life I've felt people might kill me"* Kelley, Bound Notebook of Interview Notes.

85 *"and it is extremely likely that he will"* Kelley, "Statement on Hess."

85 *The psychiatrist wrote that it was possible* Kelley to Commanding Officer.

86 *"if one considers the street as sanity"* Kelley, *22 Cells in Nuremberg*, 35.

86 *"We could have found out in two days"* Davis, "Hitler Gang Just Ordinary Thugs, Psychiatrist Says."

86 *"although in more than 1,86 such cases"* Kelley to Commanding Officer.

86 *"Hess believes or has pretended"* Ibid.

86 *rejected using it in Hess' case* Kelley, *22 Cells in Nuremberg*, 31.

86 *"Don't you remember me, Rudolf?"* Andrus, *I Was the Nuremberg Jailer*, 118.

87 *"Don't you know me? You don't recognize me?"* Overy, *Interrogations*, 406.

88 *"wanted to preserve the fiction"* Kelley, *22 Cells in Nuremberg*, 35.

88 *"completely crazy"* Overy, *Interrogations*, 121.

88 *"We knew all along that Hess wasn't really normal"* Dolibois, *Pattern of Circles*, 166.

88 *"I can smell a Jew a mile away"* Fry, *Inside Nuremberg Prison*, loc. 833.

88 *"unbelievably obscure and hazy"* Kelley, *22 Cells in Nuremberg*, 44.

89 *He told Kelley that his plan to elevate Nordic people* Anspacher, "Psychiatrist Says Hitler Was Neurotic."

89 *"This young officer is working for his country"* Dolibois, *Pattern of Circles*, 171.

89 *He looked decrepit for a fifty-two-year-old man* Andrus, *I Was the Nuremberg Jailer*, 99.

89 *"extraordinary stupidity"* Schacht, *Confessions*, 406.

89 *"a good possibility, however, that once he is sentenced"* Kelley, "Psychiatric Profiles of Nazi Defendants."

90 *"Your dark eye I have so often seen"* Schirach, "Dem Tod."

90 *Visitors to Schirach's cell* Neave, *On Trial at Nuremberg*, 97.

90 *"He had intervened to save several Jews"* "Interview with Baldur Von Schirach."

91 *nearly all of the Nazi prisoners suffered* Kelley, *22 Cells in Nuremberg*, ix.

91 *"I was to them a symbol"* Andrus, *I Was the Nuremberg Jailer*, 173.

91 *which did not include* Schacht, *Confessions*, 406.

91 *"At least we Catholics are responsible"* Sprecher, *Inside the Nuremberg Trial*, 76.

92 *He now made a point of thanking prison staff* Andrus, *I Was the Nuremberg Jailer*, 94.

92 *Frank had left the Church* Kelley, *22 Cells in Nuremberg*, 175.

92 *"He feels essentially guilty"* Kelley, "Psychiatric Profiles of Nazi Defendants."

92 *"It was obvious that Frank"* Kelley, *22 Cells in Nuremberg*, 178–182.

92 *"one of the most integrated personalities"* Kelley, "Psychiatric Profiles of Nazi Defendants."

92   *"It is my opinion that Hitler used good judgment"* Kelley, 22 *Cells in Nuremberg*, 128–129.

92   *Many wanted works by Goethe* Andrus, *I Was the Nuremberg Jailer*, 131.

93   *"Authorize death of those people"* Kelley, Bound Notebook of Interview Notes.

94   *"the most useful single technique"* Kelley, 22 *Cells in Nuremberg*, 28.

94   *"one of the advantages of having your subject always on hand"* Kelley, "Preliminary Studies of the Rorschach Records."

94   *"Perhaps if the Nazis had not so whole-heartedly curtailed"* Ibid.

95   *Kelley's interpretation of Göring's results* Kelley, "Rorschach Report on Hermann Göring."

95   *"a picture of a person of considerable intellectual endowment"* Ibid.

95   *"not knowing how revealing"* Kelley, "Hess Rorschach."

96   *"although many of [the prisoners]"* Kelley, "Preliminary Studies of the Rorschach Records."

96   *The psychiatrist advanced a diagnosis of brain damage* Ibid.

96   *"to produce the clearest possible picture"* Ibid.

97   *"There is a man, a farmer"* Kelley, "TAT Test Results: Goering."

97   *"These are men who rest in the grass"* Ibid.

98   *"shy little man"* Kelley, Bound Notebook of Interview Notes.

98   *had asphyxiated himself* "Dr. Conti Dead in Nuremberg."

98   *Kelley rushed to the scene* Klam and Kelley, "Clinical Lab Report."

98   *"I have never been a coward"* Andrus, *I Was the Nuremberg Jailer*, 87–88.

98   *ordered all chairs removed from prisoners' cells* Dolibois, *Pattern of Circles*, 180.

98   *"it was a real chore to sit and listen"* Roth, "Dr. Kelley Was Not Fooled."

98   *"did not know that the inhibitory centers"* Kelley, 22 *Cells in Nuremberg*, 156–157.

99   *Putting him and his colleagues on trial* Ley, Statement.

99   *Kelley took notes on their responses* Neave, *On Trial at Nuremberg*, 65.

99   *Göring was first* Ibid., 69–70.

100   *Informed that he could choose his own lawyer* Ibid., 71–73.

100   *Hess received the group* Ibid., 79–81.

101   *"Be a man, Funk!"* Kelley, 22 *Cells in Nuremberg*, 170.

101   *Only Dönitz appeared to expect the indictment* Tusa and Tusa, *Nuremberg Trial*, 121.

101   *"I could kick myself"* Dolibois, *Pattern of Circles*, 119.

CHAPTER 6: INTERLOPER

103   *treating what he called "misfit soldiers"* "Trial of Adolf Eichmann (Part 1)."

103   *"I had naturally been interested"* Gilbert, *Nuremberg Diary*, 3.

104   *"Psychology, above all"* "Trial of Adolf Eichmann (Part 9)."

104 *he knew little of the field's clinical applications* Zillmer et al., *Quest for the Nazi Personality*, 40.

104 *"with all due respect, Andrus would not have known"* Ibid., 40.

104 *an appointment that was never made official* Ibid., 39.

104 *"Right from the beginning, he made no secret"* Dolibois, E-mail interview.

104 *had no official description or classification* Dolibois, *Pattern of Circles*, 187.

104 *"I suppose I could have identified myself"* Dolibois, E-mail interview.

105 *"There was just one limitation on this"* "Trial of Adolf Eichmann (Part 1)."

105 *"neither at the behest of the defense counsel"* Ibid.

105 *"the trial itself as a vehicle"* Gilbert, *Nuremberg Diary*, 3–4.

105 *"because some of it was so incredible"* "Trial of Adolf Eichmann (Part 1)."

106 *"they never had anything against Jews"* "Trial of Adolf Eichmann (Part 1)."

106 *"a young man whose career might be helped"* Alice Kelley to Mandel, September 1, 1985.

106 *Kelley wrote an update of Ley's psychiatric condition* Kelley, "Mental Examination of Robert Ley"; Kelley to Donovan, October 26, 1945.

107 *"The lifeless body of the onetime leader"* Dolibois, *Pattern of Circles*, 188.

107 *"Such a death is both slow and painful"* Kelley, *22 Cells in Nuremberg*, 171.

107 *"They were trying to hum a funeral march"* Sprecher, *Inside the Nuremberg Trial*, 121.

107 *"What a way to die"* Dodd and Bloom, *Letters from Nuremberg*, 181.

108 *"could not be allowed to happen again"* Andrus, *I Was the Nuremberg Jailer*, 91.

108 *after a package arrived for one of the trial witnesses* Ibid., 127.

108 *"It's just as well"* Kelley, *22 Cells in Nuremberg*, 73–74.

108 *"could never have successfully been tried"* Kelley, "Nuremberg Trial."

108 *"kindly made . . . available for post mortem examination"* Kelley, "Preliminary Studies of the Rorschach Records."

109 *"long-standing degenerative process"* Zillmer et al., *Quest for the Nazi Personality*, 31.

109 *a finding that microscopic study confirmed* Kelley, "Preliminary Studies of the Rorschach Records."

109 *"were of a lesser scope"* Zillmer et al., *Quest for the Nazi Personality*, 32.

110 *"All of this bespeaks impotence"* Gilbert, *Psychology of Dictatorship*, 128–129.

110 *"much better than the stuff"* Tusa and Tusa, *Nuremberg Trial*, 130.

110 *Keitel similarly complained* Gilbert, "Keitel Interview."

111 *"I can't tell"* Gilbert, "Hess Thematic Apperception Test."

111 *"Any financial wizard who is good at arithmetic"* Tusa and Tusa, *Nuremberg Trial*, 130.

111 *"IQ dictates nothing but the mere intellectual efficiency"* Gilbert, *Nuremberg Diary*, 32.

111 *"From what I've seen of them"* Tusa, *Nuremberg Trial,* 130.

112 *"It wouldn't be too bad"* "Interview with Hans Fritzsche."

112 *"gentlemen who called themselves psychiatrists"* Tusa and Tusa, *Nuremberg Trial,* 129.

112 *he expressed his dissatisfaction with the legality* Neave, *On Trial at Nuremberg,* 220.

112 *who professed certainty that Göring was completely innocent* Tusa and Tusa, *Nuremberg Trial,* 122.

112 *Five days after Kelley's last letter-carrying mission* Göring, *My Life with Goering,* 136.

112 *Emmy had been arrested at her residence* Dolibois, *Pattern of Circles,* 169.

112 *His daughter Edda was separated* Lebert and Lebert, *My Father's Keeper,* 202.

112 *"one of the darkest days of my life"* Göring, *My Life with Goering,* 137.

113 *A separation of mother and daughter was not good care* Kelley to Donovan, November 9, 1945.

113 *seven weeks passed* Göring, *My Life with Goering,* 139.

113 *"his mental and physical health"* Andrus to Commanding General.

113 *A former Luftwaffe officer scrounged up a straw mattress* Göring, *My Life with Goering,* 139.

113 *secretly passed to her* Lebert and Lebert, *My Father's Keeper,* 204.

113 *"I was pleased for myself"* Kelley, *22 Cells in Nuremberg,* 35–36.

114 *"You see, I was right"* Ibid., 56.

114 *"You know I shall hang"* Ibid., 71.

114 *"I do not recognize the trial's legal jurisdiction"* Ibid., 75.

115 *"It was not cowardly of Hitler"* Ibid., 73.

115 *"He naturally denied any perversions"* Ibid., 61.

115 *Göring told Kelley and translator Triest* Fry, *Inside Nuremberg Prison,* loc. 635–643.

116 *"Göring hasn't changed a bit"* Schurr, "Gods Come Down."

116 *"He readily admitted that the writing"* Kelley, "Rudolf Hess."

116 *showing him newsreel films* Andrus, *I Was the Nuremberg Jailer,* 118; Tucker, "Hess Gloomily Views Newsreels of Himself."

117 *"by a tightening of the hands"* Kelley, *22 Cells in Nuremberg,* 33.

117 *"a part of the memory loss is simulated"* Andrus, *I Was the Nuremberg Jailer,* 120.

118 *"he obviously wanted to retain the amnesia"* Ibid., 119–120.

118 *"the right channels"* Stringer, "Hess's Aloofness Fails."

118 *"a large voluntary block"* Ibid.

118 *Kelley believed the best course* Kelley to Donovan, November 17, 1945.

118 *"he not be granted permission to conduct examinations"* Andrus, Memorandum: "Psychiatric Consultation on Rudolf Hess."

119   *scornfully noted that Hess once forcefully replied, "No"* Andrus, *I Was the Nuremberg Jailer,* 120.

119   *"I was able to see through him"* Ibid., 121–122.

119   *"Do you know about the studies of the size of the pupil of the eye?"* Kelley, *22 Cells in Nuremberg,* 21–22.

119   *Kelley faced a medical conundrum of a different sort* Ibid., 134; Kelley, "Psychiatric Profiles of Nazi Defendants."

120   *would have required a quarantine* Tusa and Tusa, *Nuremberg Trial,* 145.

120   *a spinal puncture revealed* Kelley, *22 Cells in Nuremberg,* 134; Kelley, "Medical Status of Prisoner Ernst Kaltenbrunner."

120   *"Ernest Kaltenbrunner, the man who had terrified millions"* Andrus, *I Was the Nuremberg Jailer,* 116.

120   *"may well prove fatal"* Kelley, "Psychiatric Profiles of Nazi Defendants."

120   *Kelley and translator Howard Triest traveled together* Fry, *Inside Nuremberg Prison,* loc. 498–500.

121   *"He states that Halifax received this letter"* Kelley to Donovan, November 10, 1945.

122   *"When Major Kelley dictated his report"* J. E. S., Memorandum.

123   *Göring claimed to have written* Fry, *Inside Nuremberg Prison,* loc. 651–658.

123   *"will prove a trying hardship"* Kelley to Donovan, November 13, 1945.

123   *Donovan left the team* Waller, *Wild Bill Donovan,* 343–346.

124   *"Sometimes they know what you're thinking"* Schaefer, "Virginia's Reel."

CHAPTER 7: THE PALACE OF JUSTICE

125   *He instituted a new round of security measures* Andrus, *I Was the Nuremberg Jailer,* 125.

125   *"And still we were finding contraband"* Ibid., 125–127.

126   *In Ribbentrop's messy cell* Ibid., 125–127.

126   *"There is so much that they do not want exposed"* Tusa and Tusa, *Nuremberg Trial,* 145–146.

126   *A set of new high-intensity ceiling lights* Urban, *Nuremberg Trials,* 25.

127   *"optical confusion"* Schacht, *Confessions,* 411.

127   *about fifteen hundred lunches* Sprecher, *Inside the Nuremberg Trial,* 143.

127   *"We do not want them to be in a condition"* Tusa and Tusa, *Nuremberg Trial,* 148.

127   *He made sure their uniforms* Andrus, *I Was the Nuremberg Jailer,* 38, 144.

127   *"very inferior material"* Tusa, *Nuremberg Trial,* 148.

128   *The order matched the listing* Andrus, *I Was the Nuremberg Jailer,* 144.

128   *Göring devised a clever procedure* Ibid., 59.

128   *Andrus feared the prospect* Ibid., 114.

129 *"the professional mask of geniality"* West, *Train of Powder*, 6.

129 *"has fallen away till it is nothing"* Dos Passos, "Report from Nurnberg."

129 *"plainly mad; so plainly that it seemed shameful"* West, *Train of Powder*, 5.

130 *"a horrible cartoon of a Foxy Grandpa"* Dos Passos, "Report from Nurnberg."

130 *"like a woman in a way not common"* West, *Train of Powder*, 5.

130 *in his checkered jacket* Tusa and Tusa, *Nuremberg Trial*, 148.

130 *eighty-seven million bottles of champagne* Neave, *On Trial at Nuremberg*, 240–241.

131 *he knew nothing about them* Gilbert, *Nuremberg Diary*, 36.

132 *"If Göring swore under his breath"* Andrus, *I Was the Nuremberg Jailer*, 128.

132 *"Damn it, I just wish"* Gilbert, *Psychology of Dictatorship*, 110.

132 *"When the trial began he demonstrated his peculiar abilities"* Kelley, 22 *Cells in Nuremberg*, 69.

133 *"You men knew the Führer"* Gilbert, *Nuremberg Diary*, 70.

133 *in their minds, these were purely criminal acts* Tusa and Tusa, *Nuremberg Trial*, 241.

133 *"Of course we rearmed"* Kelley, *22 Cells in Nuremberg*, 63.

134 *"Oh, but you will. You wait and see"* Gilbert, "Trial Notes."

135 *Streicher seemed keenly engrossed* Tusa and Tusa, *Nuremberg Trial*, 160.

135 *"remained seated, as if turned to stone"* Neave, *On Trial at Nuremberg*, 247.

135 *"I don't believe it"* Tusa and Tusa, *Nuremberg Trial*, 160.

135 *"Don't let everyone tell you that they had no idea"* Gilbert, *Nuremberg Diary*, 47–49.

135 *"It was such a good afternoon"* Gilbert, *Psychology of Dictatorship*, 110.

136 *"You're having a hard time keeping your group"* Gilbert, "Trial Notes."

136 *Chief prosecutor Jackson added* Neave, *On Trial at Nuremberg*, 248–249.

136 *"He is in the volunteer class"* Tusa and Tusa, *Nuremberg Trial*, 162.

137 *high-pitched voice that suggested barely repressed excitement* Long, "Hess Tells Court He Faked."

137 *"Henceforth my memory will again respond"* Hess, "Statement before the IMT at Nuremberg."

137 *Rohrscheidt laughed* Tusa and Tusa, *Nuremberg Trial*, 162.

137 *"I'm glad you're not going to fake anymore"* Tucker, "Hess Gloomily Views Newsreels of Himself."

138 *"How did I do? Good, wasn't I?"* Kelley, 22 *Cells in Nuremberg*, 32–34.

138 *"Hess, the Hess we have here?"* Gilbert, "Notes on Rudolf Hess."

138 *Göring felt resentful* Kelley, "Rudolf Hess."

139 *"as he looked around the courtroom"* Gilbert, *Nuremberg Diary*, 53

139   *"but it is obvious he has been using amnesia"* Long, "Hess Tells Court He Faked."

139   *"he was too insane to testify"* Kelley, "Nuremberg Trial."

139   *"since he felt that to be denied a trial"* Kelley, "Rudolf Hess."

139   *"This man is competent"* Kelley, "Psychiatric Evaluations."

140   *"He was furious to be eating alone"* Gilbert, *Nuremberg Diary*, 141.

140   *"Hess and Ribbentrop were put together"* Tusa and Tusa, *Nuremberg Trial*, 242.

140   *"Gott im Himmel!"* Gilbert, *Nuremberg Diary*, 102; Andrus, *I Was the Nuremberg Jailer*, 136.

140   *"Please let me talk to you"* Gilbert, "Keitel Interview."

141   *"good mental health"* "Nazis No Longer Swagger at Trial."

141   *"He wanted to know if an individual"* Kelley, "Rudolf Hess."

142   *"the General Staff Doctor, Major Kelley"* Rosenberg to Douglas Kelley.

142   *Göring described a conversation* Kelley, "Rudolf Hess."

142   *he broke down and wept* Zillmer et al., *Quest for the Nazi Personality*, 82.

143   *to replace Kelley as Nuremberg jail psychiatrist* Wyllie, *Warlord and the Renegade*, 198.

144   *"practically lived with Hess"* Davis, "Hitler Gang Just Ordinary Thugs."

144   *"He might have been addressing"* Neave, *On Trial at Nuremberg*, 255.

145   *"Somehow he makes me think of a captured lion"* Dodd and Bloom, *Letters from Nuremberg*, 263.

145   *"His fellow prisoners followed him"* Neave, *On Trial at Nuremberg*, 257.

145   *Göring's obvious contempt* Ibid., 259.

145   *"When the former Reichsmarschall strode"* Dodd and Bloom, *Letters from Nuremberg*, 267.

145   *he lost his temper on the witness stand* Neave, *On Trial at Nuremberg*, 263.

146   *"oral and incipient overt aggression"* Gilbert, *Psychology of Dictatorship*, 115.

146   *Göring spun around in the dock* Neave, *On Trial at Nuremberg*, 272.

146   *"he could not ask for drugs now"* Gilbert, *Psychology of Dictatorship*, 115.

146   *"was no longer news"* Manvell and Fraenkel, *Goering*, 334.

146   *"It is against such a background"* Ehrenfreund, *Nuremberg Legacy*, 73.

147   *"I should like to state clearly"* Andrus, *I Was the Nuremberg Jailer*, 174

147   *"I do not regret anything"* Ehrenfreund, *Nuremberg Legacy*, 85.

147   *so far from a school* Lebert and Lebert, *My Father's Keeper*, 204–205.

147   *"I am submitting herewith a great request"* Andrus, *I Was the Nuremberg Jailer*, 161–162.

148   *He consistently refused to let Emmy or other relatives* Neave, *On Trial at Nuremberg*, 267.

148   *"Whatever I thought about Göring"* Andrus, *I Was the Nuremberg Jailer*, 162.

148 *"meant one more chance to pass"* Ibid., 174.

148 *"You've grown"* Lebert and Lebert, *My Father's Keeper,* 205–206.

149 *"The sentence probably won't be carried out"* Ibid., 206.

149 *"Death sentences for insane persons"* Kelley, *22 Cells in Nuremberg,* 36–37.

149 *"A nice long prison term"* Anspacher, "SF Psychiatrist for Doomed Nazi Tells How They'll Die."

150 *"You don't have to worry about the Hitler legend"* Bosch, *Judgment on Nuremberg,* 61.

150 *Gerecke, hearing from Göring* Andrus, *I Was the Nuremberg Jailer,* 185.

150 *Andrus was among the first* Ibid., 191.

151 *"To the Commandant"* Ibid., 201.

151 *As recently as 2005* Ehrenfreund, *Nuremberg Legacy,* 90–91.

152 *"He'll never weaken"* "SF Doctor Predicts How 11 Nazis Will Die."

152 *"demonstrates how ingeniously clever"* "S.F. Psychiatrist Is Amazed at Goering Suicide."

152 *"Göring, however, went a step further"* Kelley, *22 Cells in Nuremberg,* 76.

153 *"showed some courage at the very end"* Kelley, *22 Cells in Nuremberg,* 113.

153 *would "hang happy"* "S.F. Psychiatrist Is Amazed at Goering Suicide."

153 *"a macabre request"* Andrus, *I Was the Nuremberg Jailer,* 168.

CHAPTER 8: THE NAZI MIND

155 *"We don't know about war crimes"* Bosch, *Judgment on Nuremberg,* 203.

155 *"We have high hopes"* Ibid., 218.

156 *"was anxious to forget the war years"* Alice Kelley to Selzer.

156 *"a number of people urged him"* Alice Kelley to Mandel, September 1, 1985.

156 *books that their Nazi authors had signed* Ibid.

157 *"behind big desks"* Kelley, *22 Cells in Nuremberg,* 238–239.

158 *"because we look with disgust and hatred"* Kelley, "Nuremberg Trial."

158 *"Insanity is no explanation"* Kelley, *22 Cells in Nuremberg,* 4.

158 *"It is an established scientific fact"* Ibid., 6–7.

159 *"They all worked for incredibly long hours"* Schurr, "Gods Come Down."

159 *"Hitler had a profound conviction"* Kelley, *22 Cells in Nuremberg,* 211.

159 *"Hitler was just as normal"* Ibid., 212.

159 *Cambridge professor Joseph MacCurdy* "WWII Adolf Hitler Profile Suggests 'Messiah Complex.'"

160 *"no more than a nervous bellyache"* Kelley, *22 Cells in Nuremberg,* 201.

160 *Kelley had learned* Ibid., 217.

160 *One of Hitler's doctors, Karl Brandt* Ibid., 218.

160 *Hitler's fear of death* Ibid., 215.

161 *Another factor in the attraction of death* Ibid., 202, 205.

161 *"With the exception of Dr. Ley"* Zillmer et al., *Quest for the Nazi Personality,* 80.

161 *"were not special types"* Kelley, *22 Cells in Nuremberg*, 238.

162 *"They are people who exist in every country"* Kelley, "Nuremberg Trial."

163 *"there is little in America today"* Kelley, *22 Cells in Nuremberg*, 238.

163 *American politicians, like white supremacists* Ibid., 242–243.

163 *"our thoughts and our education"* Ibid., 13.

164 *"Americans are only [now] getting it ground in"* Kelley, "Nuremberg Trial."

164 *To combat this threat* Kelley, *22 Cells in Nuremberg*, 245.

164 *While professing faith in America's traditions* Brunner, "'Oh Those Crazy Cards Again.'"

164 *Lecturing around the state* Lecturing Contracts 1946.

165 *He ended up signing a contract* Greenberg to Kelley.

165 *"was offered an instructorship"* Fabing to Byron.

166 *Visitors entered the fifty-acre estate* Forsyth County Historic Resources, "Graylyn."

166 *Doctors could even experiment with lobotomy* Davis, "Civilization Now Offers Hope to Victims."

167 *"A neurotic person invariably thinks"* Summers, "Graylyn Ready for Treatment."

167 *"will fight through the effects"* McIlwain, "Liquor Can Curb Its Own Problems."

168 *"We actually will retrain"* Summers, "Graylyn Ready for Treatment."

170 *"wouldn't act so nutty"* "Semantics Held Key to Clarity in Thought."

170 *He traveled through the Carolinas* Lecture Contracts 1947.

170 *"The average emotional age level"* Anspacher, "Nuernberg Psychiatrist Fears Nazism in U.S."

171 *"are not very bright"* Rogers, "Faster Mental Cures Found."

171 *"myth that psychiatrists are always trying to interpret"* "Mental Health Held Serious U.S. Problem."

171 *He replied that he did not know for certain* Alice Kelley to Mandel, September 1, 1985.

171 *all politicians and statesmen would undergo psychological scrutiny* "Politicians Should Get Mental Exams."

171 *"The main thing to do"* Blank, "Nuremberg Psychiatrist Has Test for Nazis."

172 *"was in no way sympathetic"* Alice Kelley to Mandel, September 1, 1985.

172 *Gilbert's book steered clear of directly referencing* Brunner, "'Oh Those Crazy Cards Again.'"

173 *Gilbert explained Göring's loyalty* Koehli, "Ponerology 101."

173 *Göring's suicide, Gilbert maintained* Brunner, "'Oh Those Crazy Cards Again.'"

174 *In March 1947, he spent four days* "Dr. Kelley Broadcasts in New York."

175 *"Nobody will anymore be interested"* Loosli-Usteri to Kelley.

177 *Kelley accepted consulting work* Holstrom to Kelley.

177 *"If he is competent to determine"* "Cherry Answers Kelley Comment."

177 *"Take a whiff"* McEwen, "Somnoform Promises Magic Aid."

178 *"After a few whiffs"* Barton, "How Drug Released Inhibitions Told."

178 *The drugs, Kelley and other proponents maintained* Ibid.

179 *"seriously considering the offer"* "Head of Graylyn Offered University Post."

179 *"It would be an exclusive teaching and research position"* Ibid.

179 *He had supervised the care* "Dr. Kelley Resigns Post on Medical School Faculty."

179 *22 Cells in Nuremberg had gone out of print* Greenberg to Kelley.

CHAPTER 9: CYANIDE

181 *a princely annual salary* Malloy to Kelley.

181 *"Do you accept armchair detectives"* Abramson to Kelley.

181 *Kelley taught courses* Wilson to Kelley.

182 *"All the students come to class"* Hansen, Professor Uses Tricker in Class."

183 *"contained nobody but us chickens"* Fabing to Byron.

183 *A former chemist with the Manhattan Project* Farrell, *Shallow Grave in Trinity County*, 107.

184 *"About one-third to one-half of the policemen"* Kelley and Hansen, "Dumb Cops Are Dangerous."

186 *"The Rorschach method has come fast"* Kelley, "Clinical Reality and Projective Technique."

186 *"I'm hunting a drug"* "U.C. Man Develops New 'Truth Serum' Method."

187 *"Do you collect coins?"* Walker, A Trail of Corn, 155.

187 *"Hermann Göring and Burton Abbott were the most self-centered"* Farrell, *Shallow Grave in Trinity County*, 83.

187 *Abbott grew to dislike and fear* Walker, *A Trail of Corn*, 162, 106.

187 *"He's all wet"* Farrell, *Shallow Grave in Trinity County*, 177.

188 *director Nicholas Ray contacted Kelley* Rathgeb, *Making of Rebel Without a Cause*, 73.

189 *One nascent show he discussed with friends* Fabing to Byron.

190 *"bring about a better understanding by the public"* KQED, "Application for a Grant."

190 *"Why shouldn't all educational programs"* Newton, "Criminal Man."

192 *"a motherly, maiden female"* Kelley, 22 Cells in Nuremberg, 226.

192 *Schroeder accused Kelley* Schroeder to Kelley.

196 *"swim across the Bay"* Randebaugh, "Theories."

197 *"a little high as I interpret the ethics"* Kelley to Chief Administrator.

204   *"I am amazed by the number of activities"* Terman to Kelley.
205   *"preparation for a speech or paper ordinarily takes"* Kelley to Terman.
205   *"was feeling the weight of his exceptional workload"* Dreher to Alice Kelley.
207   *dead upon arrival at 4:56 p.m.* "UC Criminologist Dr. Douglas Kelley Killed by Poison."
207   *"I never did know why"* Ryan, "Mysterious Suicide."
208   *"Dr. Kelley had once said"* "Private Rites Mark Funeral for Dr. Kelley."
208   *"as far as anyone knew"* "Mystery in UC Suicide Deepens."
209   *"if that's the sort of thing these accusers"* Alice Kelley to Mandel, September 1, 1985.
209   *"nuts!"* Mandel to Alice Kelley.
209   *"I never saw the container"* Alice Kelley to Mandel, September 1, 1985.
209   *"burns painfully"* Randebaugh, "Theories."
210   *"For almost 30 years we were extremely close"* Fitzkee, "Obituary."

CHAPTER 10: POST MORTEM
213   *including crystals* Alice Kelley, "Inventory of Items for Sale."
216   *"schizophrenic and . . . without any access"* Walsh, *War and the Human Race*, 77.
216   *"was affable and pleasant"* Walsh, Memorandum: "Interview with Prisoner #7."
216   *"had a latent schizophrenia"* Walsh, "Historical Responsibility of the Psychiatrist."
217   *"forbidden by the American Military"* Walsh, *War and the Human Race*, 76–77.
217   *the Soviet Union resisted making changes* Neave, *On Trial at Nuremberg*, 81.
217   *"From an oblique angle"* Dolibois, *Pattern of Circles*, 176.
217   *Many psychologists pointed out problems* Brunner, "'Oh Those Crazy Cards Again,'" 234.
218   *Gustave Gilbert was the early standard-bearer* Zillmer et al., *Quest for the Nazi Personality*, 178, 187.
218   *"worried about, you know, could the Holocaust happen"* Freakonomics, "Fear Thy Nature."
219   *Even as late as the 1970s* Brunner, "'Oh Those Crazy Cards Again,'" 249.
219   *"It can happen here"* Harrower, "Were Hitler's Henchmen Mad?"
220   *Dukie put him off* Alice Kelley to Selzer.
220   *Her actual reason for keeping the records* Alice Kelley to Mandel
220   *"some of the tests through an interpreter"* Miale and Selzer, *The Nuremberg Mind*, xiii.

220 Gilbert's preface was one of his last Williams, "Dr. Gustave Gilbert Dead at 65."

220 *"have not persuaded us that the major Nazi war criminals"* Miale and Selzer, *The Nuremberg Mind,* 14.

221 *certain large and prominent groups* Brunner, "'Oh Those Crazy Cards Again,'" 247.

221 *"their interpretations of the Rorschach results"* Harrower, "Rorschach Records of the Nazi War Criminals."

221 *applied a quantitative and statistically based criterion* Brunner, "'Oh Those Crazy Cards Again,'" 251–252.

221 *researcher Reneau Kennedy discovered those records* Zillmer et al., *Quest for the Nazi Personality,* 87.

222 *as do about 20 percent of the American public* Ibid., 98.

222 *"the differences among the members of this group"* Ibid., 99.

BIBLIOGRAPHY

"Abbreviated Clinical Record: Hermann Goering." 1945. MS. Douglas M. Kelley Personal Papers.

Abrahamsen, David. *Crime and the Human Mind.* Montclair, CA: Patterson Smith, 1969.

Abramson, Paul D., to Douglas McGlashan Kelley, March 6, 1950. MS. Special Collections, University of California, Santa Cruz.

Alexander, Leo. "Medical Science under Dictatorship." *New England Journal of Medicine* 14 (July 1949): 39–47.

Andrus, Burton C. *I Was the Nuremberg Jailer.* New York: Coward-McCann, 1969.

———. Memorandum to William Donovan, November 2, 1945. MS. Donovan Nuremberg Trials Collection, Cornell University Law Library.

———. Memorandum: "Psychiatric Consultation on Rudolf Hess." 1945. MS MLR P 20, Box 4. National Archives and Records Administration.

———. "Prison Regulations." 1945. MS. Douglas M. Kelley Personal Papers.

———. "SOP, for Reception of Visitors." 1945. MS. Douglas M. Kelley Personal Papers.

———. "Statement on Ley's Suicide." 1945. MS MLR P 20. National Archives and Records Administration.

———, to Commanding General, Third Army, November 3, 1945. MS. Douglas M. Kelley Personal Papers.

Anspacher, Carolyn. "Nazi Has Plan to Save Youth He Corrupted." *San Francisco Chronicle*, October 17, 1946.

———. "Nuernberg Psychiatrist Fears Nazism in U.S." *San Francisco Chronicle*, n.d. Douglas M. Kelley Personal Papers.

———. "Psychiatrist Says Hitler Was Neurotic, Not Insane." *San Francisco Chronicle*, October 12, 1946.

———. "SF Psychiatrist for Doomed Nazi Tells How They'll Die." *San Francisco Chronicle*, 1946. Douglas M. Kelley Personal Papers.

"Army Psychiatrist Gives Picture of Nuernberg Trials Principals." *Bakersfield Californian*, December 2, 1946.

"Autopsy Shows Dr. Kelley Didn't Have Fatal Illness." *San Francisco Chronicle*, January 3, 1958.

Barnes, John W., and Douglas McGlashan Kelley. "Combat Neurosis." n.d. MS 229, Box 3:2. Special Collections, University of California, Santa Cruz.

Barton, William S. "How Drug Released Inhibitions Told." *Los Angeles Times*, May 21, 1950.

"Berkeley Zanies Drive Cops Crazy." 1951. Douglas M. Kelley Personal Papers.

Blank, Gerald. "Nuremberg Psychiatrist Has Test for Nazis." *World*, March 26, 1947.

Book Contract. MS File 1946. Douglas M. Kelley Personal Papers.

Bosch, William J. *Judgment on Nuremberg; American Attitudes Toward the Major German War-crime Trials*. Chapel Hill: University of North Carolina Press, 1970.

Brickner, Richard M. *Is Germany Incurable?* Philadelphia: J.B. Lippincott, 1943.

"Bride of Dr. Douglas Kelley, of San Francisco." *Chattanooga Express*, October 20, 1940.

Bromberg, Walter. *Crime and the Mind: A Psychiatric Analysis of Crime and Punishment*. New York: Macmillan, 1965.

Brunner, Jose. "'Oh Those Crazy Cards Again': A History of the Debate on the Nazi Rorschachs, 1946–2001." *Political Psychology* 22, no. 2 (2001): 233–261.

Case, Bill. "Army Doctors' New System Salvages 'Mentally Wounded.'" *Chattanooga Free Press*, 1945. Douglas M. Kelley Personal Papers.

"Cherry Answers Kelley Comment." *Winston-Salem Journal*, November 18, 1947.

Crassweller, Robert D. *Trujillo: The Life and Times of a Caribbean Dictator*. New York: Macmillan, 1966.

Curnutte, Mark. "Interrogator Recalls Talks with Hitler's Inner Circle." *Cincinnati Enquirer*, November 15, 2009.

"Daughter of Truckee Historian Is Dead." October 11, 1955. Douglas M. Kelley Personal Papers.

Davidson, Eugene. *The Trial of the Germans: An Account of the Twenty-two Defendants before the International Military Tribunal at Nuremburg*. Columbia: University of Missouri, 1966.

Davis, Chester S. "Civilization Now Offers Hope to Victims of 'Civilization'" *Winston-Salem Journal and Sentinel*, September 26, 1948.

———. "How Graylyn Is Reviving Some of Our Sick Minds." *Winston-Salem Journal and Sentinel*, September 16, 1948.

Davis, Louise. "Hitler Gang Just Ordinary Thugs, Psychiatrist Says." *Nashville Tennessean*, January 29, 1946.

Dodd, Christopher J., and Lary Bloom. *Letters from Nuremberg*. New York: Crown Publishing, 2007.

Dolibois, John. E-mail Interview with Author, February 2012.

———. *Pattern of Circles: An Ambassador's Story*. Kent, OH: Kent State University Press, 1989.

Dos Passos, John. "Report from Nurnberg." *LIFE*, December 10, 1945.

"Dr. Conti Dead in Nuremberg." n.d. Douglas M. Kelley Personal Papers.

"Dr. Conti Suicide Revealed by Army." n.d. Douglas M. Kelley Personal Papers.

"Dr. D. McG. Kelley Arrives to Take Post at Bowman Gray" [Winston-Salem]. 1947. Douglas M. Kelley Personal Papers.

"Dr. George Frank Kelley Dies at 91." November 19, 1971. Douglas M. Kelley Personal Papers.

"Dr. Kelley Broadcasts in New York." *Winston-Salem Journal*, March 24, 1947.

"Dr. Kelley Is Star Witness for the Defense." *Statesville Daily*, May 28, 1947.

"Dr. Kelley Kills Self." n.d. Douglas M. Kelley Personal Papers.

"Dr. Kelley Leaves Post at Graylyn" [Winston-Salem], 1949. Douglas M. Kelley Personal Papers.

"Dr. Kelley Made News in Sensational Cases." *San Francisco Chronicle*, January 2, 1958.

"Dr. Kelley Named Officer of Semantics Institute." *Winston-Salem Journal*, June 28, 1947.

"Dr. Kelley Resigns Post on Medical School Faculty." *Winston-Salem Journal*, August 1, 1949.

"Dr. Kelley Suicide Laid to Overwork." January 2, 1958. Douglas M. Kelley Personal Papers.

Dreher, George E., to Alice Vivienne Kelley, January 4, 1958. MS. Douglas M. Kelley Personal Papers.

Early, Don, to Douglas McGlashan Kelley, February 18, 1947. MS. Douglas M. Kelley Personal Papers.

Ehrenfreund, Norbert. *The Nuremberg Legacy: How the Nazi War Crimes Trials Changed the Course of History*. New York: Palgrave Macmillan, 2007.

Essig, E. O. "Charles Fayette McGlashan." *Pan-Pacific Entomologist* (January 1931): 97–99.

Everts, William H., to Alice Vivienne Kelley, May 19, 1945. MS. Douglas M. Kelley Personal Papers.

Executive Command. "Carrier Sheet, HQ Com Z, to Senior Consultant in Neuropsychiatry." 1945. MS. Douglas M. Kelley Personal Papers.

"Experts on Semantics Deliver SF Lecture." *San Francisco Examiner*, August 11, 1952.

Fabing, Howard D., to Edward A. Byron, May 9, 1953. MS. Special Collections, University of California, Santa Cruz.

"Faculty Will Not Examine Float Entries." *Daily Californian* [Berkeley], February 26, 1932.

Farrell, Harry. *Shallow Grave in Trinity County*. New York: St. Martin's, 1997.

"File on Douglas McGlashan Kelley." n.d. MS. Federal Bureau of Investigation.

Fitzkee, Dariel. "Obituary, Douglas M. Kelley." n.d. Douglas M. Kelley Personal Papers.

"Former Local Boy Given Major Scholarship in East." *Sierra Sun* [Truckee], August 10, 1939.

Forsyth County Historic Resources. "Graylyn," November 15, 2012. http://www.cityofws.org/Assets/CityOfWS/Documents/Planning/HRC/Local_Landmarks/LHL_Sheets/72_Graylyn.pdf.

Freakonomics Radio Podcast. "Fear Thy Nature." Transcript. September 14, 2012. http://www.freakonomics.com/2012/09/14/fear-thy-nature-a-new-freakonomics-radio-podcast/.

Freeman, Walter. *The Psychiatrist; Personalities and Patterns*. New York: Grune & Stratton, 1968.

Friedman, Howard S., and Leslie R. Martin. *The Longevity Project: Surprising Discoveries for Health and Long Life from the Landmark Eight-decade Study*. New York: Hudson Street, 2011.

Fry, Helen. *Inside Nuremberg Prison: A Biography of Howard Triest*. n.p.: Kindle Ebook, 2011.

Gaillard, Ernest, Jr. Certificate. 1944. MS. Douglas M. Kelley Personal Papers.

Gelles, Michael. Telephone Interview with Author, October 2009.

"General Semantics—Science of the Effect of Words." *San Francisco News*, August 7, 1952.

Gilbert, Gustave Mark. "Goering." 1945. MS. Douglas M. Kelley Personal Papers.

———. "Hess Test Notes." 1945. MS. Douglas M. Kelley Personal Papers.

———. "Hess Thematic Apperception Test." 1945. MS. Douglas M. Kelley Personal Papers.

———. "Keitel Interview." 1945. MS. Douglas M. Kelley Personal Papers.

———. "Ley's Final Psychiatric Interview." 1945. MS. Douglas M. Kelley Personal Papers.

———. "Notes on Rudolf Hess." 1945. MS. Douglas M. Kelley Personal Papers.

———. *Nuremberg Diary*. New York: Da Capo, 1995.

———. *The Psychology of Dictatorship: Based on an Examination of the Leaders of Nazi Germany*. Westport, CT: Greenwood, 1979.

———. "Trial Notes." 1945. MS. Douglas M. Kelley Personal Papers.

"Goering Interview Notes." 1945. MS. Douglas M. Kelley Personal Papers.

"Goering Was Child in Adult World, Says Brain Expert." 1946. Douglas M. Kelley Personal Papers.

Göring, Emmy. *My Life with Goering.* London: David Bruce and Watson, 1972.

———, to Hermann Göring, October 10, 1945. MS. Douglas M. Kelley Personal Papers.

Göring, Hermann. Autobiographical Statement, 1945. MS. Douglas M. Kelley Personal Papers.

———, to Douglas McGlashan Kelley, September 9, 1945. MS. Douglas M. Kelley Personal Papers.

———, to Emmy Göring, October 10, 1945. MS. Douglas M. Kelley Personal Papers.

———, to Emmy Göring, October 28, 1945. MS. Douglas M. Kelley Personal Papers.

Green, Edwin. "General Semantics and Human Affairs." *Los Angeles Daily News,* March 16, 1942.

Greenberg Publisher to Douglas McGlashan Kelley, January 20, 1949. MS. File "1949." Douglas M. Kelley Personal Papers.

Gregor, Neil. *Haunted City: Nuremberg and the Nazi Past.* New Haven, CT: Yale University Press, 2009.

Gunkel, Christoph. "How a Top Nazi's Brother Saved Lives." *Der Spiegel,* May 2, 2012. http://www.spiegel.de/international/germany/new-book-on-herman n-goering-good-brother-albert-goering-a-830893.html.

Hale, Nathan G. *The Rise and Crisis of Psychoanalysis in the United States: Freud and the Americans, 1917–1985.* New York: Oxford University Press, 1995.

Halleck, Seymour L., ed. *Psychiatric Aspects of Criminology.* Springfield, IL: Charles C. Thomas, 1968.

Hansen, Ken. "Professor Uses Tricker in Class." *Daily Californian* [Berkeley], December 5, 1950.

Harrower, Molly. "Rorschach Records of the Nazi War Criminals: An Experimental Study after Thirty Years." *Journal of Personality Assessment* 40, no. 4 (1976).

———. "Were Hitler's Henchmen Mad?" *Psychology Today* (July 1976): 76–78.

Hastings, Donald W., and David G. Hastings. *Psychiatric Experiences of the Eighth Air Force: First Year of Combat, July 4, 1942 to July 4, 1943.* New York: Josiah Macy Jr. Foundation, 1944.

"Head of Graylyn Offered University Post." 1949. Douglas M. Kelley Personal Papers.

"Here and There with *Newsweek* Correspondents." *Newsweek* 1945. Unidentified magazine clipping in Douglas M. Kelley Personal Papers.

Hess, Rudolf. "Statement before the IMT at Nuremberg." 1945. MS MLR P 20, Box 6. National Archives and Records Administration.

"Hitler Gang's Personalities Are Discussed." *Richmond News Leader,* April 5, 1947.

"Hitler's Own Physician Never Expected Trial for War Crimes, Dr. Douglas Kelley Reveals." n.d. Douglas M. Kelley Personal Papers.

Holstrom, J. D., to Douglas McGlashan Kelley, July 5, 1950. MS. Douglas M. Kelley Personal Papers.

Hoover, J. Edgar. "Hermann Göring, Ingestion of Paracodeine Tablets." 1945. MS. Douglas M. Kelley Personal Papers.

"Immaturity Threatens Nation, Noted Psychiatrist Declares." *Hazelton Standard-Sentinel*, January 27, 1948.

"Ink Blots Test Hess's Sanity." *Philadelphia Inquirer*, October 14, 1945.

"Interview with Baldur Von Schirach." 1945. MS. Douglas M. Kelley Personal Papers.

"Interview with Hans Fritzsche." 1945. MS. Douglas M. Kelley Personal Papers.

J. E. S. Memorandum to William Donovan, n.d. MS. Donovan Nuremberg Trials Collection, Cornell University Law Library.

Joyce, Nick. "In Search of the Nazi Personality." *Journal of the American Psychological Association* 40, no. 3 (2009): 18.

Juchli, Rene H. "Emergency Call for Dr. Robert Ley." 1945. MS. Douglas M. Kelley Personal Papers.

Kaempffert, Waldemar. "New Test for Drunks." *New York Times*, November 16, 1941.

Kelley, Alice Vivienne. "Faux Invitation." 1942. MS. Douglas M. Kelley Personal Papers.

———. "Inventory of Items for Sale." 1958. MS. Douglas M. Kelley Personal Papers.

———. Memorandum. n.d. MS. Douglas M. Kelley Personal Papers.

———, to Bill Mandel, September 1, 1985. MS. Douglas M. Kelley Personal Papers.

———, to Bill Mandel, February 4, 1986. MS. Douglas M. Kelley Personal Papers.

———, to Michael Selzer, n.d. Douglas M. Kelley Personal Papers.

———, to Melody Starr. January 25, 1959. Douglas M. Kelley Personal Papers.

Kelley, Alicia, to Alice Vivienne Kelley, 1958. Douglas M. Kelley Personal Papers.

Kelley, Doug, Interviews with Author, August 2008, September 2009, March 2012, and June 2012.

Kelley, Douglas McGlashan. "Annual Ward Report." 1943. MS. Douglas M. Kelley Personal Papers.

———. "Appraisals of Prisoners." 1945. MS. Douglas M. Kelley Personal Papers.

———. Bound Notebook of Interview Notes. 1945. MS. Douglas M. Kelley Personal Papers.

———. "Clinical Reality and Projective Technique." *The American Journal of Psychiatry* 107, no. 10 (1951): 753–757.

———. "Clinical Summary of Neurological and Psychiatric Examination of Internee #31G 350013." 1945. MS. Douglas M. Kelley Personal Papers.

———. "Conjuring as an Asset to Occupational Therapy." *Occupational Therapy and Rehabilitation* 19, no. 2 (1940): 71–82.

———. "Examination of Hermann Goering." 1945. MS. Douglas M. Kelley Personal Papers.

———. "Gifted Children Followup." 1955. Douglas M. Kelley Personal Papers.

———. "Gravatt's Four-ace Trick." *GENII* (n.d.).

———. Handwritten Note. 1927. MS. Douglas M. Kelley Personal Papers.

———. "Hess Rorschach." 1945. MS. Douglas M. Kelley Personal Papers.

———. "History of Psychiatric Service." 1945. MS. Douglas M. Kelley Personal Papers.

———. "Mania and the Moon." *The Psychoanalytic Review* 29, no. 4 (1942): 406–426.

———. "Medical Report on Rudolf Hess." 1945. MS File "Prison Psychiatric Reports." ARC 6291444, MLR P 20. National Archives and Records Administration.

———. "Medical Status of Prisoner Ernst Kaltenbrunner." 1945. MS. Douglas M. Kelley Personal Papers.

———. "Memorandum on the Death of Leonardo Conti." 1945. MS. Douglas M. Kelley Personal Papers.

———. "Mental Examination of Robert Ley." 1945. MS. Douglas M. Kelley Personal Papers.

———. "The Nuremberg Trial." Lecture. 1946. Douglas McGlashan Kelley Archival Collection, University of California, Santa Cruz.

———. "Personal File, to 1937." n.d. MS. Douglas M. Kelley Personal Papers.

———. Personal letter. "File to 1937." Douglas M. Kelley Personal Papers.

———. "Preliminary Studies of the Rorschach Records of the Nazi War Criminals." 1945. TS. Douglas M. Kelley Personal Papers.

———. "Prison Psychiatric Reports." 1945. ARC 6291444, MLR P 20. National Archives and Records Administration.

———. "Psychiatric Evaluations." 1945. MS. Douglas M. Kelley Personal Papers.

———. "Psychiatric Profiles of Nazi Defendants." In "Prison Psychiatric Reports." 1945. MS. ARC 6291444, MLR P 20. National Archives and Records Administration.

———. "Psychiatric Service." 1943. MS. Douglas M. Kelley Personal Papers.

———. "Record of Professional Assignments." 1946. MS. Douglas M. Kelley Personal Papers.

———. "Rorschach Report on Hermann Göring." 1945. MS. Douglas M. Kelley Personal Papers.

———. "Rorschach Report on Joachim Von Ribbentrop." 1945. MS. Douglas M. Kelley Personal Papers.

———. "Rorschach Technique." 1943. MS. Douglas M. Kelley Personal Papers.

———. "Rudolf Hess." 1945. MS. Douglas M. Kelley Personal Papers.

———. "Statement on Hess." 1945. MS. MLR P 20, Box 4. National Archives and Records Administration.

———. "TAT Test Results: Goering." 1945. MS. Douglas M. Kelley Personal Papers.

———, to Alice Vivienne Kelley, August 20, 1935. MS. File "To 1937." Douglas M. Kelley Personal Papers.

———, to Burton C. Andrus, October 26, 1945. "Mental Examination of Prisoner [Ley] to Commanding Officer." Douglas M. Kelley Personal Papers.

———, to C. C. Carpenter, July 26, 1949. MS. Douglas M. Kelley Personal Papers.

———, to Chief Administrator, July 18, 1955. MS. Special Collections, University of California, Santa Cruz.

———, to Commanding Officer, Internal Security Detachment, October 14, 1945. "Psychiatric Status of Internee." MS. Douglas M. Kelley Personal Papers.

———, to J. D. Holstrom, January 30, 1950. MS. Douglas M. Kelley Personal Papers.

———, to Lewis Terman, July 6, 1955. MS. File "To 1937." Douglas M. Kelley Personal Papers.

———, to William Donovan, October 26, 1945. Donovan Nuremberg Trials Collection, Cornell University Law Library.

———, to William Donovan, November 9, 1945. Douglas M. Kelley Personal Papers.

———, to William Donovan, November 10, 1945. Donovan Nuremberg Trials Collection, Cornell University Law Library.

———, to William Donovan, November 13, 1945. Donovan Nuremberg Trials Collection, Cornell University Law Library.

———, to William Donovan, November 17, 1945. Douglas M. Kelley Personal Papers.

———, to William Donovan, November 22, 1945. Donovan Nuremberg Trials Collection, Cornell University Law Library.

———, to William Donovan, November 26, 1945. Donovan Nuremberg Trials Collection, Cornell University Law Library.

———. *22 Cells in Nuremberg; a Psychiatrist Examines the Nazi Criminals*. New York: Greenberg, 1947.

———. "Use of General Semantics and Korzybskian Principles as an Extensional Method of Group Psychotherapy in Traumatic Neurosis." *The Journal of Nervous and Mental Disease* 114, no. 3 (1951): 189–220.

———. "The Use of Narcosis Therapy in the ETO." 1943. MS. Douglas M. Kelley Personal Papers.

———. "Von Schirach." 1945. MS. Douglas M. Kelley Personal Papers.

Kelley, Douglas McGlashan, and Gordon Waldear. "The Criminal." 1957. MS. Douglas M. Kelley Personal Papers.

Kelley, Douglas McGlashan, and Howard Whitman. "Squeal, Nazi, Squeal!" *Collier's*, August 31, 1946.

Kelley, Douglas McGlashan, and Terry Hansen. "Dumb Cops Are Dangerous." n.d. Douglas M. Kelley Personal Papers.

"Kelley Says Dictatorship Is Danger." *Winston-Salem Sentinel*, March 27, 1947.

"Kelley Suicide Mystery Deepens." January 3, 1958. Douglas M. Kelley Personal Papers.

"Kelley Teaches Battle Psychiatry." *Chattanooga Free Press*, April 7, 1944.

Kirkland, E. H., to Douglas McGlashan Kelley, January 26, 1946. "Promotion." MS. Douglas M. Kelley Personal Papers.

Kitchin, Thurman, to Douglas McGlashan Kelley, August 13, 1946. MS. Douglas M. Kelley Personal Papers, File "1946."

Klam, Najeeb, and Douglas McGlashan Kelley. "Clinical Lab Report on Leonardo Conti." 1945. MS. Douglas M. Kelley Personal Papers.

Kodish, Bruce I. *Korzybski: A Biography*. Pasadena, CA: Extensional Publishing, 2011.

Koehli, Harrison. "Ponerology 101: Psychopathy at Nuremburg—Science of the Spirit—Sott.net." *SOTT.net*, September 6, 2010. http://www.sott.net/articles/show/214764-Ponerology-101-Psychopathy-at-Nuremburg#.

Koopman, John. "Gordon Waldear–State's Film Chronicler." *San Francisco Chronicle*, April 27, 2002.

KQED Television. "Application for a Grant from the Educational Television and Radio Center." n.d. MS. Douglas M. Kelley Personal Papers.

"KQED Wins TV Award." January 29, 1959. Douglas M. Kelley Personal Papers.

"Lawmen Hear Crime Cause from Savant." [Logan, Utah], 1951. Douglas M. Kelley Personal Papers.

Lebert, Stephan, and Norman Lebert. *My Father's Keeper: Children of Nazi Leaders*. New York: Little, Brown, 2000.

Lecture Contracts 1947. MS File "1947." Douglas M. Kelley Personal Papers.

Lecture Engagements 1947–1949. TS File "1947." Douglas M. Kelley Personal Papers.

Lecturing Contracts 1946. MS File "1946." Douglas M. Kelley Personal Papers.

Ley, Robert. Last Will and Testament. n.d. MS. Douglas M. Kelley Personal Papers.

———. Statement. n.d. MS. Douglas M. Kelley Personal Papers.

"Ley's Brain Sent to U.S. for Study." *San Francisco Chronicle*, November 1, 1945.

Long, Tania. "Hess Tells Court He Faked Illness as 'Tactical' Move." *New York Times*, December 1, 1945.

Loosli-Usteri, Marguerite, to Douglas McGlashan Kelley, December 8, 1953. Douglas M. Kelley Personal Papers.

"Magic and Mickey Mouse." *Time*, November 24, 1941.

"Magic Helps Treat Insane." *San Francisco News*, November 17, 1941.

"Magicians Will Present Stunt at 10 Today." *Daily Californian* [Berkeley], February 24, 1932.

Malloy, George D., to Douglas M. Kelley, June 28, 1952. Douglas M. Kelley Personal Papers.

Mandel, William, to Alice Vivienne Kelley, August 2, 1985. "Kelley Project: Notes On: Description of Suicide." Douglas M. Kelley Personal Papers.

Manvell, Roger, and Heinrich Fraenkel. *Goering: The Rise and Fall of the Notorious Nazi Leader*. New York: Skyhorse, 2011.

McEwen, Jim. "Somnoform Promises Magic Aid to Victims of Amnesia." *Winston-Salem Journal and Sentinel*, July 3, 1949.

McGlashan, M. Nona. *Give Me a Mountain Meadow: The Life of Charles Fayette McGlashan, 1847–1931, Imaginative Lawyer-editor of the High Sierra, Who Saved the Donner Story from Oblivion and Launched Winter Sports in the West*. Fresno, CA: Pioneer, 1977.

McIlwain, Bill. "Liquor Can Curb Its Own Problems." *Twin City Sentinel*, August 6, 1949.

"Mental Health Held Serious U.S. Problem." *Wilkes-Barre Record*, January 28, 1948.

Miale, Florence R., and Michael Selzer. *The Nuremberg Mind: The Psychology of the Nazi Leaders*. New York: Crown Group, 1976.

Miles, Steven, Interview with Author, October 2009.

Miller, Clint L. "Hermann Göring, Progress in Reduction of Paracodeine." 1945. MS. Douglas M. Kelley Personal Papers.

———. "Medical Report on PWS with Serious Illness." 1945. MS. Douglas M. Kelley Personal Papers.

"Miss Alice Hill Weds Dr. Kelley." n.d. Douglas M. Kelley Personal Papers.

"Modernism Blamed for Delinquency." *San Francisco Chronicle*, April 7, 1951.

Mosley, Leonard. *The Reich Marshal; a Biography of Hermann Goering*. Garden City, NY: Doubleday, 1974.

Moss, Frank L., to Alice Vivienne Kelley, February 4, 1961. MS. Douglas M. Kelley Personal Papers.

"Mrs. Pelton Not Insane, Declares UC Psychiatrist." 1952. Douglas M. Kelley Personal Papers.

Muir, Jean. "Profile of Douglas M. Kelley." n.d. MS. Archives and Special Collections, University of California, Santa Cruz.

"Mystery in UC Suicide Deepens." *San Francisco Examiner*, January 3, 1958.

"Nazis No Longer Swagger at Trial." 1945. Douglas M. Kelley Personal Papers.

Neave, Airey. *On Trial at Nuremberg.* Boston: Little, Brown, 1978.

"Neurosis Victims Return to Battle." n.d. Douglas M. Kelley Personal Papers.

Newton, Dwight. "The Criminal Man." *San Francisco Examiner,* August 12, 1958.

Noyes, Arthur. "Ley Hangs Himself in Cell." *Stars and Stripes,* October 28, 1945.

The Nuremberg Nazi Trial: Excerpts from the Testimony of Hermann Goering, Albert Speer, Auschwitz Commander Rudolf Hoess, and Others. St Petersburg, FL: Red and Black, 2010.

"Nuremberg Rorschach Tests." 1945. TS. Douglas M. Kelley Personal Papers.

Outline of the Training Plan in Clinical Psychology for the Department of Psychiatry, the Bowman Gray School of Medicine of Wake Forest College. 1947. MS File "1947." Douglas M. Kelley Personal Papers.

Overy, Richard J. *Interrogations: The Nazi Elite in Allied Hands.* New York: Viking, 2001.

Palm, Henry. "Psychiatrist Says There Is No 'Criminal Type.'" *San Francisco Examiner,* July 22, 1951.

Perkin, Robert L. "Time-Benders Watch Their P's and C's." *Rocky Mountain News* [Denver], July 23, 1949.

Pick, Daniel. *The Pursuit of the Nazi Mind: Hitler, Hess, and the Analysts.* Oxford: Oxford University Press, 2012.

"Politicians Should Get Mental Exams; and So Should the Psychiatrists!" *Twin City Sentinel,* February 18, 1948.

"Private Rites Mark Funeral for Dr. Kelley." *Berkeley Gazette,* January 3, 1958.

"Psychiatrist Has Criticism for Pals." *San Francisco News,* November 12, 1951.

"Psychiatrists Using Shell Game to Treat Insane." *San Francisco Examiner,* November 18, 1941.

"Psychiatry and Crime." *Greensboro Record,* November 17, 1947.

"Quarter of U.S. Police Held Unfit." September 24, 1952. Douglas M. Kelley Personal Papers.

Randebaugh, Charles. "Theories, but Not One Fits Kelley Suicide." *San Francisco Chronicle,* January 4, 1958.

Rathgeb, Douglas L. *The Making of Rebel without a Cause.* Jefferson, NC: McFarland, 2004.

Rees, J. R., to Douglas McGlashan Kelley, December 4, 1945. MS. Douglas M. Kelley Personal Papers.

Rickman, Joel Y. "2 Deputies Balk Jail Probe Lie Test." San Jose Mercury News, September 10, 1950.

Rogers, Marian. "Faster Mental Cures Found during War, Kelley Asserts." *Tulsa World,* December 4, 1947.

Rosenberg, Alfred, to Douglas McGlashan Kelley, December 26, 1945. MS. Douglas M. Kelley Personal Papers.

Rosenberg, Lee G., to Alice Vivienne Kelley, May 30, 1960. MS. Douglas M. Kelley Personal Papers.

———, to Alice Vivienne Kelley, August 23, 1960. MS. Douglas M. Kelley Personal Papers.

Ross, Helen. "Dr. Douglas Kelley Analyzes Neuroses of Hitler, Nuremberg Trial Principals." *Cataba New Enterprise* (1947).

Roth, Marschal, Jr. "Dr. Kelley Was Not Fooled by Hess's 'Faking of Amnesia.'" *Chattanooga Daily Times*, January 31, 1946.

"Rudolf Hess: Report of British Observation and Findings." n.d. MS. Douglas M. Kelley Personal Papers.

Ryan, Joan. "Mysterious Suicide of Nuremberg Psychiatrist." *San Francisco Chronicle*, February 6, 2005.

Sauckel, Fritz, to Douglas McGlashan Kelley, 1945. MS. Douglas M. Kelley Personal Papers.

Schacht, Hjalmar Horace Greeley. *Confessions of "the Old Wizard"; Autobiography*. Boston: Houghton Mifflin, 1955.

Schaefer, Virginia Chumley. "Virginia's Reel" [Chattanooga], 1945. Douglas M. Kelley Personal Papers.

Schirach, Baldur von. "*Dem Tod*." ["To Death"]. 1945. MS. Douglas M. Kelley Personal Papers.

Schroeder, Christa, to Douglas McGlashan Kelley, April 1, 1952. MS. Douglas M. Kelley Personal Papers.

Schurr, Cathleen. "The Gods Come Down." 1946. MS 229, Box 3:9. Special Collections, University of California, Santa Cruz.

Schwarz, Wolfgang. "Hermann Rorschach, M.D.: His Life and Work." *Rorschachiana: Journal of the International Society for the Rorschach* 21, no. 1 (1996): 6–17.

Sears, Robert R., to William Mandel, September 8, 1985. Douglas M. Kelley Personal Papers.

"Semantics Held Key to Clarity in Thought." Denver Post, July 21, 1949.

"SF Doctor Predicts How 11 Nazis Will Die." *San Francisco Examiner*, October 15, 1946.

"S.F. Psychiatrist Is Amazed at Goering Suicide." *San Francisco Chronicle*, October 16, 1946.

Shurkin, Joel N. *Terman's Kids: The Groundbreaking Study of How the Gifted Grow Up*. Boston: Little, Brown, 1992.

Sprecher, Drexel A. *Inside the Nuremberg Trial: A Prosecutor's Comprehensive Account*. Vols. I–II. Lanham, MD: University of America, 1999.

Stack, Robert I. "The Capture of Goering." n.d. 36th Infantry Division Association. http://www.kwanah.com/36division/ps/ps0277.htm.

"Streicher's Lewd Sex Library May Play Part in Trial." October 20, 1945. Douglas M. Kelley Personal Papers.

Stringer, Ann. "Hess's Aloofness Fails: Talks to Old Partners in World Crime." *Dunkirk Evening Observer*, November 20, 1945.

Summers, Scott. "Graylyn Ready for Treatment of Mental Ills." August 17, 1947. Douglas M. Kelley Personal Papers.

Teich, Frederick. "Inventory: Alfred Rosenberg." 1945. MS MLR P 20, Box 3. National Archives and Records Administration.

———. "Inventory: Hermann Goering." 1945. MS MLR P 20. National Archives and Records Administration.

———. "Inventory: Rudolf Hess." 1945. MS MLR P 20, Box 4. National Archives and Records Administration.

"Tells Need of Training People to Grow up." *Los Angeles Evening Herald Express*, April 1, 1952.

Terman, Lewis, to Douglas McGlashan Kelley, June 23, 1955. MS. File "1955." Douglas M. Kelley Personal Papers.

"Therapeutic Progress." *The American Practitioner* 48 (1914): 601–602.

"They Can't Tie Him." *Oakland Post-Inquirer*, February 24, 1932.

"Time-Bender Idea Bodes Ill for Russ." *Associated Press*, 1947. Douglas M. Kelley Personal Papers.

"Totalitarianism Discussed." *Winston-Salem Sentinel*, June 26, 1947.

"The Trial of Adolf Eichmann (Session 55, Part 1)." n.d. *Nizkor.org*, http://www.nizkor.org/hweb/people/e/eichmann-adolf/transcripts/Sessions/Session-055–01.html.

"The Trial of Adolf Eichmann (Session 55, Part 9)." n.d. *Nizkor.org*, http://www.nizkor.org/hweb/people/e/eichmann-adolf/transcripts/Sessions/Session-055–09.html.

Triest, Howard. Telephone interview with author. January 2012.

Tucker, George. "Doctors Seek Way to Clear Hess's Mind, Put Him on Trial." *Fresno Bee*, November 5, 1945.

———. "Hess Gloomily Views Newsreels of Himself." *San Francisco Examiner*, November 9, 1945.

———. "'I Feel Better,' Hess Says after Confessing Ruse." *Los Angeles Times*, November 30, 1945.

Tusa, Ann, and John Tusa. *The Nuremberg Trial*. New York: Atheneum, 1984.

"UC Criminologist Dr. Douglas Kelley Killed by Poison." *Berkeley Gazette*, January 2, 1958.

"UC Doctors Use Drug to Aid Psychiatric Test." *San Francisco Examiner*, January 22, 1942.

"U.C. 'Houdini' Sirkus Stunt." *Oakland Post-Inquirer*, February 24, 1932.

"UC Man Develops New 'Truth Serum' Method." *Berkeley Gazette*, 1950. Douglas M. Kelley Personal Papers.

"UC Man Reports Better Truth Serum." 1949. Douglas M. Kelley Personal Papers.

"UC's Dr. Kelley, Crime Expert, Commits Suicide." *San Francisco Chronicle*, January 2, 1958.

University of California. "U.S. Neglects Mental Disease Research." 1942. Douglas M. Kelley Personal Papers.

University of California, Berkeley. School of Criminology. Press Release. September 30, 1954. Douglas M. Kelley Personal Papers.

Untitled News Clip. 1945. Douglas M. Kelley Personal Papers.

Urban, Markus. *The Nuremberg Trials: A Short Guide*. Nürnberg: Sandberg, 2008.

"U.S. Experts to Study Dr. Ley's Damaged Brain." *Chicago Daily Tribune*, November 1, 1945.

Volz, Matt. "Montana Pilot, 99, Recalls Flying Goering." *Azcentral.com*, January 29, 2011. http://www.azcentral.com/offbeat/articles/2011/01/29/20110129montana-pilot-recalls-goering-flight-ON.html.

Waggoner, Walter H. "Walter Langer Is Dead at 82; Wrote Secret Study of Hitler." *New York Times*, July 10, 1981.

Walker, James. "Lessons of War Will Help Now." *Greenville News*, February 19, 1947.

Walker, Keith. *A Trail of Corn*. Santa Rosa, CA: Golden Door, 1995.

Waller, Douglas C. *Wild Bill Donovan: The Spymaster Who Created the OSS and Modern American Espionage*. New York: Free, 2011.

Waller, James. *Becoming Evil: How Ordinary People Commit Genocide and Mass Killing*. Oxford: Oxford University Press, 2002.

Walsh, Maurice N. "Historical Responsibility of the Psychiatrist." Archives of General Psychiatry 11, no. 4 (1964): 355–359.

———. Memorandum: "Interview with Prisoner #7." 1948. MS. History of Medicine Collection, the Mayo Clinic.

———. *War and the Human Race*. New York: Elsevier, 1971.

"Wedding Announcement." n.d. Douglas M. Kelley Personal Papers.

Wertham, Frederick. "A Psychiatrist Examines the Master-criminals at Nuremberg: Review of *22 Cells at Nuremberg*." *New York Times*, February 2, 1947.

West, Rebecca. *A Train of Powder*. New York: Viking, 1955.

Whitman, Howard. "Blots on Your Character." *Woman's Home Companion* (January 1947). Douglas M. Kelley Personal Papers.

"Wife Who Killed Sons Called Insane." 1952. Douglas M. Kelley Personal Papers.

Williams, Lena. "Dr. Gustave Gilbert Dead at 65; Trial Psychologist at Nuremberg." *New York Times*, February 7, 1977.

Wilson, O. W., to Douglas McGlashan Kelley, July 26, 1949. MS. File "1949." Douglas M. Kelley Personal Papers.

"WWII Adolf Hitler Profile Suggests 'Messiah Complex.'" BBC News, April 4, 2012. http://www.bbc.co.uk/news/world-europe-17949037.

Wyllie, James. *The Warlord and the Renegade: The Story of Hermann and Albert Goering*. Stroud, UK: Sutton, 2006.

Zillmer, Eric A., Molly Harrower, Barry A. Ritzler, and Robert P. Archer. *The Quest for the Nazi Personality: A Psychological Investigation of Nazi War Criminals*. Routledge, 1995.

INDEX

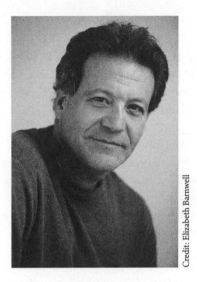

Credit: Elizabeth Barnwell

Jack El-Hai is the author of *The Lobotomist* and is a widely published journalist who covers history, medicine, and science. He has contributed more than five hundred articles to such publications as *The Atlantic, Scientific American Mind, Wired,* the *Washington Post Magazine,* and the *History Channel Magazine.* He is the winner of the June Roth Memorial Award for Medical Journalism, as well as fellowships and grants from the McKnight Foundation, the Jerome Foundation, and the Center for Arts Criticism. A faculty member of the MFA program in creative writing at Augsburg College, he lives in Minneapolis.